Renault 6 1968-76 Autobook

By Kenneth Ball

and the Autobooks Team of Technical Writers

Renault 6—850 1968-75
Renault 6—1100 1970-73
Renault 6L 1975-76
Renault 6TL 1973-76

AUTOBOOKS

Autobooks Ltd. Golden Lane Brighton BN1 2QJ England

The AUTOBOOK series of Workshop Manuals is the largest in the world and covers the majority of British and Continental motor cars, as well as all major Japanese and Australian models. For a full list see the back of this manual.

CONTENTS

ISBN 0 85147 614 7

First Edition   1971
Second Edition, fully revised   1972
Third Edition, fully revised   1973
Fourth Edition, fully revised   1975
Fifth Edition, fully revised   1976

728

Printed and bound in Brighton England for Autobooks Ltd by G. Beard & Son Ltd   C

ACKNOWLEDGEMENT

We wish to thank Renault Ltd for their co-operation and also for supplying data and illustrations. Considerable assistance has also been given by owners, who have discussed their cars in detail, and we would like to express our gratitude for this invaluable advice and help.

INTRODUCTION

This do-it-yourself Workshop Manual has been specially written for the owner who wishes to maintain his car in first class condition and to carry out his own servicing and repairs. Considerable savings on garage charges can be made, and one can drive in safety and confidence knowing the work has been done properly.

Comprehensive step-by-step instructions and illustrations are given on all dismantling, overhauling and assembling operations. Certain assemblies require the use of expensive special tools, the purchase of which would be unjustified. In these cases information is included but the reader is recommended to hand the unit to the agent for attention.

Throughout the Manual hints and tips are included which will be found invaluable, and there is an easy to follow fault diagnosis at the end of each chapter.

Whilst every care has been taken to ensure correctness of information it is obviously not possible to guarantee complete freedom from errors or to accept liability arising from such errors or omissions.

Instructions may refer to the righthand or lefthand sides of the vehicle or the components. These are the same as the righthand or lefthand of an observer standing behind the car and looking forward.

CHAPTER 1

ENGINE

1 : 1 Description

The two engines fitted in the cars described in this manual are similar in design and construction, but vary in dimension and specification details. They are both four-cylinder units with the cylinders disposed vertically in-line and having pushrod operated overhead valves actuated by a side mounted camshaft, chain driven from a crankshaft sprocket.

Replaceable wet liners are used for the cylinder bores and the crankshaft runs in three whitemetal bearings in the case of the 845cc engine while the 1108cc unit has five main bearings.

Coil and distributor ignition is used with a centrifugal automatic advance mechanism. A vacuum control mechanism is also fitted but to the 1108 cc units only. The firing order is 1–3–4–2, No. 1 being at the clutch (front) end of the engine.

The gearbox and differential assembly is bolted to the front end of the engine from which it can be removed without disturbing the engine if necessary.

Sections through the engine are shown in **FIGS 1 : 1** and **1 : 2** while full specifications may be found in **Technical Data** at the end of the book.

On later models a disposable full-flow oil filter is fitted, this should be changed every 9000 miles (15,000 km).

Using a strap spanner or Tool No. MOT.445 loosen the filter from underneath the car, and unscrew it by hand. Discard the old gasket.

Wet the new gasket with engine oil and position in its groove in the block. Screw the filter up by hand until it touches the gasket, then turn a further quarter turn with the strap spanner, and then unscrew, check that the gasket is properly seated. Screw the filter up again until it touches and with the strap spanner screw a further half to three quarters of a turn.

1 : 2 Servicing with engine in or out of car

Many of the servicing jobs which the owner/driver may wish to do for himself may be carried out with the engine in position in the car. These operations include cylinder head removal for decarbonizing or attention to the valves or valve gear, oil pump overhaul, or servicing such ancillaries as carburetter, generator, starter motor and ignition.

Operations such as the removal of the timing gear or the crankshaft and flywheel require the removal of the engine from the car. Since all these jobs may be carried out best with the engine on the bench, the removal of the engine will be described and it is left to the operator to decide whether removal is desirable for the work he intends to do.

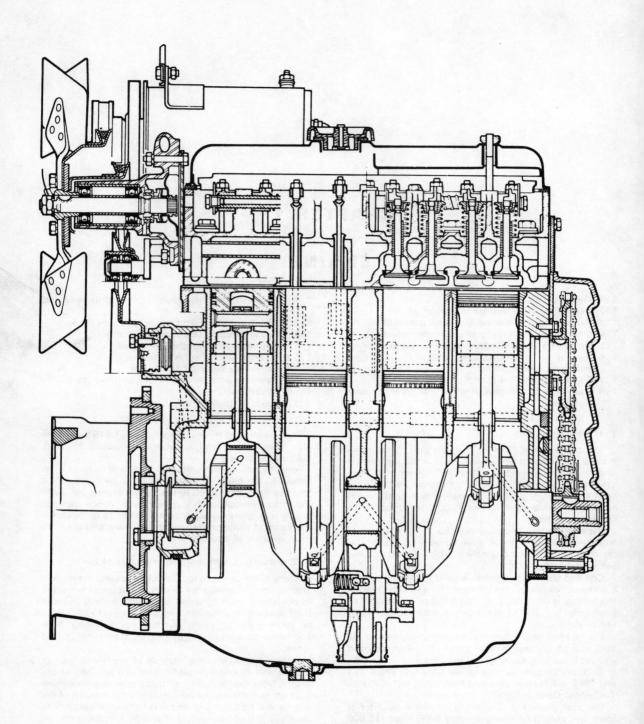

FIG 1:1   Longitudinal section through 845 cc engine. The 1108 cc engine is similar but with five main bearings

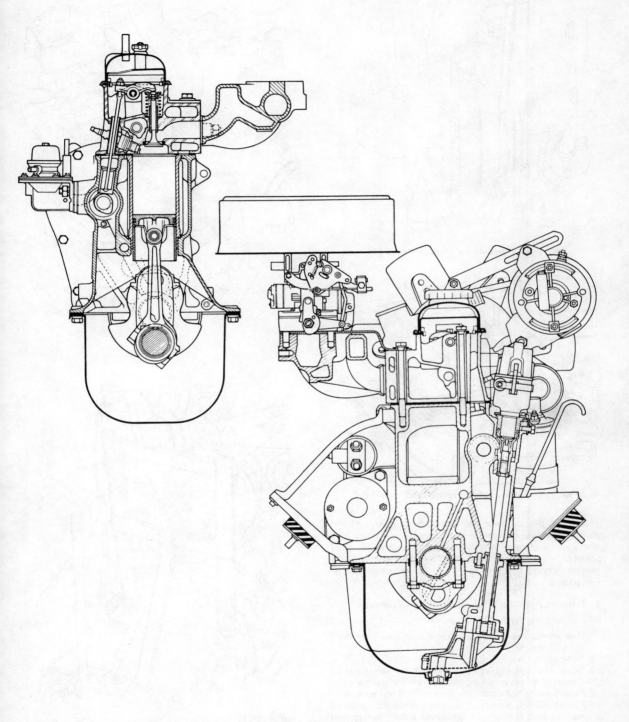

FIG 1:2   Transverse section through engine

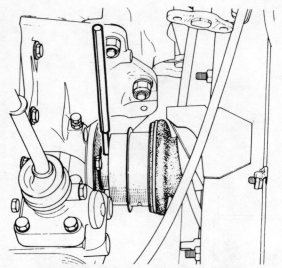

FIG 1:3 Removing a drive shaft rollpin

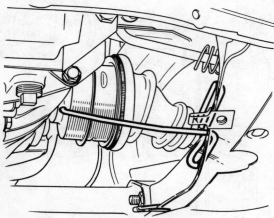

FIG 1:4 Drive shaft coupling retainer clamp

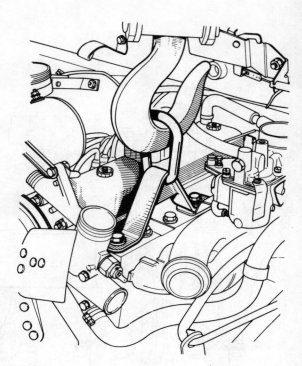

Normally the complete assembly of the engine/gearbox/transmission will be removed from the car as a single unit and separated later on the bench if necessary. It is possible, however, to take out the gear/transmission section leaving the engine in the car as described in **Chapter 6**.

1:3 Removing the engine/gearbox assembly

845 cc engine with BV334 gearbox:

1 Disconnect the battery and remove the air filter from the carburetter.
2 Remove the bonnet.
3 Drain the cooling system by making reference to **Chapter 4** and retaining the coolant for further use.
4 Remove two bolts from the gear control rod assembly.
5 Push back the gear control rod towards the inside of the car and remove the gearlever return spring and push out the rollpin.

FIG 1:5 Lifting adaptors for 845 cc engine, top, and 1108 cc engine, bottom

6 Withdraw the two securing screws from the gear control rod bracket on top of the radiator.

7 Remove the radiator stay and the second part of the gear control rod.

8 Remove the clutch swivel lever after having disconnected the arm at the fork end.

9 Withdraw the gearbox earth strap bolt.

10 Remove the exhaust manifold/pipe clamp and after unscrewing the clamp at the silencer end, ease the exhaust pipe round towards the front of the car.

11 Disconnect the choke cable, the water temperature gauge lead and the hose clips between pump and radiator and on the heater hose.

12 Disconnect the starter cable at the solenoid.

13 Unhook the handbrake return spring.

14 Withdraw the bolts from the steering column flexible joint.

15 Disconnect the following electrical leads: dynamo, low-tension from the coil, oil pressure switch.

16 Disconnect the accelerator cable and return spring.

17 Uncouple the fuel pipe at the fuel pump inlet union and the heater hose at the water pump end.

18 Jack up the front of the car and place securely on stands or chocks. Remove the road wheels.

19 Remove the gearbox undertray and drain the gearbox, retaining the oil for future use.

20 Remove the steering arm bolts at the steering box end.

21 Mark the position of the steering box shims (see **Chapter 9**).

22 Withdraw the two steering box securing bolts and then take off the steering box and remove the radiator.

23 Disconnect the speedometer cable.

24 Pull back the protective rubber sleeves from the points of exit of the transmission shafts from the gearbox and using a suitable drift push out the transmission shaft rollpins as shown in **FIG 1 : 3**.

25 A suitable retaining rod (Tool No. AV.49A) should now be fixed to each shaft to prevent the transmission shaft joint coming out of position. These retaining rods may be simply made from a length of mild steel hooked and secured to the shaft by means of worm drive hose clips or exhaust pipe clips. The type of retaining rod is shown in **FIG 1 : 4**.

26 Disconnect the upper suspension ball joints using suitable wedges or a ball joint removing tool.

27 Pull the transmission shafts out of engagement with the gearbox sun wheels and then replace the upper suspension ball joints to hold in place the stub axles.

28 Remove the front gearbox and side engine mounting pad nuts.

29 Lift the engine/gearbox unit complete from the car using a suitable hoist, taking care that the steering column and accelerator control lever are not fouled (see **FIG 1 : 5**—Tool No. Mot.86).

845 cc engine with BV.354 gearbox:

1 When withdrawing the drive shafts at the gearbox end, tap out the brake hose retaining clips but do not disconnect.

2 Fit Tool No. AV.560 as shown in **FIG 1 : 6** and compress the drive shaft as much as possible by turning the knurled nut **A**.

Take care not to damage the adjusting ring oil seals when withdrawing the drive shafts.

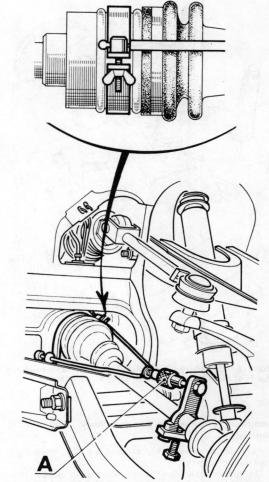

FIG 1 : 6 Compressing drive shaft with BV.354 gearbox

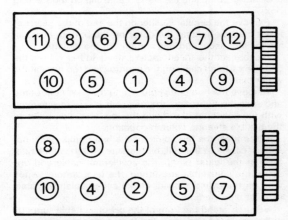

FIG 1 : 7 Cylinder head bolt tightening sequence. Top, 845 cc engine; bottom, 1108 cc engine

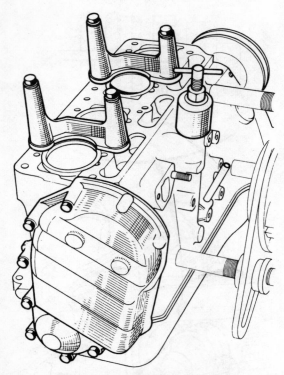

FIG 1:8   Cylinder liner clamps (Tool MOT.12) in position and Tool MOT.04, distributor drive shaft extractor

Removing engine/gearbox assembly, 1108cc engine:

Remove the bonnet, battery and air filter, then drain the cooling system.

Disconnect the pipe to the expansion bottle, temperature switch wires on the radiator, fan motor cables, gearshift lever return spring, top radiator hose and bottom hose at the pump and the starter cable clip on the steering box.

Remove the circular washer on the end of the gearshift lever, the bolt holding the collar on the bottom hose, all the radiator securing bolts and lift out the radiator.

Disconnect the speedometer cable and free it from the clip, the earthing cable on the gearbox and top hose at the water pump.

Remove the two bolts connecting the gear control rod and split the two parts, the gearshift lever crossmember with the gear control rod and the top hose, two bolts on the flexible steering column coupling.

Disconnect the inlet pipe on the fuel pump, generator cables, cables to the coil, oil pressure switch wire, heater hose at the water pump, the accelerator cable and unscrew the adjustable end fitting, the temperature switch wire on the cylinder head, choke cable, solenoid cable, exhaust pipe clamp.

Securely stand the front of the car on suitable supports and remove the undertray and then drain the oil from the gearbox/transmission.

Fit Tool No. AV.560 as shown in **FIG 1:6** and compress the drive shaft as much as possible by turning the knurled nut **A**.

Remove the brake calipers without disconnecting the fluid hoses, then disconnect the steering arms at the adjustable rack end fittings and also the suspension upper ball joints. Tilt the stub axle carriers and at the same time extract the ends of the drive shafts from the sun wheels, being careful not to foul the lip on the differential adjusting ring with oil seals.

Mark the position of the steering box setting shims then take out the two securing bolts and remove the steering box.

Take out the two clutch housing securing bolts and fit the lifting hook MOT.498 as shown in **FIG 1:5**, then take the weight of the engine on suitable lifting tackle.

Remove the two nuts from the engine side mounting brackets. Disconnect the clutch cable at the lever on the gearbox. Remove the gearbox front mounting pad and support.

Taking steps to see that the choke flap is closed so as to prevent the control rod fouling the scuttle, lift out the engine/gearbox/transmission assembly and lay it in a convenient place for further operations or on an engine stand.

1:4 Lifting and replacing the cylinder head

(a) Lifting:

1 Drain the cooling system as detailed in **Chapter 4**, retaining the coolant for further use.
2 Loosen the water cooling and heater hose connections and remove the distributor and the two driving belts.
3 Disconnect the battery connection to earth, the LT and HT plug and ignition leads.
4 Detach the inlet/exhaust manifold complete with carburetter after having uncoupled fuel pipes and accelerator and choke controls and the exhaust pipe flange.
5 Remove the rocker box cover, air filter and generator noting that on 1108cc engines it is necessary to divide the gearshift control.
6 Loosen the cylinder head retaining bolts, a little at a time and in the reverse order shown in **FIG 1:7**. A special tool (MOT.15) is available to unscrew the bolts lying between the pushrods on the 845cc engine.
7 Remove the cylinder head bolts and the head complete with rocker gear, valves and springs may be lifted away, being careful not to disturb the cylinder liners. Should the head remain stuck to the block, tap the head gently with a block of wood, never use a sharp instrument as a lever in the joint as this will ruin the mating surfaces (alloy) and cause a leak.
8 Place the cylinder head on one side pending servicing, which is fully described in the next section.
9 Withdraw the eight pushrods, carefully removing them to avoid disturbing the tappet blocks and keep them in order for exact replacement to their original positions. As already mentioned, wet or removable type cylinder liners are used in this engine and in consequence liner retaining clamps must be fitted whenever the cylinder head is removed, to maintain an effective bottom liner seal. These clamps may be purchased (Part No. MOT. 12 or MOT.521) or simple flat-shaped plates made up with distance pieces for fitting under the cylinder head studs (see **FIG 1:8**).

(b) Replacing:

1 Ensure both the cylinder head and cylinder block mating surfaces are completely free from scale, dirt and grit and the surface is not scored or distorted. A rotary wire brush carefully used will give the most suitable finish on the block surface but the softer alloy cylinder head must only be carefully scraped with a blunt tool. Avoid scratching.

2 Wirebrush the cylinder head bolt threads, remove the liner clamps.

3 Fit a new gasket, dry, with the 'HAUT-TOP' mark facing upwards, using locating dowels, Tool No. MOT.104, if available.

4 Insert the pushrods in their original order and slacken the rocker arm clearance screws.

5 Lower the cylinder head into position. It will be observed that the inner valve rockers may be pushed aside against their shaft springs in order to avoid contact with a pushrod which may be in the raised position. This cannot be done with the outer four rockers and therefore the engine should be rotated until the ideal pushrod/rocker relationship is established for ease of cylinder head fitting.

6 Screw in the cylinder head retaining bolts (noting in 845 cc engines the different lengths as shown in **FIG 1:9**) finger tight, and then using a torque wrench, tighten progressively in the order shown in **FIG 1:7** to a torque figure of 40 to 50 lb ft. It is important to loosen each bolt a quarter of a turn after it has reached the correct torque figure and then tighten again to the final torque figure of 40 to 50 lb ft.

7 Adjust the rocker arm clearances COLD using feeler gauges, inlet .006 inch (.15 mm), exhaust .008 inch (.20 mm) The simplest method to carry out this operation is to rotate the engine with the starting handle until number one piston is at TDC (finger on plug hole will indicate compression stroke) then rotate engine slightly until piston just begins to descend on power stroke. Both valves will now be fully closed and the tappets at lowest point of the cam.

Repeat the procedure for remaining valves, remembering firing order is 1—3—4—2. Counting from the front of the engine, inlet valves are number 2—3—6—7, exhaust valves are number 1—4—5—8.

8 After 600 miles running the cylinder head bolt torque settings should be checked and the rocker clearances reset. This may be carried out either with a cold or warm (50 minutes after switching off) **not** hot engine. If the latter, then the bolt tightening torque should be as for cold engines but the rocker clearances should be INLET .007 inch (.18 mm) and EXHAUST .010 inch (.25 mm).

9 Replace distributor, driving belts (see **Chapter 4, Section 4:2**), generator, air filter and rocker cover, manifold, carburetter, connect all controls, fuel line, battery connection and hoses.

10 Refill the cooling system as described in **Chapter 4**, fit the spark plugs and reconnect the HT and LT leads.

11 Start the engine and test for leaks.

The distributor drive shaft has large and small segments which automatically ensure correct replacement when refitting.

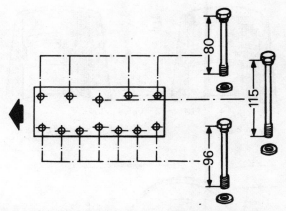

FIG 1:9 Showing location of head bolts, 845 cc engine, dimensions in millimetres

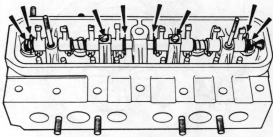

FIG 1:10 Components for removal before withdrawing rocker shaft, 845 cc engine

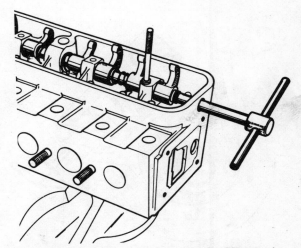

FIG 1:11 Withdrawing the rocker shafts, 845 cc engine

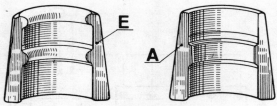

FIG 1:12 Valve collets

Key to Fig 1:12   A Inlet   E Exhaust

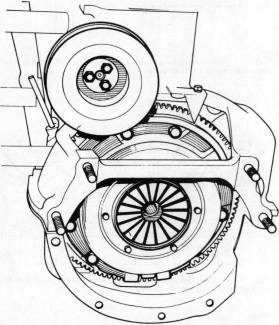

FIG 1:13 Showing the clutch and camshaft pulley

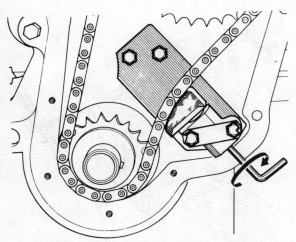

FIG 1:14 Removing the timing chain tensioner

1:5 Servicing the cylinder head, and valve gear

1 Remove the cylinder head as fully described in the previous section.

2 Unscrew and remove the spark plugs, the fan and pulley, the water pump and its backplate and the cylinder head end plate and rubber plug.

3 Dismantle the rocker gear on the 845 cc engine by removing the four clips, the two end springs and the two shaft lockbolts as indicated by arrows in **FIG 1:10**. Remove the two rocker shafts and component parts of the rocker gear as shown in **FIG 1:11**, using a suitable tool or screwed rod. As the shaft is withdrawn so the rocker arms and springs may be taken off in rotation.

4 On 1108 cc engines the rocker shaft is removed by unscrewing the bearing bracket nuts and lifting off the rocker shaft assembly. Remove the spring clips and slide off the rockers, springs, and bearing brackets. The shaft end plugs cannot be removed.

5 Using a suitable type valve spring compressor, compress the valve springs.

6 Remove the collets, spring seats, valve springs and lower washers.

Keep all the component parts in order so that they may be reassembled in their original locations.

The collets for inlet and exhaust valves are of differing type as shown in **FIG 1:12**. Great care must be taken to assemble the correct collets to the correct valve stems.

7 Remove all carbon deposits from inside the cylinder head and from the valve heads by gently scraping with a blunt tool, finally finishing with metal polish or impregnated wadding.

8 Remove the valves, keeping them in strict sequence for exact replacement and remove any carbon or scale from the surfaces.

9 Apply a suction cup to a valve head and using a small quantity of first coarse, then fine, grinding paste, grind each valve into its respective seat.

To correctly grind a valve, the grinding tool should be rotated back and forth between the palms of the hands without any downward pressure being applied. When a unbroken band of frosty grey appearance without any pitting or black spots is to be seen on both the valve and seat faces, then the valve is correctly ground in. Wash away all trace of grinding compound with petrol.

10 Repeat the operation on the remaining seven valves.

11 In the event of the valves or valve seats being burnt or damaged beyond the ability of grinding to rectify then new valves should be fitted or the seats recut. If the seats are to be recut, then standard cutters (90 deg.) should be used. There is no provision for renewing valve seats.

12 In the event of new valve guides being required (this can be checked by inserting a new valve in the guide) various oversizes are available as listed in **Technical Data** but as reaming and press facilities are required, it is recommended that valve guide renewal be left to a service station.

13 Lightly oil the valves, guides, washers and collets and use a set of new springs if the old ones have been in operation for more than 15,000 miles.

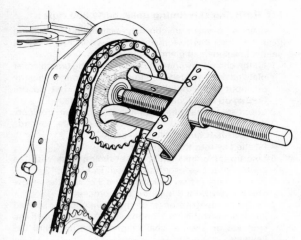

FIG 1:15 Removing the camshaft sprocket (800 engine)

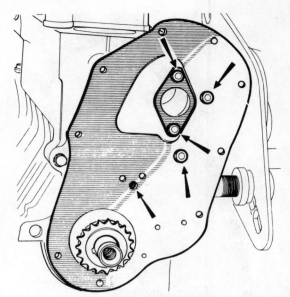

FIG 1:16 The camshaft flange, coverplate and gauze filter (800 engine)

14 Fit the valves in their original order together with spring lower washers, the valve springs and the seat washers.

15 Using the compressor, compress the valve spring and insert the collets, noting the differing type (see Operation 6).

16 On 845 cc engines. Insert the rocker arm shafts, ensuring that the set bolt holes are in line with the holes in the brackets. Fit the rocker arms and springs in turn as the rocker shaft enters. Screw in the two shaft set bolts and lock them by bending the tabwashers over. Fit the end springs and clips. Place the rubber plug in the cylinder head end plate and fit the end plate, water pump, the pulley and fan.

17 On 1108 cc engines. Fit the valve springs with the closed coil downwards towards the cylinder head. Assemble the rocker shaft in the reverse order to dismantling, ensuring that the holes in the rocker arm shaft are in line with those in the support brackets.

18 Replace the pushrods, gasket and cylinder head all as described in previous **Section 1:4**.

1:6 Removing, checking and refitting the timing gear and camshaft

(a) Removal, with head, pushrods and tappets removed as previously described:

1 Withdraw the camshaft pulley located at the front of the engine by withdrawing the three retaining setscrews (see **FIG 1:13**) and remove the timing chain cover, located at the rear of the engine.

2 Remove the chain tensioner by bending back the locking tabs and unscrewing the retaining bolts shown in **FIG 1:14**.

3 Insert a 3mm Allen key into the cylinder and turn the key in a clockwise direction until the pad carrier assembly is no longer under tension. Remove the tensioner and its thrust plate and the oil input plate.

4 Remove the camshaft sprocket with a puller similar to the one shown in **FIG 1:15** (800 engine).

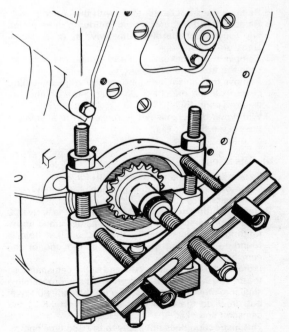

FIG 1:17 Removing the crankshaft sprocket

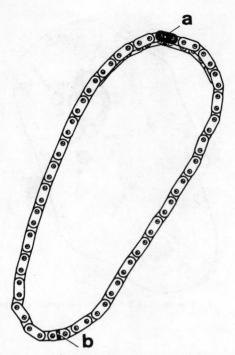

FIG 1:18 Identification marks on timing chain (800 engine)

Key to Fig 1:18　　　**a** Yellow link　　　**b** Scribed line

5 Remove the sprocket together with the chain.
6 Remove the distributor sleeve, oil pump drive pinion and top part of the distributor drive as described in **Section 1:15**.
7 Remove the sprocket key and withdraw the camshaft from the front end of the engine.
8 Remove the camshaft end mounting flange, the timing coverplate and the chain tensioner gauze oil filter, all as arrowed in **FIG 1:16**.
9 Withdraw the crankshaft sprocket with a suitable puller (see **FIG 1:17**).

(b) Checking:

1 Inspect the camshaft sprocket teeth for wear.
2 Carry out a component inspection and renew any worn parts.
3 Before refitting the camshaft sprocket on the early 800 type engine a screwed rod is used as described under refitting procedure later in this section if a hole is found to be drilled and tapped in the end of the camshaft.

If there is no hole drilled in the end of the camshaft, use the drilling in the end of the crankshaft and proceed in a similar manner to that described for the early 800 type but draw on the crankshaft sprocket instead of the camshaft sprocket.

This instruction does not apply to the 688 type engine (see **Section 1:16**).

(c) Refitting the timing gear, early 800 type:

In order to assist in correctly assembling the timing gear the chain has two marks as shown in **FIG 1:18**, a yellow link shown at **a** and a scribed line **b**.

1 Fit the chain tensioner gauze filter and the timing cover plate gasket smeared with jointing compound, also the oil input plate together with its gasket, but do not tighten up the securing screws at this stage.
2 Lubricate the camshaft bearings and place in position.
3 Fit the camshaft end flange with the chamfer towards the camshaft and tighten the screws.
4 Fit the key into the camshaft.
5 Line up the crankshaft sprocket timing mark with the centres of the camshaft as shown in **FIG 1:19**.
6 Fit the chain on the crankshaft sprocket with the yellow link **a** opposite the mark on the sprocket.
7 Fit the camshaft sprocket on the chain with the scribed line **b** against the mark on the sprocket, then push the sprocket on the camshaft aligning the key with the keyway.
8 Refer to **FIG 1:20**. Screw the threaded rod 1 into the camshaft and fit a washer 2 and nut 3 on to the rod. The inside diameter of the washer must be greater than the diameter of the shoulder on the camshaft to ensure the correct position of the sprocket on the shaft (see **FIG 1:21**).
9 Screw up the nut to press the sprocket on to the camshaft. The correct end float is obtained when the washer touches the outside face of the camshaft.

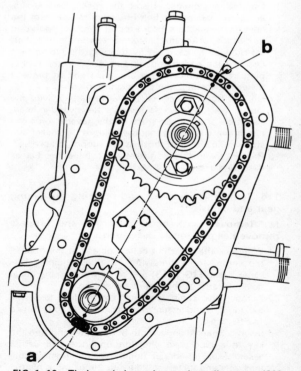

FIG 1:19 Timing chain and sprocket alignment (800 engine). The 688 engines have V-marks which line up from inboard side of sprockets (see FIG 1:43)

10 Fit the tensioner with its thrust plate. Tighten the two bolts. Insert a 3 mm Allen key and turn it in a clockwise direction until the pad touches the timing chain. Tighten and lock the retaining bolt.

11 Tighten the timing coverplate screws and the oil input plate screws. Fit the timing cover and gasket using a little jointing compound.

1 : 7 The sump and oil pump

Access to the oil pump is obtained by removal of the sump.

845 cc engines :

1 Drain off the engine oil into a suitable container.
2 Remove the front nuts (see **FIG 1 : 22**) and tap out the bolts holding the tubular crossmember. Remove the rear nuts and remove the crossmember over the rear bolts. Remove the anti-roll bar.
3 Progressively loosen the securing bolts and lower the sump. Replace the bottom bolt to prevent oil leaking from the transmission unit.

1108 cc engines :

1 Drain the engine oil, then remove the anti-roll bar and the clutch shield.
2 Unscrew the two engine pad securing nuts as far as possible on the sidemembers, and raise the engine by jacking up the clutch housing.
3 Remove the bolts securing the sump, lower it as far as it will go and then turn the engine until the crankshaft balance weights are in the position shown in **FIG 1 : 23**. Remove the sump and clean off all traces of old gasket or jointing compound.

Remove the three oil pump retaining bolts and withdraw the pump complete with the drive shaft which is geared to the camshaft. It will be noted that the upper end of the oil pump drive shaft is slotted with uneven segments to provide a drive for the distributor.

Overhauling the oil pump :

845 cc engines :

The oil pump is shown in exploded form in **FIG 1 : 24**. It has a valve ball and spring retained by a disc retainer on the early type, on the later type a screwed plug is used. The earlier disc retainer is not available as a spare part.

1 Remove the pressure relief valve plug, spring and ball.
2 Remove the cover securing bolts arrowed in **FIG 1 : 25**.
3 Withdraw the two gearwheels and shaft.
4 Clean all component parts and check for wear in the drive shaft splines, the valve seats.
5 Check that the clearance between gearwheels and the pump body does not exceed .008 inch (.20 mm). If it does then the gearwheels should be renewed.
6 If the oil pressure has previously been considered low a new pressure relief valve spring should be fitted at this time but of course a low oil pressure may be due to other factors including worn engine bearings. Before Nov. 1970 the free length of the spring was 1.144 inch (29.5 mm) with disc retainer this has since been changed to 1.498 inch (38.5 mm) with screwed plug. Reassembly and refitting is a reversal of removal and dismantling procedures. Use a new paper gasket when fitting the oil pump to the crankcase.

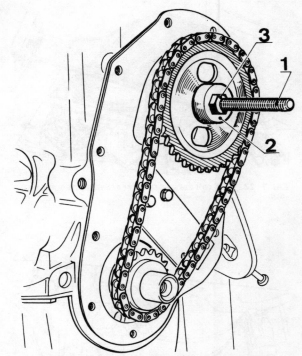

FIG 1 : 20   Pressing on the camshaft sprocket

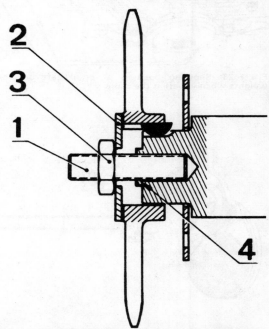

FIG 1 : 21   Sectional view of camshaft sprocket installation. The inside diameter of 2 must be greater than the camshaft shoulder 4 (800 engine)

Key to Fig 1 : 21   1 Screwed rod   2 Thrust washer
3 Nut   4 Shoulder on camshaft

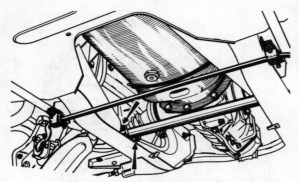

FIG 1:22 Anti-roll bar and tubular crossmember mountings

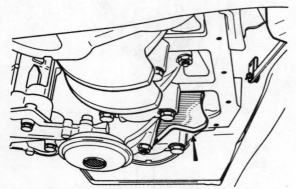

FIG 1:23 Showing position of crankshaft balance weights when lowering the sump

1108 cc engines:

The construction is slightly different in that the pressure relief valve is held in position by the bottom cover.

1 Remove the cover retaining screws, taking care to release the pressure of the relief valve spring slowly.
2 Withdraw the gears and shaft.
3 Clean and check all parts for excessive wear, the clearance between the gears and the body should not exceed .008 inch (.20 mm).

Reassembling and fitting is a reversal of the removal and dismantling procedures but do not use a gasket between the pump and the block.

Refitting the sump:

845 cc engines:

1 Clean all mating surfaces on the sump, crankcase and gearbox. Smear surfaces with jointing compound which will help to retain the gaskets in position.
2 Smear the ends of the rear main bearing gasket with good quality jointing compound.
3 Fit the side gaskets to overlap the rear main bearing gasket and to locate on the crankcase studs as shown in **FIG 1:26A**. Apply jointing compound where the gaskets overlap each other.
4 Fit the front main bearing gasket so that its ends overlap the side gaskets. Apply jointing compound at the point of overlap (see **FIG 1:26B**).
5 Fit the rear end of the sump in position so that its locating area is in line with the gasket on the rear main bearing. Take care not to shift the gaskets.
6 Pull up the front part of the sump until it is parallel with the gasket face on the cylinder block.
7 Push the sump upwards onto the locating studs. Place the two securing bolts in position on either side of the sump and check with your hand to ensure that the rear bearing gasket is still correctly positioned.
8 Secure the sump in place by fitting the remainder of the bolts. (The two bolts with screwdriver slots are positioned one each side at the rear of the sump, see **FIG 1:27**.)
9 Refit the tubular crossmember and the anti-roll bar.

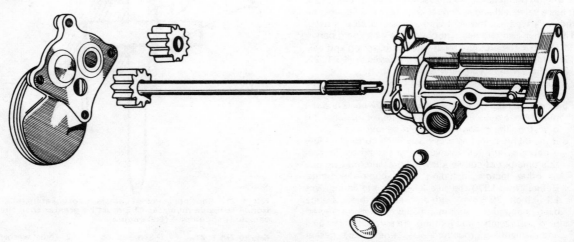

FIG 1:24 Components of oil pump on early 845 cc engines

1108 cc engines:

1 Fit the main bearing rubber seals in position and also the side gaskets using a little jointing compound and hold them in place with four studs one screwed in each corner of the cylinder block (see **FIG 1 : 28**).

2 Make sure that the crankshaft balance weights are still in the right position and fit the sump, being particularly careful not to displace the gaskets and seals.

3 Fit the bolts and tighten them, noting that the two slotted bolts are fitted at the rear of the block.

4 Lower the engine to its normal position and tighten up the side mounting pad securing nuts.

5 Refit the clutch shield and anti-roll bar.

Fill the sump with the recommended grade of engine oil. Refer to Technical Data for quantities.

Normal oil pressures are as follows:

	600 rev/min	4000 rev/min
845 cc	17 lb/sq inch	34 lb/sq inch
1108 cc	10 lb/sq inch	50 lb/sq inch

1 : 8 Removal and replacement of the clutch and flywheel

As previously mentioned, the gearbox is mounted at the front end of the engine and access to the clutch and fly-wheel may be obtained by (i) removing the engine/gearbox as a complete unit as fully detailed in **Section 1 : 3** and then removing the gearbox or (ii) by removing the gearbox and leaving the engine in position in the car as fully described in **Chapter 6, Section 6 : 3**.

(a) Removal:

1 Mark the position of the clutch pressure plate in relation to the flywheel and then unscrew the retaining bolts, progressively, a little at a time to avoid distortion of the plate.

2 Remove the pressure plate and friction disc (driven plate).

3 Mark the position of the flywheel in relation to the crankshaft for exact replacement.

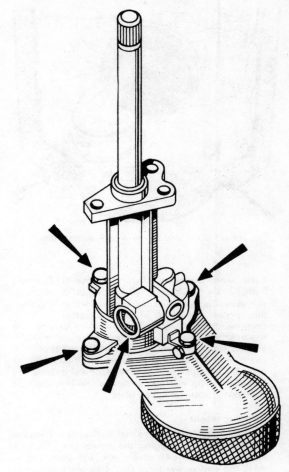

FIG 1 : 25   Oil pump securing bolts

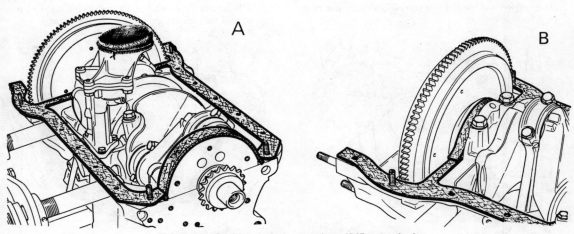

FIG 1 : 26   Positions of sump gaskets (845 cc engine)

Key to Fig 1 : 26   **A** Rear main bearing gasket   **B** Front main bearing gasket

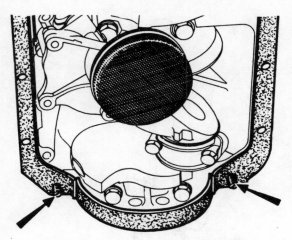

FIG 1:27 Slotted crankcase/sump studs

4 Bend back the locking tabs and remove the flywheel bolts. On the 688 engine self-locking bolts are used.

5 Withdraw the flywheel complete with starter ring gear, taking great care not to damage the gear teeth.

6 Examine the condition of the flywheel surface and starter ring gear and if in a scored or worn condition exchange the flywheel for a reconditioned unit.

7 Examine the clutch pressure plate and friction disc in accordance with the recommendations contained in **Chapter 5**. Do not dismantle the pressure plate or attempt to reline the driven plate.

(b) Replacement:

1 Fit the flywheel to the crankshaft in the correct original relative position engaging the dowel pins. Fit new locking plates on 845 cc engines and these are to mask the two dowel pins. On 1108 cc engines use new self-locking bolts.

2 Position the friction plate and then offer up the pressure plate again in a position to correspond with the one prior to dismantling.

3 Tighten the pressure plate retaining bolts finger tight and evenly and then insert a mandrel or tube which is a sliding fit in the friction plate splines in order to centralize the plate (see **FIG 1:29**). When this is achieved, fully tighten progressively and evenly the pressure plate bolts and withdraw the mandrel. The centring mandrel or tube (Tool No. EMB.319) is of stepped type to engage in the centre crankshaft spigot bush.

1:9 Servicing the big-ends, connecting rods and pistons

(a) Dismantling:

1 Remove the sump, cylinder head and oil pump as previously described in this Chapter.

2 Mark the position of the flywheel in relation to the crankshaft.

3 Unlock and unscrew the flywheel bolts and remove the flywheel.

4 Check the connecting rod reference numbers:
No. 1 is at the clutch end and on the opposite side to the camshaft (see **FIG 1:30**).

5 Bend down the tabs and unscrew the nuts on the big-end caps.

6 Remove the big-end caps and shells.

7 Remove the cylinder liner retaining clamps.

8 Remove each individual liner-piston-connecting rod assembly through the top of the cylinder block. Keep the assemblies in order for exact replacement.

9 Carefully withdraw the piston and connecting rod from each liner.

10 Remove the piston rings, using a twisting action to avoid snapping them.

11 Remove the gudgeon pin retaining circlips and push out the gudgeon pins. If they are stiff immerse the piston in boiling water.

12 From engine No. 11210 (800-02) a larger diameter gudgeon pin (.63 inch (16 mm)) is fitted, and to extract it special equipment is used. Also fitting involves heating the small-end to 250°C and fitting the new pin with the same equipment. This instruction also applies to the gudgeon pins in the 688 engine which have a diameter of .71 inch (18 mm). This work should be given to your local service garage.

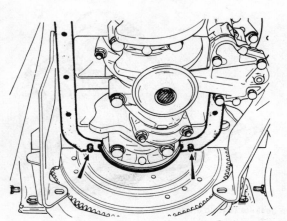
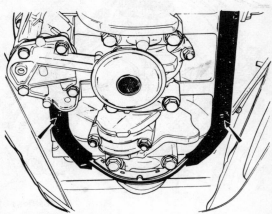

FIG 1:28 Fitting the sump gaskets (1108 cc engine)

(b) Checking:

1 Examine the connecting rods for bow or twist and renew if any is present.

2 Check the clearance between the gudgeon pin and the connecting rod small-end and use a new gudgeon pin as a guide. If wear is apparent, exchange the connecting rod for a factory reconditioned unit and fit a new gudgeon pin.

3 Check the big-end bearings. These are of renewable shell type and are available in oversizes as listed in **Technical Data** for use when the crankshaft bearings have been reground. See **Section 1:10** for grinding detail.

4 It will be obvious that with 'wet' or renewable liners, new piston-liner-rod assemblies or component parts are available dependent upon the bore wear. Inspection will normally indicate the necessity for replacement parts and new pistons and liners will of course be matched in size. Oversizes will not therefore apply.

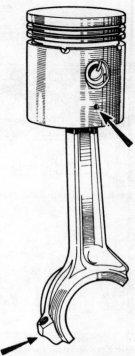

FIG 1:31   Piston and connecting rod assembly

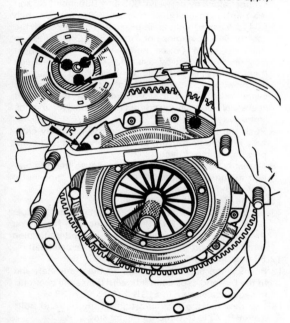

FIG 1:29   Clutch driven plate alignment

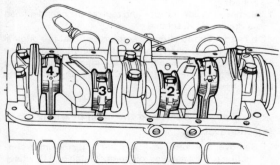

FIG 1:30   Big-end fitting sequence

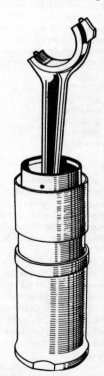

FIG 1:32   Liner, piston and rod assembly

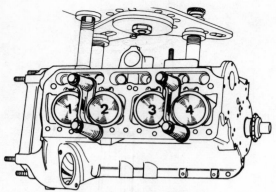

FIG 1:33   Piston fitting sequence (No. 1 at front of engine)

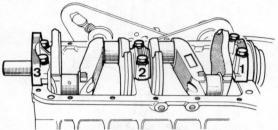

FIG 1:34   Main bearing fitting sequence, 845 cc engine

5 The difference in weight between the heaviest and lightest connecting rod should not exceed 8 grammes. To identify connecting rods within these tolerances a colour marking is daubed on the rod. Check the colour codes and ensure they are all the same. The following is a list of weights and colour codes:

Weight			Colour
341 to 350 grammes	..	..	Blue
351 to 359 grammes	..	..	White
360 to 368 grammes	..	..	Red
369 to 377 grammes	..	..	Yellow
378 to 386 grammes	..	..	Green
387 to 395 grammes	..	..	Black

(c)   Assembling:

1 Fit a new circlip to a piston.
2 Immerse the piston in boiling water. Push the gudgeon pin into the piston and connecting rod by hand ensuring that they are fitted the correct way round.
3 The hole in the piston skirt should be visible when the big-end identification number is on the lefthand side as shown in FIG 1:31.
4 Fit the second circlip.
5 Fit the piston rings to the piston, using a twisting motion and narrow strips of tin to enable the rings to ride over the lands. Stagger the ring gaps at three different points of a circle. Commencing from the top groove, the piston rings are two compression rings and an oil control ring. The rings are supplied with correct gaps, never grind the ends of the piston rings to alter these gaps.
6 Fit new liner seals to the lower ends of the liners. There are two types of seal for each engine size. The 845 cc engine uses copper or impregnated paper seals. Copper seals are available in four thicknesses, .036 inch (.90 mm), .038 inch (.95 mm), .040 inch (1 mm) and .042 inch (1.05 mm). Impregnated paper seals are available in three thicknesses. Blue spot, .003 inch (.07 mm), Red spot, .004 inch (.10 mm), and Green spot, .0055 inch (.14 mm). The 1108 cc engine uses impregnated paper or 'Excelnyl', each available in three thicknesses, the impregnated paper seals are the same as for the 845 cc engine, the 'Excelnyl' seals are Blue spot, .0032 inch (.08 mm), Red spot, .004 inch (.1 mm), and Green spot, .005 inch (.12 mm).
Select a .036 inch (.90 mm) copper seal, or a seal with a Blue spot, as applicable.

7 Place each liner into the cylinder block in turn pressing down with the hand to ensure it is seating properly on its seal. Maintaining this pressure it is now essential that each liner projects above the top face of the cylinder block by between .003 and .006 inch (.08 and .15 mm) with a copper seal or .0015 to .005 inch (.04 to .12 mm) with an impregnated paper seal in the case of 845 cc engines or .0015 to .005 inch (.04 to .12 mm) on 1108 cc engines. The measurement may be carried out by using feeler gauges between the top face of the cylinder block and a suitable machined block resting upon the top surface of the cylinder liner. Use a seal of different thickness if necessary to obtain the correct projection. Remove the liners.
8 Push the piston-ring-connecting rod assembly carefully into the liner using plenty of oil and a ring compression clamp if necessary.
9 Correctly position the connecting rod so that the big-end identification number is on the side opposite to that of the camshaft.
10 Fit the big-end shell bearings.
11 Fit each liner-piston-rod assembly into the cylinder block as shown in FIG 1:32, making sure No. 1 is at the clutch end of the engine and big-end indentification numbers are on the sides away from the camshaft.
12 Fit liner retaining clamps.
13 Position the big-end bearings on the crankshaft and fit the big-end caps complete with their shell bearings, in sequence shown in FIGS 1:30 and 1:33.
14 Use new locking tabs and tighten the big-end bolts evenly to 25 lb ft. Bend up the locking tabs.
15 Check the engine for freedom of rotation.
16 Replace the oil pump and sump as previously described.
17 Remove the liner clamps and replace the cylinder head as previously described.

It cannot be too strongly emphasized that the original fitting location of liners, rods, pistons and bearings must at all times be maintained. Make sketches or notes during dismantling and mark component parts with quick drying paint if necessary.

1:10   The crankshaft and the main bearings

(a)   Removal:

1 Remove the sump, cylinder head, piston-liner-connecting rod assemblies, oil pump, clutch and flywheel, timing gear, all as previously described.

2 Mark the main bearing caps so that they will be replaced in their original positions and the correct way
round on replacement as shown in **FIG 1 : 34**.

3 Unscrew the bearing cap bolts and withdraw them.

4 Remove the bearing caps together with the shell
bearings.

5 Lift out the crankshaft complete with end float flanges.

6 Remove the lower halves of the main shell bearings.

(b) Checking:

1 Examine the clutch spigot bush which is located in the
flywheel end of the crankshaft. If this is worn it may
be extracted by tapping a thread into it and then
screwing in an appropriate bolt.

2 Clean the crankshaft oil pressure holes with a wire
probe.

3 The crankshaft journals and crankpins may be tested
for wear and ovality by using a micrometer. Oversize
shell bearings are available when the nominal diameters have been reground by the following amounts:

	845cc	1108cc
Journals	.010 inch (.25 mm)	.010 inch (.25 mm)
Crankpin	.010 inch (.25 mm)	.009 inch (.23 mm)

The permissible grinding tolerances are:

Journals	.00035 to .001 inch (.009 to .025 mm)	0 to .001 inch (0 to .025 mm)
Crankpin	.001 to .0016 inch (.025 to .041 mm)	0 to .001 inch (0 to .025 mm)

Always carry out a check to ensure that a crankshaft
has not already been reground. On no account should
the recommended undersizes be exceeded.

(c) Reassembly:

1 Place the lower halves of the main shell bearings in
position in the cylinder block. On 1108 cc engines,
bearings 1 and 3 are the same, and 2, 4 and 5 are the
same. They may easily be identified as they have the
oil holes.

2 Oil the bearings and crankpins and fit the crankshaft
carefully into place.

3 Fit the end float flanges with their white-metalled faces
against the crankshaft.

4 Fit the upper shell bearings to their caps.

5 Fit the bearing caps to their locations.

6 Tighten the retaining bolts evenly to a torque of 50
lb ft.

7 Ideally a dial gauge should now be used to measure
the crankshaft end float but the use of feeler gauges
and a suitable distance piece between the crankshaft
flange and the cylinder block web will provide a good
alternative.

The end float should be between .002 and .009 inch
(.05 to .23 mm) on 845 cc engines or .002 and .006
inch (.05 to .16 mm) on 1108 cc engines, any devia-
tion will necessitate changing the end float flanges
which are available in various thicknesses.

On 1108 cc engines, fit the main bearing oil seal, using
Tool No. MOT.131-02, being extremely careful not to
damage the lip of the seal. If a new crankshaft is being
fitted, fit the seal in its original position, but if the same
crankshaft is being refitted, push the seal in an extra
$\frac{1}{8}$ inch (3 mm) so that the lip for the seal does not bear
on the same position. Fit a $\frac{1}{8}$ inch (3 mm) distance
washer so that it is flush with the crankcase face.

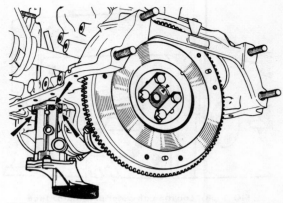

**FIG 1:35 Flywheel securing bolts and alignment marks,
845 cc engine**

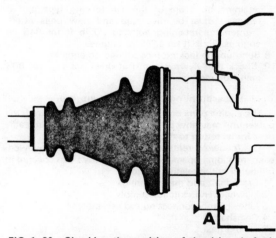

**FIG 1:36 Checking the position of the drive shafts in
relation to the gearbox. A = $\frac{19}{32}$ to $\frac{51}{64}$ inch (15 to 20 mm)**

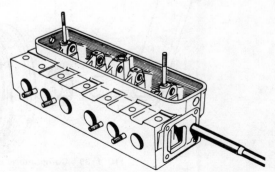

FIG 1:37 Extracting the water circulation tube

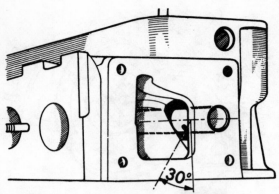

FIG 1:38 Location of water distributor tube

8 Fit the flywheel in its original position relative to the crankshaft and position new locking plates on 845 cc engines so as to mask and retain the dowel pins (see **FIG 1:35**). On 1108 cc engines the flywheel retaining bolts are of the self locking type and if removed must be discarded and new ones fitted. Tighten the retaining bolts to 30 lb ft for 845 cc engines, 35 lb ft for 1108 cc engines.
9 Bend up the locking tabs on 845 cc engines.
10 Check that flywheel run-out does not exceed .003 inch (.06 mm).

1:11 Reassembling the stripped engine

The engine parts having been checked or renewed, the power unit may now be completely reassembled in readiness for its return to the car.

The following refitting sequence should be followed, each individual operation having already been covered in full detail in the relative sections.
1 Crankshaft and main bearings.
2 Flywheel and clutch assembly.
3 Liner-piston-connecting rod assembly.
4 Camshaft.
5 Timing gear.
6 Oil pump and sump.
7 Tappets.

8 Cylinder head and valve gear.
9 Manifolds and auxiliaries which will not obstruct refitting the engine to the car.

Always use new gaskets and use plenty of oil when fitting component parts.

1:12 Replacing the engine in the car

It will be found more convenient to assemble the gearbox to the engine before reinstallation and then the procedure is a reversal of that given in **Section 1:3**, paying attention to the following points on the respective engines.

Ensure that the rollpin holes (see **FIG 1:3**) in the transmission shafts and the gearbox splined drive shafts are correctly aligned with each other. Then push in the rollpin and fill the ends of the holes with a suitable sealing compound.

When refitting the drive shafts on 1108 cc models take care not to foul the lip of the oil seals on the differential adjusting nuts. Check the position of the drive shafts in relation to the gearbox in accordance with the dimension given in **FIG 1:36**.

Make sure that the steering box setting shims are correctly located.

Adjust the clutch to the clearances given in **Chapter 5**.

Refill the engine gearbox and cooling system. Reconnect the battery and run the engine, checking for correct function, leaks and the tightness of all nuts and bolts when hot.

1:13 Internal water tube renewal

After a considerable mileage or if water without inhibitors or antifreeze has been used in the cooling system, the internal water distribution pipe in the cylinder head may need renewal.

Push the old pipe out using a suitable mandrel as shown in **FIG 1:37**.

When replacing the new pipe make sure that the holes in the pipe are pointing towards the exhaust pipe valve seat at the correct angle as shown in **FIG 1:38**. The end of the pipe which has two holes close together must be at the cylinder block plate end. The ends of the pipe should be peened to prevent rotation or lateral movement.

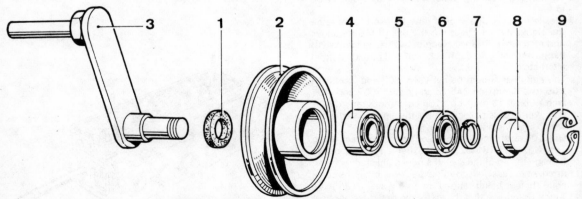

FIG 1:39 Components of belt tensioner on 845 cc engine

Key to Fig 1:39 1 Felt seal   2 Pulley   3 Shaft   4 Bearing   5 Spacer   6 Bearing   7 Circlip   8 Grease cap   9 Circlip

1 : 14 Servicing the belt tensioner

Two driving V-belts are fitted. One driving the generator from the water pump pulley, the other driving the water pump from the front camshaft pulley and running over a tensioner pulley. Adjustment of both belts is described in **Chapter 4**, **Section 4 : 2**.

Should it be necessary to overhaul the tensioner then proceed as follows :

1 Withdraw the tensioner from its support. On 845 cc engines the tensioner locknut if plain has a righthand thread, if grooved on the flats has a lefthand thread. The pulley bearings on both engines are similar.

2 See **FIG 1 : 39** and remove the circlip 9, cap 8 and circlip 7.

3 Press out the shaft 3 and the two bearings 4 and 6 and spacer 5 from the pulley 2.

4 Examine the bearings for wear and renew if necessary.

5 Renew the felt seal 1 and position in the groove in the pulley.

6 Refit the component parts in reverse order to dismantling and fill the cap with high melting point grease before fitting it and the final circlip 9.

7 Fit the tensioner to the engine and adjust as described in **Chapter 4**.

1 : 15 The oil pump and distributor drive gear

The driving gear is meshed to the camshaft and as mentioned in **Section 1 : 6**, before the camshaft can be withdrawn the distributor sleeve, the oil pump drive pinion and top part of the distributor drive shaft must be removed using Tool No. MOT.04 obtainable from your dealer and shown in position in **FIG 1 : 8**.

Refitting :

1 Refit the drive gear for the oil pump and distributor.

2 On 845 cc engines insert the guide of Tool No. MOT.468 in the distributor sleeve. Position the sleeve on the block with the chamfer facing the block. Fit the tool drift on the sleeve, and using a tube, drive the sleeve in until the drift touches the block. Using the bolt from Tool No. MOT.04 check that there is a clearance between the sleeve and the gear of .006 to .022 inch (.15 to .55 mm).

3 Turn the engine until No. 1 piston is in the firing position.

4 Engage the distributor drive shaft end fitting ensuring that it is correctly positioned with the drive slot set 60 deg. (90 deg. on the 688 type engine) to the longitudinal line of the engine and the largest segment towards the clutch end of the engine (see **FIG 1 : 40**). The distributor may be pushed into position so that the large and small segments of the drive locate automatically.

1 : 16 Modifications

The camshaft :

On the 688 type of engine the fitting of the camshaft sprocket differs to that described in **Section 1 : 6** for the 800 type. Referring to **FIG 1 : 41** it will be seen that a spacer washer is fitted between the flange plate and the

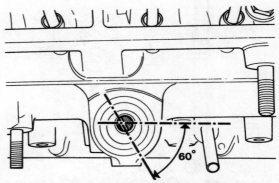

FIG 1 : 40 Distributor and oil pump drive gear alignment, 845 cc engine

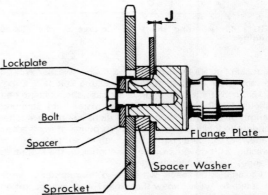

FIG 1 : 41 Camshaft sprocket locking arrangement on the later 688-10 engines. J = .002 to .005 inch (.06 to .11 mm)

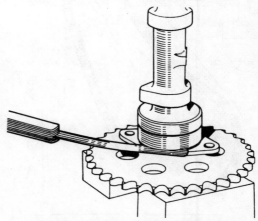

FIG 1 : 42 Checking the camshaft end float

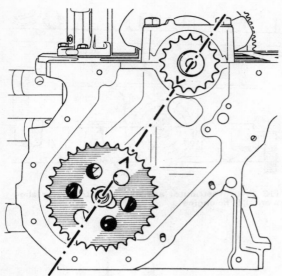

FIG 1:43 Aligning the timing marks on the 688-10 engines

sprocket. In some instances the spacer washer will be 5 mm (.197 inch) thick instead of the standard 4 mm (.157 inch) thickness. If this is the case, the retaining bolt should be 30 mm (1.18 inch) long instead of a standard length of 20 mm (.79 inch) and there will be no washer under the locking plate. Bear these points in mind when renewing the parts, particularly with regard to the spacer washer, as it governs (in conjunction with the mounting flange) the camshaft end float.

1 Examine the spacer washer and the mounting flange plate for wear; renew them if any wear is apparent on the bearing faces.

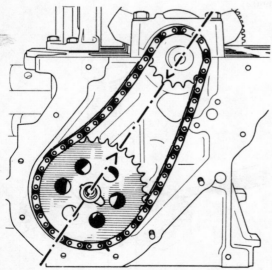

FIG 1:44 The timing chain in position

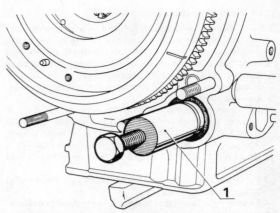

FIG 1:45 Removing the camshaft front oil seal with special tool MOT 500 (1)

2 Fit the mounting flange, the key and the spacer washer to the camshaft.
3 Fit the sprocket, washer (if standard), and the lockplate and bolt. If the bolt is a standard 20 mm tighten to a torque of 15 lb ft (2 kgm). If it is a special 30 mm length tighten to 22 lb ft (3 kgm). Do not lock the bolt at this stage.
4 With feeler gauges check the clearance J as shown in FIG 1:42. It should be between .002 and .005 inch (.06 and .11 mm).
5 Remove the sprocket wheel.
6 Lubricate the camshaft bearings and fit the camshaft in position. Fit and tighten the camshaft mounting flange bolts.
7 Locate the camshaft sprocket on the camshaft. Ensure the timing mark on the sprocket face is presented outwards and align the timing marks as shown in FIG 1:43.
8 Without disturbing the camshaft position, carefully remove the sprocket. Fit the timing chain over the crankshaft sprocket and around the camshaft sprocket, maintaining the timing mark alignment, fit the camshaft sprocket in the camshaft (see FIG 1:44).
9 Secure the camshaft sprocket as described in operation 3 and lock the bolt head with the tag on the lockplate.
10 Fit the chain tensioner assembly. Insert a 3 mm hexagon key into the retaining cylinder and turn it clockwise to release the pad into the chain.
11 Fit the timing cover with a new cork gasket.

Camshaft oil retainer:

Before fitting the camshaft pulley at the front of the engine renew the camshaft seal. A special tool, MOT 500, is necessary to do this as shown in FIG 1:45. Push the tool fully home to force the lips of the seal over the flange of the tool. Screw the bolt down onto the camshaft to extract the seal.

To fit a new seal, use the taper sleeve of the special tool to stretch the seal over the camshaft and then use the collar bush to push the seal into position (see FIG 1:46).

1:17 Fault diagnosis

(a) Engine will not start

1 Defective coil
2 Faulty capacitor (condenser)
3 Dirty, pitted or maladjusted contact breaker points
4 Ignition wires loose or insulation faulty
5 Damp spark plug leads
6 Battery discharged or terminals corroded
7 Faulty or jammed starter
8 Spark plug leads wrongly connected
9 Vapour lock in fuel pipes
10 Defective fuel pump
11 Overchoking
12 Underchoking
13 Blocked petrol filter or carburetter jets
14 Leaking valves
15 Sticking valves
16 Valve timing incorrect
17 Ignition timing incorrect

(b) Engine stalls

Check 1, 2, 3, 4, 10, 11, 12, 13, 14 and 15 in (a)
1 Spark plugs defective or gaps incorrect
2 Retarded ignition
3 Mixture too weak
4 Water in fuel system
5 Petrol tank vent blocked
6 Incorrect valve clearance

(c) Engine idles badly

Check 1 and 6 in (b)
1 Air leak at manifold joints
2 Slow-running jet blocked or out of adjustment
3 Air leak in carburetter
4 Over rich mixture
5 Worn piston rings
6 Worn valve stems or guides
7 Weak exhaust valve springs

(d) Engine misfires

Check 1, 2, 3, 4, 5, 8, 10, 13, 14, 15, 16, 17 in (a); 1, 2, 3 and 6 in (b)
1 Weak or broken valve springs

(e) Engine overheats (see Chapter 4)

(f) Compression low

Check 14 and 15 in (a); 5 and 6 in (c) and 1 in (d)
1 Worn piston ring grooves
2 Scored or worn cylinder bores

(g) Engine lacks power

Check 3, 10, 11, 13, 14, 15, 16 and 17 in (a); 1, 2, 3 and 6 in (b); 5 and 6 in (c) and 1 in (d). Also check (e) and (f)
1 Leaking joint washers
2 Fouled spark plugs
3 Automatic advance not operating

(h) Burnt valves or seats

Check 14 and 15 in (a); 6 in (b) and 1 in (d). Also check (e)
1 Excessive carbon around valve seat and head

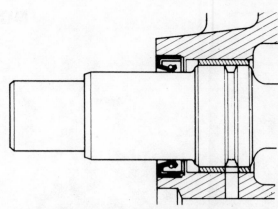

FIG 1:46 The new oil seal assembled in position

(j) Sticking valves

Check 1 in (d)
1 Burnt valve stem
2 Scored valve stem or guide
3 Incorrect valve clearance

(k) Excessive cylinder wear

Check 11 in (a) and see **Chapter 4**
1 Lack of oil
2 Dirty oil
3 Piston rings gummed up or broken
4 Badly fitting piston rings
5 Connecting rods bent

(l) Excessive oil consumption

Check 5 and 6 in (c) and check (k)
1 Ring gaps too wide
2 Oil return holes in piston choked with carbon
3 Scored cylinders
4 Oil level too high
5 External oil leaks

(m) Crankshaft and connecting rod bearing failure

Check 1 in (k)
1 Restricted oilways
2 Worn journals or crankpins
3 Loose bearing caps
4 Extremely low oil pressure
5 Bent connecting rod

(n) Internal water leakage (see Chapter 4)

(o) Poor circulation (see Chapter 4)

(p) Corrosion (see Chapter 4)

(q) High fuel consumption (see Chapter 2)

(r) Engine vibration

1 Loose generator bolts
2 Fan blades out of balance
3 Exhaust pipe mountings too tight
4 Rubber mounting pads hardened or bonding ineffective

NOTES

CHAPTER 2

FUEL SYSTEM

2 : 1   The fuel pumps

A mechanical fuel pump is fitted to the 850 cc models but on the 1100 cc models an electric fuel pump may be used.

The mechanical pump is bolted to the engine block on the righthand side (see FIG 2 : 1). It is driven from the camshaft via an eccentric operating the pump lever.

The electric pump (type SU, AUF 200 series) is located inboard of the righthand rear road wheel.

2 : 2   Routine maintenance (mechanical)

The only maintenance required periodically is to clean the sediment chamber (see FIG 2 : 2).

1 Unscrew the bolt 14, lift off the cover 16 and remove the gauze from its seating. Wash the gauze in petrol. Loosen sediment in the body with a screwdriver and remove. Avoid damaging the valve 23.

2 Refit the parts in the reverse order of dismantling, using a new joint 17 if the original one has deteriorated. Do not overtighten the lid screw.

3 Check the inlet and outlet unions for tightness.

2 : 3   Dismantling (mechanical)

1 Disconnect the inlet and outlet fuel pipes and plug the fuel line from the tank.

2 Remove the pump from the engine by unscrewing the two retaining nuts and spring washers.

3 Clean the exterior of the pump and file a mark across the mating flanges of top and bottom halves of the pump to facilitate exact replacement.

4 See FIG 2 : 2 and remove the lid assembly and filter gauze, then unscrew the screws 19 and withdraw the top part of the pump body.

5 Withdraw the diaphragm and valve assembly 1.

6 This may be further dismantled into its component parts 2, 3, 4 and 5.

7 The spring 8 may then be withdrawn and all components will be accessible.

8 Renew the diaphragm and valves if necessary.

2 : 4   Reassembly (mechanical)

1 Reassembly is a reversal of dismantling instructions but remember to give the valves particular attention when fitting, ensure that the inlet valve points towards the diaphragm and the outlet valve points away from the diaphragm as shown in FIG 2 : 2.

2 When refitting the pump to the engine block fit a new gasket and tighten the nuts evenly a few threads at a time, to prevent locking and distortion.

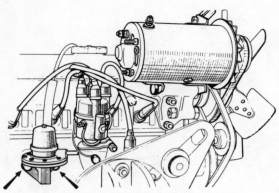

FIG 2:1 The location of the fuel pump

2:5 Testing the pump (mechanical)

1 Uncouple the fuel feed pipe where it connects with the carburetter.
2 Either by using the priming lever 9 on the pump, operating the starter or by turning the engine by the starting handle, a well defined spurt of petrol should be ejected from the disconnected fuel line.

3 If the pump has been dismantled then before refitting to the engine, place a thumb over the inlet port and operate the operating lever. A good suction noise should be heard which will indicate correct reassembly.

2:6 The electric fuel pump

Removal:

1 Disconnect the battery terminals
2 Disconnect both leads at the pump and the two hoses.
3 Remove the securing bolts and withdraw the pump.

Dismantling:

1 Refer to FIG 2:3 and remove terminal parts 30 to 33 and seal 43 if fitted. Take off cover 29. Remove contact blade 22.
2 Remove housing screws 7 and earthing screw 9. Part housing 6 from body. Unscrew diaphragm 2 anticlockwise, holding the assembly over the bench to catch the eleven brass rollers 3. Do not attempt to remove the diaphragm from its spindle.
3 Remove washer 21 and nut 20. Cut away lead washer 19. Release pedestal 16 (two screws 28). Remove earth tag 13, tip the pedestal and withdraw terminal

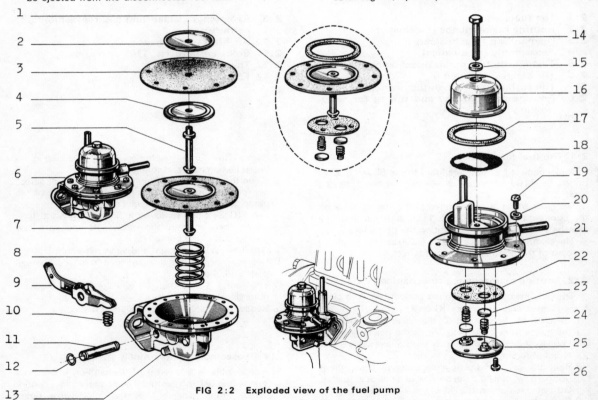

FIG 2:2 Exploded view of the fuel pump

Key to Fig 2:2   1 Diaphragm and valve assembly   2 Diaphragm plate   3 Diaphragm   4 Diaphragm plate
5 Diaphragm operating rod   6 Petrol pump complete   7 Diaphragm complete   8 Diaphragm spring
9 Petrol pump operating lever   10 Pump lever spring   11 Lever spindle   12 Lever spindle circlip   13 Pump lower casing
14 Pump lid retaining bolt   15 Gasket   16 Pump lid   17 Filter gasket   18 Filter   19 Pump case retaining screw
20 Washer   21 Pump upper casing   22 Gasket   23 Valve   24 Valve spring   25 Valve plate   26 Valve plate retaining screw
Parts 1 to 5 are components (not additional to) assembly 7

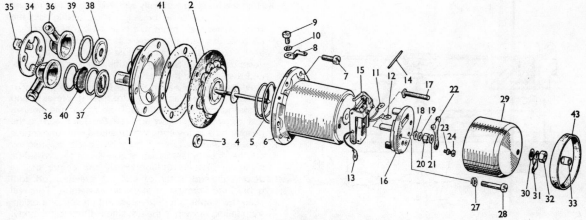

FIG 2:3 Exploded view of the AUF 200 type pump components

Key to Fig 2:3   1 Pump body   2 Diaphragm and spindle assembly   3 Armature centralizing roller   4 Impact washer   5 Armature spring   6 Coil-housing   7 2BA setscrew   8 Earth connector   9 4BA setscrew   10 Spring washer   11 Terminal tag for 5BA   12 Terminal tag for 2BA   13 Earth tag for 2BA   14 Rocker pivot pin   15 Rocker mechanism   16 Pedestal   17 Terminal stud   18 Spring washer   19 Lead washer   20 Terminal nut   21 End cover seal washer   22 Contact blade   23 Washer 5BA   24 Contact blade screw   27 2BA spring washer   28 2BA screw   29 End cover   30 Shakeproof washer   31 Lucar connector   32 2BA nut   33 Insulating sleeve   34 Clamp plate   35 2BA screw   36 Inlet and outlet nozzle   37 Inlet valve   38 Outlet valve   39 Sealing washer   40 Filter   41 Gasket   43 Seal

stud 17 from the terminal tag. Take away the pedestal complete with rocker mechanism.

4 Push out pin 14 to release the rocker mechanism, which cannot be further dismantled.

5 Remove clamp plate 34 (two 2BA screws). Remove nozzles 36, filter 40 and valves 37 and 38.

Examination of pump:

1 Clean all the parts and inspect for cracks, damaged joint faces and threads. Suck and blow at the valve assemblies to check that they are seating properly. The narrow retaining tongue on the valve cage should allow a valve lift of approximately $\frac{1}{16}$ inch.

2 Look for damage or corrosion in the valve recesses in the body. If the valve seating is pitted the body will need renewal.

3 Clean the filter with a brush and not with a piece of fluffy tag. If it is cracked, renew it. Check all electrical leads and tags for damage to insulation and security.

4 If the contact points are badly burned or pitted, renew the rocker assembly and blade.

5 Examine the diaphragm for signs of deterioration. Be prepared to renew all washers and gaskets, remembering that a new lead washer 19 will be needed.

Reassembling pump:

1 Fit the rocker assembly to the pedestal as in **FIG 2:4** so that the final position is as shown by the inset. **Note that the pin is hardened and must only be renewed by fitting a genuine SU part.** If the rockers are not perfectly free in action, apply a tiny drop of oil to the pivots and set the arms with a pair of long-nosed pliers if necessary.

2 Fit terminal 17 to the pedestal and then assemble the following parts in this order. Fit spring washer 18 and

then put the terminal stud through the 2BA terminal tag. Follow this with the new lead washer 19 and coned nut 20 with its coned face to the washer. Tighten the nut and lastly add washer 21.

3 Fit the pedestal to the housing with screws 28. The lefthand screw must be threaded through the earthing tag 13 and then the spring washer is fitted, so that the tag is immediately under the head of the screw. When tightening the screw see that the tag does not turn or it may strain the lead. **Do not overtighten or the pedestal will crack. Do not fit the contact blade yet.**

4 Assemble impact washer 4 to the diaphragm spindle and fit spring 5 into the coil housing with the large diameter first. Screw the diaphragm clockwise so that the spindle enters the trunnion in the middle of the rocker assembly. **Do not put jointing compound on the diaphragm.** Screw in the diaphragm until the rocker will not throw-over, but be careful not to confuse this with jamming the armature in the coil housing.

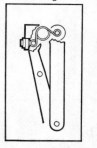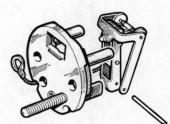

FIG 2:4 Fitting the rocker assembly to the pedestal. The inset shows the correct position of the toggle spring

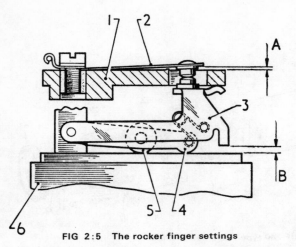

FIG 2:5 The rocker finger settings

Key to Fig 2:5   1 Pedestal   2 Contact blade   3 Outer
rocker   4 Inner rocker   5 Trunnion   6 Coil housing
A = .035 inch (.9 mm)   B = .070 inch (1.8 mm)

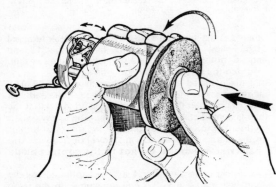

**FIG 2:6 Unscrewing the diaphragm until the rocker
just 'throws out'**

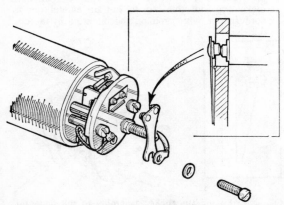

**FIG 2:7 Setting the correct relative position of blade
and rocker contact points**

5 Hold the housing vertically with the diaphragm upper-most and fit the eleven brass rollers by turning back the edge of the diaphragm. On later-type rocker mechanisms with adjustable fingers as depicted in **FIG 2:5**, fit the contact blade and adjust the finger settings as described under 'Setting modified rocker assemblies' and then remove the blade.

6 Hold the assembly as in **FIG 2:6** and push firmly but steadily on the diaphragm. Unscrew it, pressing and releasing the diaphragm until the rocker mechanism just 'throws-over'. Now unscrew the diaphragm to the nearest hole in the edge which aligns with one on the housing flange. From there, turn back or unscrew another four holes, which is equivalent to two-thirds of a complete revolution. Press the centre of the diaphragm and fit the official SU retaining-fork tool behind the trunnion of the rocker assembly. This will keep the diaphragm depressed and prevent the rollers from falling out while the housing is fitted to the body.

Assembling the body:

1 Inlet and outlet valves are identical. The recess in the body for the inlet valve is deeper to accommodate the filter and an extra washer. With tongue side uppermost, place the outlet valve in the recess marked 'OUTLET', place a joint washer on top and fit the outlet nozzle.

2 With tongue side downwards, fit the inlet valve in the 'INLET' recess, followed by a joint washer, the filter, dome side upwards, another joint washer and the inlet nozzle.

3 Settle the assemblies correctly into their recesses and clamp down with plate 34, first setting the nozzles to point in the desired direction.

Attaching body to housing:

1 **Do not put jointing compound on the diaphragm.** With the cast lugs on the coil housing at the bottom, insert the six screws finger tight. Fit the earthing screw and Lucar connector.

2 Remove the SU tool which was inserted behind the rocker trunnion and tighten the screws diametrically and evenly. Any further stretching of the diaphragm before final tightening is unnecessary.

Adjusting the contact blade:

1 Fit the contact blade and coil lead to the pedestal with 5BA screw and washer.

2 The contact points on the blade must be a little above the points on the rocker when closed, as shown in **FIG 2:7**. The blade is slotted for adjustment.

Setting rocker assemblies:

1 Use **FIG 2:5** as a guide. Check dimension **A**. It should be .035±.005 inch and adjustment is made by bending the stop finger just behind the pedestal.

2 Check the gap between the rocker finger and the coil housing face at **B**. If necessary, bend the finger to obtain a gap of .070 + .005 inch.

Fitting the end cover:

Fit seal washer 21 to the terminal stud, followed by the cover. Secure with nut 32 and fit the terminal tag or connector. Fit insulating sleeve 33. The pump will now be ready for testing.

Testing pump:

Fit the pump and switch on. If it is suspected that fuel is not reaching the carburetter(s), disconnect the fuel line from the carburetter(s) and switch on. If jets of fuel squirt from the disconnected pipe, check that the needle valve in the carburetter float chamber is not stuck.

If the flow is normal at first but diminishes rapidly, and the pump slows down, check the fuel tank venting by removing the filler cap. Reduced flow can also be caused by blocked fuel lines or by a clogged filter. Remove filter 40 in **FIG 2:3** and clean with a brush and fuel.

If the pump operates rapidly but does not pump sufficient fuel, check for an air leak on the suction side of the pump, dirt under the valves or faulty valve sealing washers.

If there is no flow, check that current is reaching the pump terminal. If current is there, remove the end cover of the pump to check the contact points. If they are touching, replace the lead on the terminal and short across the contacts with a piece of bared wire. If the pump then makes a stroke the fault is due to dirt, burning or maladjustment of the points.

If an obstructed pipeline is suspected, disconnect the inlet pipe. If the pump then works, there is a restriction in the line from the pump to the tank. Remove the fuel tank filler cap and clear the pipe with compressed air. **Do not pass compressed air through the pump or the valves will be damaged.**

If the preceding operations fail, suspect stiffening of the diaphragm or excessive friction in the rocker mechanism. Remove the coil housing and flex the diaphragm a few times, taking care that the brass rollers do not fall out. When reassembling, apply a little thin oil to the 'throw-over' spring spindles where they pivot in the brass rockers. Follow the original assembly instructions when refitting the coil housing to the body.

If the pump is noisy, suspect an air leak on the suction side. Disconnect the fuel feed to the carburetter and lead it into a container. Switch on and look for continuous air bubbles while the pipe is immersed in fuel. This confirms that there is an air leak. To cure this, check all pipe connections and unions. Also check that the coil housing screws are evenly tightened.

If the pump operates without delivering fuel, check for a serious air leak on the suction side. Another likely cause is dirt under one of the valves, particularly the inlet valve. Remove the valves for cleaning.

Contact gap setting:

1 Check that when the outer rocker is pressed back against the coil housing, the contact blade rests on the narrow ridge on the pedestal which is arrowed in **FIG 2:8**. If necessary, swing the blade clear and set it slightly. It must rest lightly on the rib as over-tensioning will restrict rocker travel.

2:7 The carburetter, operating principles

A Solex, type 32 PD1S.3 Mk. 428 downdraught carburetter, shown in **FIG 2:9**, was originally fitted to the 845 cc engines, slightly modified versions, Mk. 451 and Mk. 467 were also used, but since the beginning of 1973, models fitted with the 800-03 engine have been equipped with the Solex, type 32 E1SA 4 Mk. 570, which is a modified version of the original; but adapted to

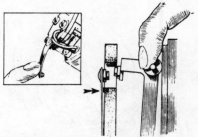

FIG 2:8 Setting the contact blade to ensure contact with the pedestal ridge

conform with the anti-pollution laws. This latest carburetter is also very similar to the type fitted to the 1108 cc models, it is the same make and type, but carries a different series number and mark. The first type fitted to the 1108 cc was the series 2 Mk. 481, this was changed later to the series 3 Mk. 525 in 1972, slightly modified versions, Mk. 512 and Mk. 560 have also been used, and from January 1973 a 32 SE1A may be fitted, the later types were designed with the anti-pollution laws in mind and, of course, the jet sizes vary from those on the series 4 Mk. 570. A list of jet sizes are given in **Technical Data**.

As the carburetters are basically very similar the PD1S 3 Mk. 428 and the EISA 2 Mk. 481 are described and the principle explained to cover all the necessary contingencies.

The carburetter comprises three main parts; the body, the float chamber and the float chamber cover which carries the choke assembly and the oil vapour breather tube.

The component parts of the carburetter are shown in **FIG 2:10** and **FIG 2:11** shows the unit in sectional form.

The Strangler. The choke ensures starting from cold, idling and the ability to drive away with a cold engine. It is remotely controlled manually. The device consists of the choke butterfly (V¹), **FIG 2:11**, which is able to close completely the main air intake of the carburetter. A lever riveted at the end of the choke spindle is held in contact with the choke cam lever by a spring.

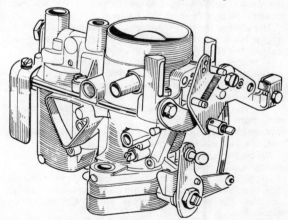

FIG 2:9 The Solex PDIS 3 Mark 428 downdraught carburetter

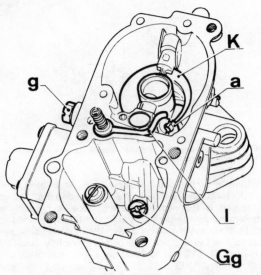

FIG 2:10 Components of the Solex carburetter

Key to Fig 2:10
a Air compensator jet
g Slow-running jet
K Choke tube
l Accelerator pump
Gg Main jet

This lever, fitted on the float chamber cover, is connected to the choke control cable and by means of a connecting rod to the fast idle lever fitted to the throttle spindle of the carburetter.

A locking device with ball and spring located behind the choke lever allows these controls to be placed in two positions.

The first gives complete closure of the choke.

The second gives complete opening of the choke. Each position of the choke corresponds to a predetermined opening (fast idle setting) of the throttle butterfly.

To start from cold at low temperatures, pull the strangler control fully out to allow the lever to pass to the locking position corresponding to the complete closure of the choke and to increase the tension of the spring on the choke butterfly as well as to permit the throttle butterfly to take the fast idle position.

Dependent upon the ambient temperature, after the engine has been running for a few minutes, progressively push in the choke control to an intermediate position.

In this new position, the tension of the spring on the choke decreases allowing the choke butterfly to open under the effect of the depression, the throttle butterfly remaining slightly open.

The rich mixture supplied by the carburetter in these conditions is to ensure the starting of the engine and provides for a fast idle which prevents the engine stalling before it has reached normal working temperatures.

When the engine has become sufficiently warm, the strangler control should be pushed fully home.

In this position (second locating position) the choke is fully open and the throttle butterfly is in the normal idling position, the starting device is therefore completely inoperative.

When starting with a warm engine, close the strangler only slightly.

When starting with a hot engine, do not use the strangler.

Slow-running. The engine is supplied with fuel for slow-running by the pilot jet (g). Emulsyfying air is supplied by two calibrated holes, the one (u^1) is located in the air intake of the carburetter, the other (u^2) located in the waist of the choke tube. The slow-running screw allows variation of the idling speed. The volume control screw (W) enables the idling mixture strength to be adjusted precisely for all engine operating conditions.

Normal running. For normal running, fuel is supplied by the main jet (Gg), screwed obliquely in the lower part of the float chamber, and air by the calibrated choke tube (K).

The automatic correction of the mixture is effected by air entering via the calibrated correction jet in (a). The emulsion tube (s) is integral with the float chamber.

Accelerator pump. The accelerator pump injects a quantity of fuel at the time of acceleration in the following manner: With the throttle butterfly closed and in the slow-running position, the membrane (M) is held in place by a spring, thus allowing the pump chamber to become charged. The membrane (M) is connected to the accelerator by a control system linked to the throttle spindle. Immediately the throttle opens, the movement of the spindle causes instantaneous displacement of the membrane (M), thus causing the fuel in the pump chamber to be discharged into the choke tube via the calibrated injector (i).

An exploded drawing showing component parts of the carburetter is given in **FIG 2:12**.

2:8 Routine maintenance and slow-running adjustment

The only regular checks which need to be carried out to the carburetter are to ensure that the jets are secure in their seats and that gaskets are in good condition. This is particularly important in the case of the inlet needle valve as a loose valve will cause flooding of the float chamber.

Occasionally unscrew the five cover retaining screws, remove the float chamber and wash out all sediment with clean fuel. Blow through the jets with a tyre pump, never use wire or probe. Clean fuel inlet filter gauze if fitted.

Slow-running adjustment:

Refer to the appropriate illustration to ascertain the positions of the volume control and slow-running throttle screws.

1 The engine must be at full operating temperature before attempting to carry out any adjustment.

2 Screw in the throttle adjusting screw until the engine is running at a very fast tickover.

3 Screw the volume adjusting screw slowly in or out until the engine runs at its most evenly without any tendency to 'hunt' or to run in a lumpy manner.

4 Now screw out the throttle adjusting screw until the desired tickover (see **Technical Data**) is attained and readjust the volume control screw for even running.

Do not attempt to obtain too low an idling speed as modern engines perform best with a slightly fast idling speed. Remember that uneven idling may not necessarily be due to the carburetter being out of adjustment but may

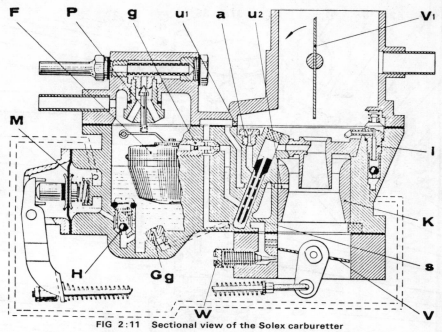

FIG 2:11   Sectional view of the Solex carburetter

Key to Fig 2:11   **a** Correction jet   **F** Float   **Gg** Main jet   **g** Pilot jet   **H** Pump inlet valve   **i** Pump injector
K Choke tube   **M** Pump membrane   **P** Needle valve with spring   **s** Emulsion tube   **u¹** Calibrated orifice   **u²** Calibrated orifice
V Throttle   **V¹** Strangler   **W** Volume control screw

be the result of incorrect valve clearances, wrong spark plug or contact breaker gaps.

The following specific points are emphasized.

Never alter the setting of the fuel inlet needle valve by adding or removing washers. Never dismantle the emulsion block. The fast idle rods are all preset at the time of manufacture and should not be altered.

2:9 Removing, dismantling and reassembling the carburetter

(a) Removal:

1 Remove the air filter.
2 Remove the fuel inlet pipe from the carburetter.
3 Detach the accelerator rod ball joint.
4 Detach the choke control cable.
5 Remove the oil mist breather tube.
6 Unscrew the two carburetter flange retaining bolts and withdraw the carburetter.

Reference to **FIG 2:13** will indicate most of the foregoing attachment points.

(b) Dismantling:

1 Remove the carburetter cover retaining screws and withdraw the cover. Avoid damage to the cover gasket.
2 Remove the float lever and spindle, noting the method of fitting then withdraw the float.
3 Unscrew the needle valve from the cover, noting the number and sequence of any washers.
4 Unscrew and detach external butterfly levers, interconnecting rods and remove springs and washers.

It cannot be too strongly emphasized that sketches and measurements should be made before dismantling to ensure exact replacement of component parts and accurate re-instatement of original settings on reassembly.

5 The throttle and strangler butterflies may be removed from their spindles but only if essential. The butterfly to spindle retaining screws should be a binding fit and too frequent removal may spoil their self-locking action.
6 Unscrew the jets using screwdrivers of appropriate individual size to avoid burring them.
7 Examine all component parts for wear. Jets may be renewed after a considerable mileage but if the throttle butterfly is worn or its spindle or bushes then an exchange carburetter should be obtained. Wear in these components will badly affect even slow-running.

(c) Reassembly:

This is largely a reversal of dismantling procedure. Ensure that all jets together with any washers are screwed into their seats securely. Use new gaskets if suspect both for cover and flange.

Never clean jets with wire, only use a tyre pump. Check their sizes are correct by reference to **Technical Data**.

2:10 Air filter maintenance

Remove the top cover by unscrewing the central nut and lifting the cover away. Renew the paper element in accordance with recommendations contained in the

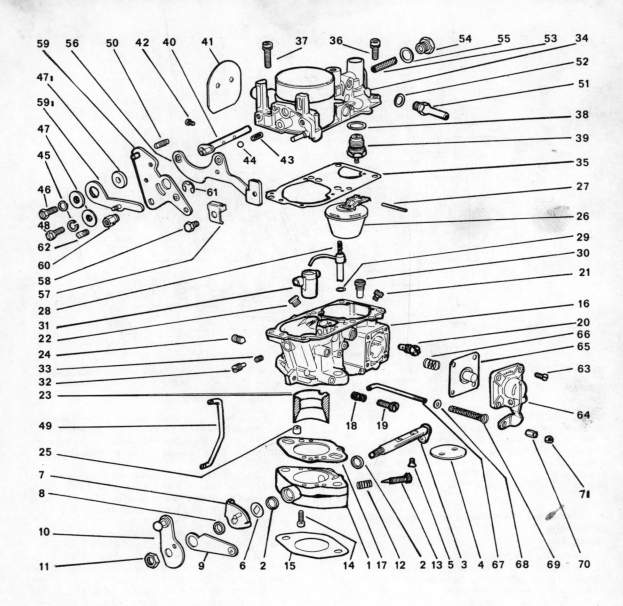

FIG 2:12 Exploded view of the Solex carburetter

Key to Fig 2:12   1 Body   2 Dust proofing   3 Throttle spindle with pump lever   4 Throttle   5 Throttle fixing screw
6 Throttle spindle washer   7 Abutment lever   8 Lever ring   9 Intermediate lever   10 Throttle lever
11 Throttle spindle end nut   12 Spring   13 Volume control screw   14 Throttle chamber fixing screw   15 Flange washer
16 Float chamber   17 Washer for throttle chamber   18 Spring   19 Slow-running adjustment screw   20 Pilot jet
21 Main jet   22 Correction jet   23 Choke tube   24 Choke tube fixing screw   25 Choke tube locating plug   26 Float
27 Float toggle spindle   28 Calibrated pump injector with spring   29 Washer   30 Non-return valve complete
31 Spraying nozzle   32 Spraying nozzle fixing screw   33 Spring   34 Float chamber cover   35 Float chamber cover gasket
36 Float chamber assembly screw   37 Float chamber assembly screw   38 Needle valve washer   39 Needle valve
40 Strangler spindle with strangler lever   41 Strangler shutter   42 Strangler fixing screw   43 Starter valve locating ball spring
44 Starter valve locating ball   45 Spring washer   46 Screw   47 Lever ring   47a Cross-piece   48 Screw
49 Connecting rod   50 Spring   51 Petrol union   52 Washer for petrol union   53 Filter gauze   54 Filter plug
55 Filter plug washer   59a Strangler intermediate lever   56 Bowden cable bracket   57 Starter cable clamp   58 Screw
59 Cam lever assembly   60 Swivel   61 Truarc ring   62 Strangler cable locking screw   63 Pump assembly fixing screw
64 Pump cover complete   65 Pump diaphragm complete   66 Pump diaphragm spring   67 Pump control rod
68 Pump control rod retaining washer   69 Pump control rod spring   70 Pump control rod adjustment nut   71 Adjustment nut locknut

owner's handbook. Renew more frequently in dusty conditions. A choked air filter element will cause increased fuel consumption and rich running.

Always check the condition of washers, collars and hoses connected or forming component parts of the air filter. Keep clips tight and renew any perished rubber parts.

2:11 Solex carburetter, 1108 cc engines

This is a similar carburetter in operating principles to that described in **Section 2:7**. The types 32 EISA and 32 SEIA have been designed and adjusted at the factory with a view to reducing air pollution as much as possible.

The throttle screw (1 in **FIG 2:14**) and the adjusting screw 2, which controls the initial throttle opening in the cold start position, are set at the factory and must not be moved. For these reasons the different parts of the carburetter body are not supplied separately, but only the complete preset body.

A list of the jet and choke sizes will be found in **Technical Data** at the end of this book and their positions are clearly shown in the cut open view of **FIG 2:15**.

Slow-running adjustment:

This is not controlled by a device to regulate the amount of throttle opening when idling, but by an air screw **A** in **FIG 2:16**, acting directly on the airflow by means of internal passages.

The fuel screw **B** is used to regulate the air/fuel mixture, and it is important to carry out this operation with great care so as to reduce the emission of carbon monoxide to a minimum.

Start up the engine and by means of the air screw **A** obtain the correct idling speed which is 725 rev/min ± 50.

Turn the fuel screw **B** until the engine speed increases and then bring the speed back to 725 by using the air screw again.

Repeat these operations until the highest possible engine speed obtained when turning the fuel screw **B** lies between 675 and 775 rev/min.

Screw in **B** in order to slightly weaken the mixture and reduce the idling speed by 20 to 25 rev/min without affecting the smoothness of the engine running.

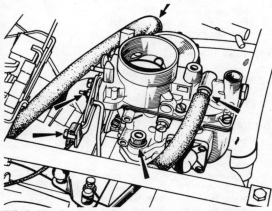

FIG 2:13 Disconnection points for carburetter removal

Check that the engine speed still lies within the specified limits.

Removing the carburetter:

Disconnect the battery and remove the air cleaner.

Disconnect the choke cable, vacuum pipe, oil fume ventilation hose, the accelerator link arm and the fuel supply pipe.

Clamp the water heating hoses at the bottom of the carburetter and disconnect them.

Remove the two securing nuts and lift off the carburetter.

When refitting reverse the above procedure and check the level in the cooling system.

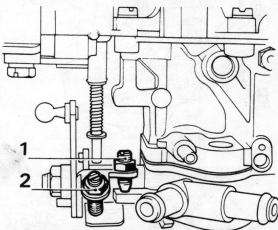

FIG 2:14 Showing position of throttle screw 1 and throttle cold start setting screws 2. These controls must not be disturbed

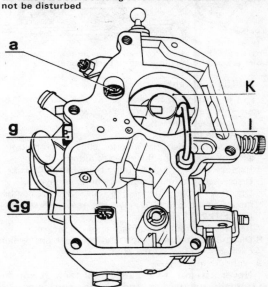

FIG 2:15 View of 32 EISA.2 carburetter showing jet locations
Key to Fig 2:15   **a** Air compensator jet   **g** Idling jet
Gg Main jet   **I** Accelerator pump   **K** Choke tube

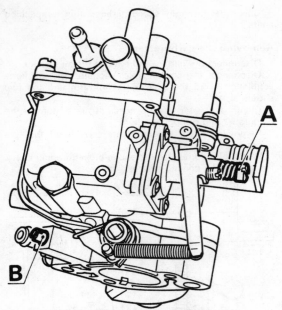

FIG 2:16 Adjusting the idling speed
Key to Fig 2:16   A Air screw   **B** Mixture control screw

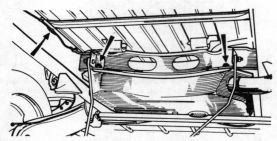

FIG 2:17 Fuel tank to rear crossmember securing bolts (two) and fuel line union, early models

2:12 The fuel tank

This is situated at the rear of the car and it may be removed for repair or renewal as follows:

1 Remove the spare wheel.
2 Empty the fuel tank.
3 Unscrew the filler hose clip, the clips which hold the air vent pipe and the filler pipe securing bolt.
4 Remove the two tank securing bolts (see **FIG 2:17**).
5 Disconnect the fuel gauge wire at its connector.
6 Unscrew on early models the four rear crossmember mounting bolts and remove the rear crossmember (see **FIG 2:18**).
7 Remove the front mounting bolt of the fuel tank.
8 Disconnect the vent pipe and the fuel line which connects the tank to the pump.
9 Withdraw the tank.

Never attempt to repair a fuel tank. It can be extremely dangerous and is, in any event, a specialists' job.

Replacement is largely a reversal of dismantling, but the following points are emphasized.

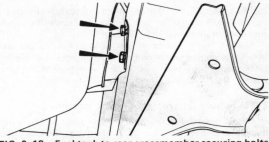

FIG 2:18 Fuel tank to rear crossmember securing bolts (two of four shown)

1 Place sealing compound between the rear crossmember and body side on early models.
2 Fit rubber spacers between the fuel tank and the securing lugs, the tank and the rear crossmember on early models and the filler tube and its securing bracket.

2:13 Fault diagnosis

(a) Leakage or insufficient fuel delivered

1 Air vent pipe in tank restricted
2 Fuel pipes blocked
3 Air leaks at pipe connections
4 Pump or carburetter filters blocked
5 Pump gaskets faulty
6 Pump diaphragm defective
7 Pump valves sticking or seating badly
8 Fuel vapourizing in pipelines due to heat

(b) Excessive fuel consumption

1 Carburetter needs adjusting
2 Fuel leakage
3 Sticking controls or choke device
4 Dirty air cleaners
5 Excessive engine temperature
6 Brakes binding
7 Tyres under-inflated
8 Idling speed too high
9 Car overloaded

(c) Idling speed too high

1 Rich fuel mixture
2 Carburetter controls sticking
3 Slow-running screws incorrectly adjusted
4 Worn carburetter butterfly valve

(d) Noisy fuel pump

1 Loose mountings
2 Air leaks on suction side and at diaphragm
3 Obstruction in fuel pipe
4 Clogged pump filter

(e) No fuel delivery

1 Float needle stuck
2 Vent pipe in tank blocked
3 Pipeline obstructed
4 Pump diaphragm stiff or damaged
5 Inlet valve in pump stuck open
6 Bad air leak on suction side of pump
7 Electrical connections to pump faulty
8 Pump contact points dirty

CHAPTER 3

IGNITION SYSTEM

3:1 Operating principle

The ignition system comprises a coil and distributor, the latter being driven by a shaft geared to the camshaft as previously described in **Chapter 1.**

Both the coil and the distributor are mounted on the righthand side of the engine and may be either SEV or Ducellier. Type and identification numbers will be found in **Technical Data**. The SEV distributor is the more widely used and that will be described in detail, but most of the following instructions will apply to both types (see **FIG 3:1**).

Mechanical advance:

The ignition spark must occur at the correct time with sufficient intensity to ignite the compressed fuel/air mixture. As the engine speed increases, the spark must occur earlier to provide a longer period for the fuel/air mixture to ignite, burn and apply its power at the beginning of the power stroke. This varying spark timing relative to engine speed is controlled by the centrifugal advance mechanism of the distributor. No vacuum advance unit is fitted to the 850 cc but one is fitted to the 1100 cc distributor. Depression in the manifold operates the vacuum unit, the suction varying with engine load. At small throttle openings, with no load on the engine, there is a high degree of vacuum in the manifold causing the vacuum unit to advance the ignition. When hill-climbing on large throttle openings, the much reduced vacuum

ensures that the unit will retard the ignition. The firing order is 1, 3, 4, 2.

An exploded drawing of the distributor is shown in **FIG 3:2** (850 cc).

3:2 Maintenance and adjustment

(a) Adjusting the contact points

1 Take off the distributor cap by removing the two retaining clips, remove the rotor arm and turn the engine until the contact breaker heel is on the highest point of the cam.

It will be found easier to turn the engine smoothly if the spark plugs are first removed.

2 See **FIG 3:3** and slacken the screw 1, insert the blade of a screwdriver into the slots and twist the screwdriver to adjust the gap 'E' between the contact breaker points which should be between .016 and .020 inch (.4 to .5 mm).

When the gap is correct, the feeler blade should just fall by its own weight.

3 Tighten the locking screw 1, recheck the gap.

4 Put two drops of engine oil on the central felt pad and put a trace of petroleum jelly on the cam high spots.

5 Replace the rotor and cap.

(b) Grinding or replacing the contact breaker points, see FIG 3:2:

1 Should the contact breaker points become badly pitted or burned, clean them by removing the nut

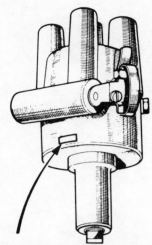

FIG 3:1 Location of the distributor identification plate

and insulating sleeve then lift the cable from the terminal pillar.

2 Lift the spring contact from the pivot after slipping off the retaining circlip. Take out the lockscrew and lift off the fixed contact.

3 Rub the points on an oilstone until all trace of pitting or pips has been removed, keeping them true and square during the process.

4 Clean the points with petrol and replace in reverse order to dismantling.

5 Adjust the contact breaker gap as previously described. Should the points have worn thin by repeated grinding, then they should be renewed.

(c) Routine care, see FIG 3:2:

1 Occasionally check the tightness of the baseplate retaining screws and the capacitor retaining screws. Looseness of these screws can cause pitting of the contact breaker points.

2 Check the condition of the distributor cap centre carbon brush and ensure that it is free on its holder.

3 Keep the inner and outer surfaces of the distributor cap clean and dry and all HT connections tight.

4 Occasionally apply oil to the centre cam felt pad 12 through the holes in the base plate (to lubricate the centrifugal advance mechanism) and apply a little petroleum jelly to the high points of the cam.

3:3 Removing and dismantling the distributor

1 Disconnect the high- and low-tension cables from the distributor and release the high-tension cables from the spark plugs.

2 Unscrew the nut securing the clamp plate of the distributor to the cylinder block and lift the distributor from the engine.

3 Remove the distributor cap and rotor arm, take out the two base plate screws and remove the contact breaker assembly and base plate complete. Do not loosen the clamp plate unless it is intended to retime the ignition.

4 See FIG 3:2 and remove the retaining circlips and the cam 6 and the flat washer.

5 Carefully remove the restraining springs 10 from the counter weights 11 and withdraw the weights.

6 Withdraw the lower circlip 14 from the shaft and remove it in an upward direction, removing the three flat washers and noting their positions.

7 Check all component parts and bushes for wear. Although end float may be rectified by the renewal of the flat washers and small internal components may similarly be renewed, should wear be apparent in the graphite bushes, then they should be renewed by a service station having the appropriate equipment or consideration given to obtaining a factory exchange unit.

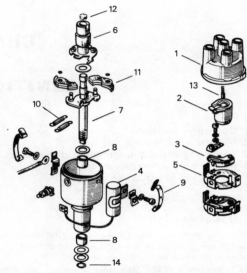

FIG 3:2 Exploded view of the distributor

Key to Fig 3:2
1 Distributor cap   2 Rotor
3 Contact breaker arms and points   4 Capacitor (condenser)
5 Contact breaker plate assembly   6 Cam   7 Drive shaft
8 Bearing bushes   9 Retaining clips   10 Weight restraining springs   11 Governor weights   12 Felt pad
13 Carbon contact brush   14 Circlip shaft

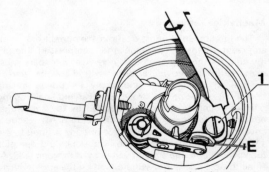

FIG 3:3 Adjusting the contact breaker gap

Key to Fig 3:3   E Gap .016 to .020 inch (.4 to .5 mm)
1 Locking screw

3 : 4 Reassembly and replacement

1 This is a reversal of the dismantling procedure and particular care should be given to the correct sequence replacement of washers as illustrated in **FIG 3 : 2**.
2 Set the points to the correct gap as previously described, replace the rotor and cap.
3 The distributor complete with clamp plate may now be pushed into the distributor pedestal. The driving gear consists of large and small segments and when engagement of the distributor head has been made, the ignition timing should automatically be correct, provided the clamp plate has not been disturbed.
4 Secure the clamp plate to the cylinder block and connect the LT and HT leads to coil and plugs.

3 : 5 Timing the ignition

In the event of the clamp plate having been loosened or the timing otherwise disturbed, proceed as follows:

Turn the engine until the mark on the flywheel is in line with the pointer as observed through the inspection hole (see **FIG 3 : 4**).

Check that the rotor arm is pointing to the segment in the cap for No. 1 cylinder.

Loosen the distributor clamp and retard the distributor by turning it slightly clockwise.

Connect a 12-volt test bulb between the LT terminal and earth. Switch on the ignition.

Slowly turn the distributor in an anticlockwise direction until the bulb just lights up. This indicates that the points have broken and the clamp should be secured.

Give the engine two more turns and check that the setting is correct.

A further slight adjustment may be found desirable after a road test, depending on engine condition and the grade of fuel used.

3 : 6 High-tension cables, coil and capacitor

The HT cables should be kept clean by wiping them periodically with a petrol soaked cloth. Ensure that the connections at both the distributor cap and spark plug ends are secure. Note carefully the fitting order of the spark plug leads before removing.

Failure of the coil and capacitor can cause a great deal of time wasting and the following guide will help to reduce the time taken to diagnose an ignition fault.

Whilst it is too complicated to carry out a coil test by standard test circuit, the best method to test the efficiency of a coil is by substitution.

Although a coil will operate quite well with the low-tension cables incorrectly connected as much as 60 per cent sparking efficiency may be lost if the connections have been wrongly made. Correct connections are coil negative terminal to distributor for negative earth electrical system.

The capacitor:

A short-circuit, resulting from the breakdown of the dielectric between the electrodes of the capacitor, which is in parallel connected across the contact breaker points, will prevent the interruption of the low-tension circuit and cause ignition failure.

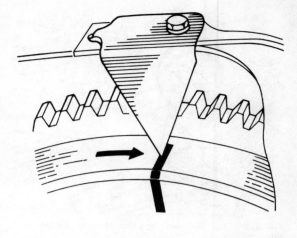

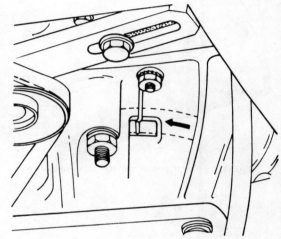

FIG 3 : 4   The ignition timing marks

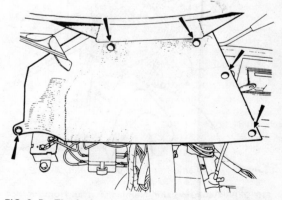

FIG 3 : 5   The facia panel lower protective panel fixings

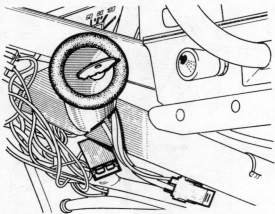

FIG 3:6 The 'Neiman' ignition-starter switch and junction box

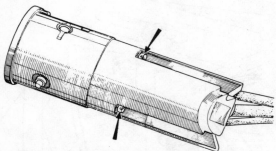

FIG 3:7 The 'Neiman' switch securing screws

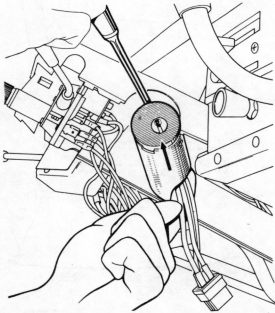

FIG 3:8 Releasing the 'Neiman' switch from its location

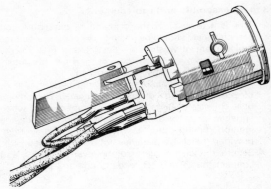

FIG 3:9 'Neiman' switch and locking fork mechanism exposed

An open circuit in the capacitor may be suspected when the points are excessively burnt and difficult starting is experienced. The capacitor is fitted to the exterior of the distributor and in the event of failure, it should be renewed.

3:7 The spark plugs

Every 6000 miles, clean and adjust the spark plugs to .025 inch gap. A plug cleaning machine is preferable but a wire brush is a good alternative.

When adjusting the gap, never bend the centre electrode but always the outer one. Keep the insulator clean and do not overtighten the plug when fitting to the cylinder head.

Every 12,000 miles fit a new set of the type recommended in **Technical Data**. It pays to check the type recommended at the time of purchase as in the light of plug development and operating experience, makers' spark plug specifications change from time to time.

A good indication of engine tune and condition can be obtained from inspecting the plugs and by making reference to the following guide.

Oil-fouled:

Wet oily deposit—causing misfiring and bad starting—results from worn or incorrectly assembled piston rings, worn valves and guides, or worn bearings.

Carbon-fouled:

Dry sooty black deposits—caused by sticking choke, carburetter float level too high, clogged air cleaner, faulty breaker points, weak coil or capacitor, plug too cold for slow stop and go driving.

Worn out:

Insulator pitted and electrodes eroded—causing inferior engine performance and high fuel consumption.

Burned electrodes:

Blistered insulator and eroded electrodes, indicating that the plug is running too hot—caused by excessive knocking, ignition too far advanced, defective cooling system, lean air/fuel mixture, sticking valves.

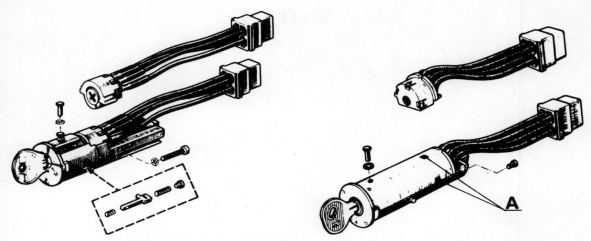

FIG 3:10   Renewing Neiman (left) or LMP (right) ignition switches

Normal:

Any deposits should be powdery and brown to greyish tan in colour, there may also be slight erosion of the electrodes. This condition indicates proper heat range and mixed periods of high and low speed driving.

3:8 The ignition and starter switch ('Neiman' type)

The 'Neiman' switch has five positions:

Stop—accessories—parking—ignition—starting.

The 'Accessories' position is for supplementary electrical accessories (radio), and the feed is taken from the spare terminal in the 'Neiman' switch junction box.

(a) Removal:

1 Disconnect the battery.
2 Remove the bottom protective panel (see **FIG 3:5**).
3 Turn the key to the 'Garage' position and withdraw the key.
4 Disconnect the junction box (see **FIG 3:6**).
5 Unscrew the switch securing screws (see **FIG 3:7**) to expose the locking fork.
6 Press on retaining catch with a scriber and press the switch from the rear in a forward direction as arrowed in **FIG 3:8**. Withdraw the switch.

(b) Refitting:

Carry out the removal operations in reverse.

Renewing switch:

1 Remove the switch and turn the key to the 'stop' position.

2 Remove the key to free the locking tumbler.
3 Remove the two retaining screws.
4 Press in the catches, shown at 'A' on the LMP switch (see **FIG 3:10**).
5 Slide the catch to the rear and withdraw

3:9 Fault diagnosis

(a) Engine will not fire

1 Battery discharged
2 Distributor points dirty, pitted or out of adjustment
3 Distributor cap dirty
4 Carbon brush inside distributor cap not in contact with rotor
5 Faulty cable or loose connection in low-tension circuit
6 Distributor rotor arm cracked
7 Faulty coil
8 Broken contact breaker spring
9 Contact points stuck open
10 Ignition/starter switch faulty

(b) Engine misfires

1 Check 2, 3, 5 and 7 in (a)
2 Weak contact breaker spring
3 High-tension plug and coil leads cracked or perished
4 Spark plug loose
5 Spark plug insulation cracked
6 Spark plug gap incorrect
7 Ignition timing too far advanced
8 Faulty capacitor

NOTES

CHAPTER 4

COOLING SYSTEM

4:1 Principle of the system

The system is of the pressurized 'no loss' sealed-type comprising a radiator where the thermo-siphon action is assisted by a water pump driven by a V-belt. A thermostat is fitted to prevent water circulation until engine operating temperature has been reached. Cooling is assisted by fan blades fitted to the water pump shaft.

A glass overflow reservoir collects excess coolant from the radiator as the coolant in the system expands with heat. The depression created as the system cools, causes the coolant to flow back from the reservoir into the radiator. The fluid level in the reservoir should be maintained as described in the next section. The normal operating temperature of the engine is 183°F (84°C) and the capacity of the system is approximately 10 pints.

4:2 Routine maintenance

It is important to keep all hose clips tight and occasionally inspect the hoses (both engine and heater) for signs of hardening or deterioration and renew if necessary.

The coolant should be maintained at the correct level (which is indicated on the glass expansion chamber by a maximum level mark) with a 40 per cent solution of good quality antifreeze (see **FIG 4:1**).

The expansion chamber may be removed as follows:
1 Pinch the radiator to chamber hose flat with a suitable clamp. Disconnect the hose from the chamber end.
2 Unscrew and remove the chamber valve cap.
3 Remove the expansion chamber strap screw.

Refitting is a reversal of dismantling procedure but screw up the chamber strap screw until the spring coils touch and then slack off one turn.

The contents of the cooling system should be drained and fresh antifreeze solution put in each autumn. (The car was originally filled with a mixture of water, glycol and rust inhibitor 'For Life' but it is unlikely that the original mixture will have been preserved during successive overhauls.)

Special procedure must be followed for draining or filling the system as follows:

(a) Draining:

1 Remove the expansion chamber valve cap.
2 Remove the radiator drain plug. The coolant will first run out slowly, then when it runs out at full flow the expansion chamber has emptied.

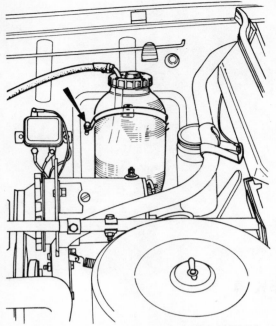

FIG 4:1   The expansion chamber and securing strap

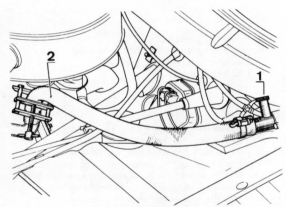

FIG 4:2   The heater bleed screw

Key to Fig 4:2 1 Heater hose 2 Fitted with compression clamp

3 Remove the radiator filler cap.

4 Open the heater bleed valve 1 (see **FIG 4:2**).

5 Set the heater control to 'HOT'.

6 Remove the cylinder block drain plug and thoroughly flush out the system with water, using a hose until the water runs clear.

(b) Filling:

1 Screw in the engine and radiator drain plugs.

2 Set the heater control to 'HOT'.

3 Pour coolant into the expansion chamber until the level is within $1\frac{3}{16}$ inch (30 mm) over the maximum level mark.

4 Fit the expansion chamber valve and screw up the cap.

5 Open the heater bleed screw.

6 Fill the system through the radiator filler cap, extremely slowly.

7 When the radiator is full, pinch the hose 2 (see **FIG 4:2**) by positioning a clamp near to the water pump.

8 Start the engine and run it at a fast tickover, at the same time continuing to fill the radiator.

9 Close the heater bleed screw when air ceases to issue from it. Do not touch it again.

10 Remove the hose clamp.

11 Top up the radiator and fit the radiator filler cap.

12 Switch off the engine after the thermostat opens.

13 Allow the engine to cool completely then check the level of the coolant in the expansion chamber. Add more coolant if required to the maximum level.

Never put cold water into a hot engine and during emptying, refilling or flushing, keep the heater controls to 'ON'. In extreme conditions of corrosion or neglect which might cause a blockage in the radiator core, then the radiator should be removed as described later in this Chapter, a hose fitted into the bottom outlet and the water turned on. This is known as back flushing.

The appearance of oil in the coolant may be indicative of an internal water leak, gasket or cylinder seal failure and either this or the opposite, occurrence of water in the sump oil, should be immediately rectified.

The procedure for filling the cooling system on 1108 cc models is described in **Section 4:6**.

Belt adjustment:

As previously mentioned, two V-belts are used on the engine. Adjustment of the camshaft to water pump belt is effected by moving the belt tensioner. To do this see **FIG 4:3** and loosen the locknut 'A' for 845 cc engines, this may be either right or lefthand thread, a lefthand thread will be indicated by a grooved nut, on 1108 cc engines unscrew the locknut on the adjusting screw. Adjust the tensioner until the belt during its longest run may be pushed on 845 cc engines $\frac{1}{8}$ to $\frac{13}{64}$ inch (3 to 5 mm) and on 1108 cc engines $\frac{1}{8}$ to $\frac{5}{32}$ inch (3 to 4 mm).

Adjustment of the water pump to generator belt is carried out by loosening the strap bolt and moving the generator until the belt can similarly be pushed on 845 cc engines with a DC generator $\frac{15}{64}$ to $\frac{9}{32}$ inch (6 to 7 mm) or with an alternator $\frac{1}{8}$ to $\frac{13}{64}$ inch (3 to 5 mm), on 1108 cc engines $\frac{1}{8}$ to $\frac{5}{32}$ inch (3 to 4 mm).

4:3 Water pump removal and refitting

845 cc engine:

Refer to **FIGS 4:4** and **4:5**.

1 Disconnect the battery.

2 Drain the cooling system as described in the previous section.

3 Disconnect the generator leads and remove the generator complete with its bracket.

4 Disconnect the lead from the temperature gauge transmitter.

5 Remove the gearshift control and radiator tie-rods and ease the radiator forward at the top.

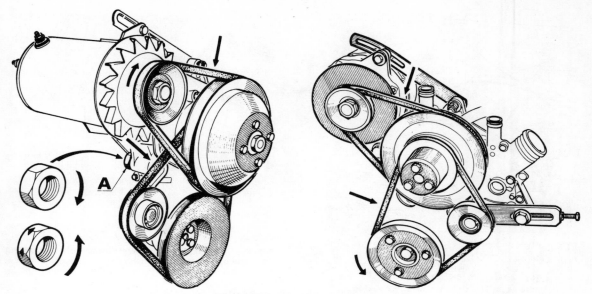

FIG 4:3   The generator fixing and adjustment points

6 Disconnect the water hoses between the radiator and the water pump.

7 Disconnect the heater hoses at their connection with the water pump.

8 Loosen the belt tensioner and remove the inner driving belt (camshaft pulley to water pump), **FIG 4:5**.

9 Unscrew the water pump securing bolts.

10 Loosen the water pump by gently tapping it with a wooden or plastic mallet and then remove it.

11 Clean the gasket faces.

The water pump is not repairable and in the event of servicing being required then the pump should be exchanged for a factory exchange unit.

Refitting the water pump is a reversal of removal operations. Use new gaskets, fitted dry. Fill the system as previously described, adjust the V-belts and run the engine to test for leaks.

1108 cc engine:

1 Disconnect the battery.

2 Drain the cooling system

3 Slacken off and remove the drive belts, turn the engine so that any two bolts of the clutch lie either side of the camshaft pulley to remove the belt.

4 Remove the water pump pulley.

5 Disconnect all hoses.

6 Unscrew the retaining bolt and unstick the pump with a soft hammer. This pump is not repairable.

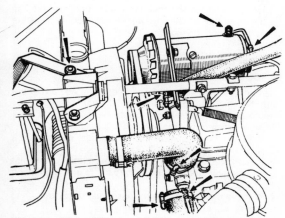

FIG 4:4   Water pump removal disconnection points, 845 cc engine

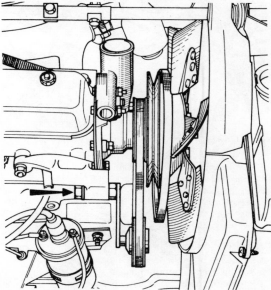

FIG 4:5   Water pump and fan driving belts—removal, 845 cc engine

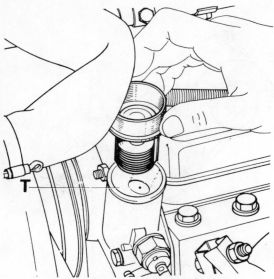

FIG 4:6 The thermostat and housing

4:4 Thermostat removal, testing and replacement

(a) Removal:

1 Drain the cooling system and retain the coolant.
2 Loosen the clips and remove the top water hose which connects the radiator to the vertical outlet of the water pump.
3 The thermostat may now be withdrawn from the water pump housing as shown in FIG 4:6.

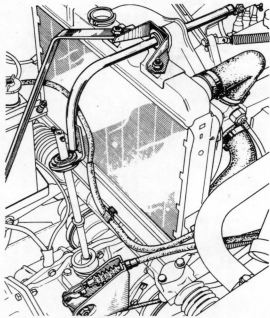

FIG 4:7 The radiator showing upper securing bolts and hose connections, 845 cc engine

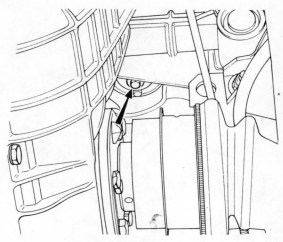

FIG 4:8 The radiator lower securing bolt to steering box (one of two only shown)

(b) Testing

The thermostat is essential to rapid warm up, maximum engine performance and heater efficiency. Although there are bypass facilities, in the event of failure of the thermostat, should this actually happen, then it should be removed until a correct replacement has been obtained.

If the thermostat is suspected to have failed, test it by heating in water together with a thermometer. Note the temperature at which the valve starts to open. It should commence to open within 3°C of the temperature marked on the thermostat flange (see **Technical Data**) and continue to rise to the fully open position (at least $\frac{1}{4}$ inch valve lift).

If the thermostat fails the test, it should be replaced by a new unit.

(c) Replacement:

1 It is essential that the thermostat is fitted in the water pump housing, the correct way round so that the water aperture T shown in FIG 4:6 is not blocked.
2 Having lowered the thermostat into position, replace the hose, tighten the clips and refill the cooling system as described previously.

4:5 Radiator removal

845 cc engine:

Although most servicing operations can be carried out with the radiator in position, the following procedure should be observed when it has to be removed for back flushing, repair or engine removal. Refer to FIG 4:7.

1 Drain the cooling system and retain the coolant.
2 Disconnect the battery.
3 Disconnect the hoses between the water pump and the radiator and the hose leading to the expansion chamber.
4 Remove the two gear control rod assembly bolts and the roll pin on top of the gearlever.
5 Remove the gear control rod support screws on top of the radiator.

6 Remove the radiator stay and the gear control rod support bracket with the gear control rod.

7 Remove the starter cable from the clips on the radiator.

8 Remove the two screws holding the clutch idle lever assembly, and take off the clutch idle lever assembly.

9 Remove the two bolts fixing the bottom of the radiator to the steering box (see **FIG 4 : 8**).

10 Remove the radiator.

Radiator replacement is a reversal of removal procedure, remember to fill the cooling system.

1108 cc engine:

1 Disconnect the battery.

2 Drain the cooling system.

3 Disconnect the radiator hoses.

4 Disconnect the radiator thermostatic switch wires (see **FIG 4 : 10**).

5 Disconnect the cooling fan motor wires at the relay.

6 Unscrew the two radiator securing nuts and remove the radiator.

4:6 Filling the cooling system, 1108 cc models

Close the drain taps on the radiator and engine. Set the heater contol to HOT.

Fill up the expansion bottle to within $1\frac{1}{4}$ inches (30 mm) above the maximum mark and fit the valve and cap.

Refer to **FIG 4 : 9** and open the bleed screws 1 and 2.

Fill the system via the radiator filler and when it is full clamp the hoses 3 and 4 as near to the water pump as possible.

Run the engine at about 1500 rev/min and continue to add water as necessary until the water issuing from the bleed screws is **free from any air**. Close the bleed screws and do not touch them again.

Remove the clamps. Top up the radiator and fit the cap. Wait until the cooling fan motor cuts in, then stop the engine.

When the engine is quite cool check that the level in the expansion bottle is correct.

4:7 Electric fan 1108 cc models

A Mosta thermostatic switch is screwed into the radiator and, depending upon water temperature, switches on or off an electrically driven fan by means of a relay. The switch is designed to cut in at 92°C and switch off when the temperature drops to 82°C.

The installation may be seen in **FIG 4 :10**. No maintenance is required other than seeing that the parts are kept clean and the wiring and connections in good condition.

4:8 Fault diagnosis

(a) Internal water leakage

1 Cracked cylinder liner wall

2 Loose cylinder head nuts

3 Cracked cylinder head

4 Faulty head gasket

5 Cracked tappet chest wall

6 Faulty cylinder liner seals

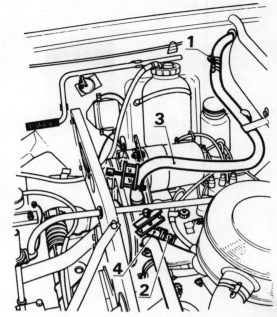

FIG 4 : 9   Filling the system, 1108 cc engines

Key to Fig 4 : 9   1/2 Bleed screws   3/4 Hoses with clamps

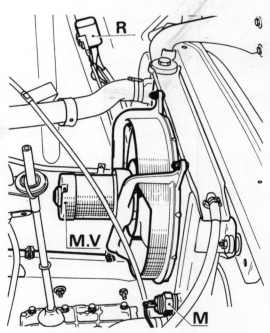

FIG 4 :10   Electric fan installation

Key to Fig 4 :10   **MV** Electric fan motor   **R** Relay
M Thermostatic switch

(b) Poor circulation

1 Radiator core blocked
2 Engine water passages restricted
3 Low water level in expansion tank
4 Loose fan belts
5 Defective thermostat
6 Perished or collapsed radiator hoses

(c) Corrosion

1 Impurities in the water
2 Old antifreeze in system

(d) Overheating

1 Check (b)
2 Sludge in crankcase
3 Faulty ignition timing
4 Low oil level in sump
5 Tight engine
6 Choked exhaust system
7 Binding brakes
8 Slipping clutch
9 Incorrect valve timing
10 Retarded ignition
11 Mixture too weak

CHAPTER 5

CLUTCH

5:1 Construction and operation

A single dry plate type clutch is fitted comprising a friction disc (driven plate) the centre splines of which are resiliently mounted against rotational shock. The pressure plate assembly is of diaphragm spring type to maintain even pressure by the pressure plate on the friction disc which is held against the flywheel face. **FIG 5:1** shows the clutch assembly in section.

The clutch release bearing is of ballbearing type and bears upon the pressure plate assembly. The pressure plate assembly is bolted to the engine flywheel while the friction disc is splined to the gearbox primary shaft.

The clutch type number is stamped on the pressure plate assembly pressed steel cover as shown in **FIG 5:2**.

When the clutch is fully engaged, the diaphragm spring exerts a powerful force on the pressure plate.

This pressure nips the friction disc by means of its linings between the faces of the flywheel and the pressure plate.

When the engine is running, the friction disc is therefore revolving with the flywheel and carries round with it the transmission primary shaft to which it is splined.

To disengage the clutch, a hinged lever connected to the clutch pedal causes the release bearing to bear upon the release plate which in turn moves the pressure plate away from the friction disc and so disconnects the drive. The friction disc and the transmission shaft are then free to revolve or come to a stop without transmitting any drive even though the engine is still rotating.

The withdrawal mechanism consists of a cable connected between the clutch pedal and a gearbox mounted swivel lever thence through a pushrod connected to the clutch withdrawal hinge lever.

In the driving condition (clutch pedal released) when the clutch pedal is released the pushrod and cable are returned to their stop by the assistance of the pedal return spring and the release lever return spring.

5:2 Routine maintenance

The only maintenance required for this type of clutch is to occasionally check and adjust the clutch pedal free movement. This clearance must be maintained to ensure that the clutch fully engages when the pedal is in the released position. Too little free movement may cause

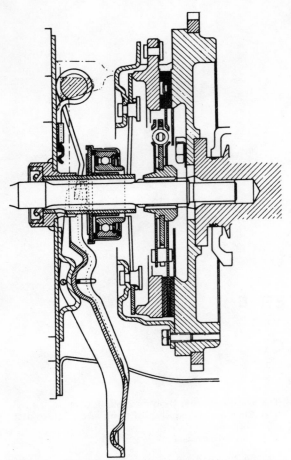

FIG 5:1 Sectional view of the clutch, 845 cc engine with BV.334 gearbox

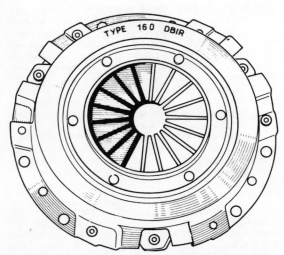

FIG 5:2 Location of clutch type identification number

clutch slip, too much free movement may cause difficulty in disengaging the clutch with consequent poor gear changing.

1 See **FIG 5:3** and loosen locknut 1 at the attachment of the clutch operating rod to the clutch release lever.
2 Screw the adjusting nut 2 in or out to obtain a clearance of $\frac{1}{8}$ to $\frac{5}{32}$ inch (3 to 4 mm) at the outer end of the fork.
3 Tighten the locknut 1.

5:3 Servicing the clutch operating mechanism

(a) Renewing the clutch release bearing:

1 Disconnect the clutch operating rod and remove the gearbox as fully described in **Chapter 6, Section 6:3**.
2 Refer to **FIG 5:4** for the 845 cc and remove the retaining spring 1. The 1108 cc type is shown in **FIG 5:8**. Unhook the springs (arrowed) to free the release bearing.
3 Withdraw the release bearing.
4 Lubricate the new bearing and the lever fork ends with Molykote BR2 grease and fit the bearing onto the gearbox primary shaft.
5 Fit the retaining spring by locating the spring ends into the holes in the support and fork.
6 Replace the gearbox and connect the clutch operating rod. Adjust the clutch free movement as previously described.

Removal or renewal of the clutch release lever (withdrawal fork) may be undertaken if required by carrying out the preceding operations and additionally removing

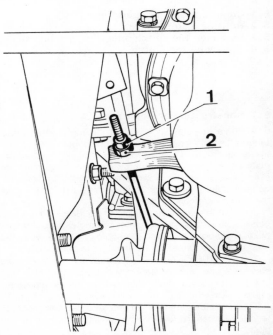

FIG 5:3 The clutch operating rod adjusting nuts (845 cc)

Key to Fig 5:3   1 Locknut   2 Adjusting nut

the spring 2 (see **FIG 5:4**) on 845 cc engines. On 1108 cc engines the fork pins have to be withdrawn with Tool No. Emb.384, and the shaft withdrawn to release the fork and spring (see **FIG 5:8**). When the pins are refitted, they should be inserted until $\frac{1}{32}$ inch (1 mm) of the shank is proud of the fork boss.

(b) Renewing the clutch operating cable:

1 Disconnect the clutch cable at the gearbox mounted swivel lever, and pull out from its securing point as shown in **FIG 5:5**. Other models at the lever. Free the cable from the sleeve stop.
2 Remove the clutch pedal, as detailed later in this Section.
3 Remove the pin from the fork end of the cable.
4 Remove the cable from its securing point on the pedal assembly (see **FIG 5:6**) and withdraw the cable complete.
5 Refitting the new cable is a reversal of the removal operations. Adjust the clutch free movement.

(c) Removing and refitting the clutch pedal

1 Disconnect the clutch cable from the swivel lever on the gearbox (see **FIG 5:5**).
2 Remove the parcel tray.
3 Unhook the brake pedal and clutch pedal return springs.
4 Remove the securing pin holding the pedal pivot pin and pull out the pedal pivot from the lefthand side as shown in **FIG 5:7** for the lefthand drive models, from the righthand side on righthand drive models.
5 Remove the clutch and brake pedals.
6 Disconnect the fork end of the cable from the pedal, and withdraw the pedal.
7 Refitting the pedals is largely a reversal of the removal procedure but make sure that the pedal return springs and washers are correctly located and that the clutch cable fork end fits securely onto the cable.
8 Adjust the clutch free play.

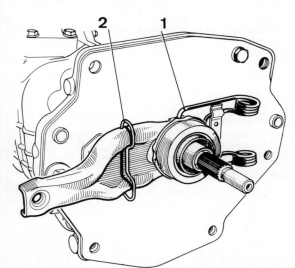

FIG 5:4   The clutch release lever and bearing (845 cc)
Key to Fig 5:4   1 Release bearing return spring
2 Release lever retaining spring

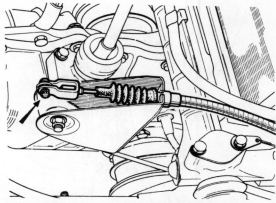

FIG 5:5   The clutch cable to gearbox mounted swivel lever connection, 845 cc engine, lefthand drive

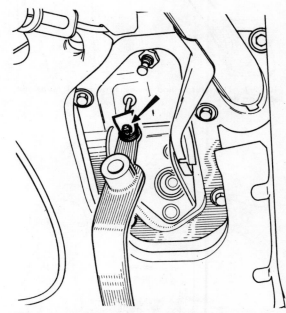

FIG 5:6   The clutch cable to clutch pedal connection

5:4 Removing the clutch

The procedure is fully described in **Chapter 1, Section 1:8**.

5:5 Clutch dismantling and inspection

(a) The friction disc (driven plate):

If, on inspection, the friction disc linings are worn down to or nearly down to the rivets, it should be renewed.

Similarly, oil staining or severe discolouration should be investigated and the reason or source ascertained and again the disc should be renewed. Do not attempt to reline the friction disc yourself.

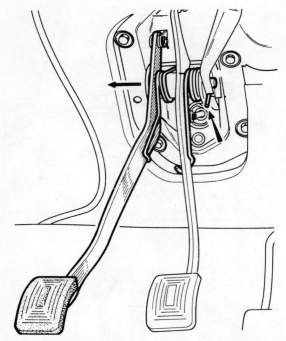

FIG 5:7 The clutch and brake foot pedal pivot pin, lefthand drive

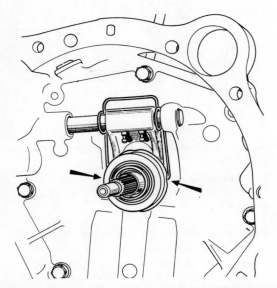

FIG 5:8 The release mechanism of the 160.DBR.260 type clutch (R1181 models)

(b) The pressure plate:

Examination should include checking for broken diaphragm spring segments, distortion and scoring of the release bearing and friction disc bearing surfaces.

Never dismantle a pressure plate, always exchange it for a factory reconditioned unit.

5:6 Clutch reassembly, refitting and friction disc alignment

These operations are fully described in **Chapter 1, Section 1:8.**

5:7 Fault diagnosis

(a) Drag or spin

1 Oil or grease on friction disc (driven plate) linings
2 Bent engine backplate
3 Misalignment between the engine and transmission unit
4 Friction disc hub binding on input shaft splines
5 Binding of input shaft spigot bearing
6 Distorted clutch friction disc
7 Warped or damaged pressure plate or cover assembly
8 Broken friction disc linings
9 Dirt or foreign matter in the clutch
10 Worn operating linkage

(b) Fierceness or snatch

1 Check 1, 2, 3 and 4 in (a)
2 Worn clutch linings

(c) Slip

1 Check 1, 2 and 3 in (a)
2 Check 2 in (b)
3 Weak pressure plate spring diaphragm
4 Seized or binding linkage

(d) Judder

1 Check 1, 2 and 3 in (a)
2 Pressure plate not parallel with flywheel
3 Contact area of friction disc linings not evenly distributed
4 Bent input shaft
5 Buckled friction disc
6 Faulty engine transmission unit rubber mountings

(e) Rattle

1 Check 3 in (c)
2 Worn release mechanism
3 Excessive backlash in transmission and final drive unit
4 Wear in transmission bearings
5 Release bearing loose on its release lever

(f) Tick or knock

1 Worn input shaft spigot or bearings
2 Badly worn splines in friction disc hub
3 Withdrawal lever out of line or bent
4 Faulty starter motor drive
5 Loose flywheel

(g) Friction disc fracture

1 Check 2 and 3 in (a)

CHAPTER 6

GEARBOX AND TRANSMISSION

6:1 Description

Two types of gearbox will be described in this chapter, the early type 334.04 which is fitted to cars with the original 845 cc engine, and the type 354.00 as fitted to those models with the larger 1108 cc engine, and the later version 845 cc.

The construction of both types is similar in that the unit is made up of two cast aluminium half sections, with the crownwheel and pinion final drive and differential unit integral with the gearbox. This combined unit is mounted in front of the engine where it drives the front wheels through two halfshafts. Further details will be found in **Technical Data** at the end of the book.

Both types have four forward speeds and a reverse with synchromesh engagement on all four forward ratios. Change of gear is effected in the conventional manner by shift lever fork which is shown later in this chapter.

The integral transmission assembly comprises two sun wheels, two planet gears, a crownwheel and pinion. The complete assembly is shown in the sectional diagrams of **FIGS 6:1** and **6:2**.

6:2 Routine maintenance

This consists of periodically checking the gearbox bolts for tightness, and draining, checking and topping up the gearbox oil in accordance with the servicing periods recommended in the owners handbook.

The gears are splash lubricated and it is important that the level be maintained up to the filler orifice which also acts as an oil level indicator. Type 334.04 gearboxes have in addition to the filler orifice two drain plugs located underneath the casing as shown in **FIG 6:3**. Type 354.00 boxes have only one drain plug.

Oil of grade EP.80 is recommended, and draining is best carried out after a run when the oil is warm. Oil capacity is $2\frac{1}{4}$ pints for the smaller type and 3 pints for the larger.

6:3 Gearbox/transmission removal, leaving the engine in position in the car

Removal of the complete engine/gearbox unit for later separation is fully described in **Chapter 1, Section 1:3**. Removal of the gearbox/transmission unit alone is carried out as follows:

845 cc engine:

1 Disconnect the battery.
2 Raise the front of the vehicle on stands.
3 Remove the undertray and drain the gearbox, retaining the oil for further use if required.
4 Refer to **FIG 6:4** and remove the two-gear control rod assembly bolts, and separate the two parts.

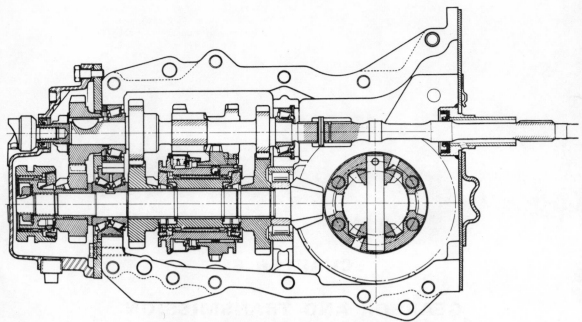

FIG 6:1 Longitudinal section through gearbox/transmission

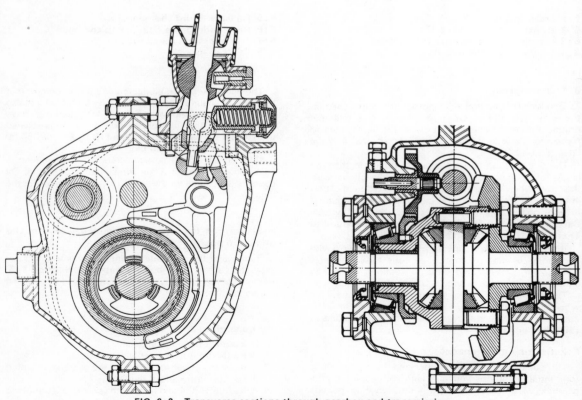

FIG 6:2 Transverse sections through gearbox and transmission

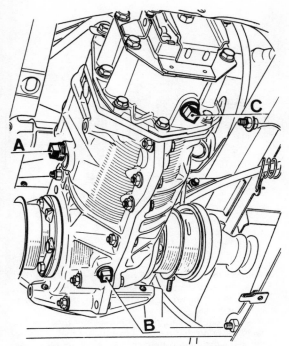

FIG 6:3   Drain and filler plug location

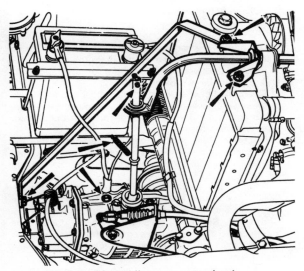

FIG 6:4   Dismantling gear control rod

9 Remove the clutch swivel assembly and disconnect the clutch rod at the fork end.

10 Remove the speedometer cable.

11 Using a suitable drift, knock out the drive shaft rollpins and fit the shaft retaining clips as described and illustrated in **Chapter 1, Section 1 : 3.**

12 Disconnect the steering arms at the steering box end and the upper front suspension ball joints (see **Chapter 1**).

13 Pull out the drive shafts from the differential and replace the nuts on the upper suspension ball joints to hold the stub axles in place.

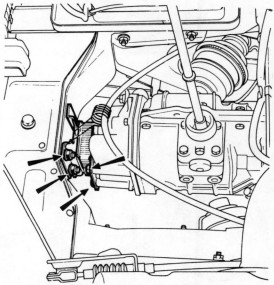

FIG 6:5   Gearbox front mounting

5 Remove the two screws from the gear control rod support bracket on top of the radiator.

6 Remove the radiator stay.

7 Push out the rollpin on top of the gearlever, and remove the front part of the gear control lever.

8 Unhook the gearlever return spring and remove the bolt securing the gearbox earth wire.

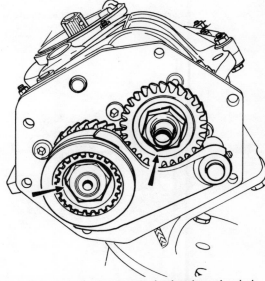

FIG 6:6   Fourth-speed gearwheel and synchro hub

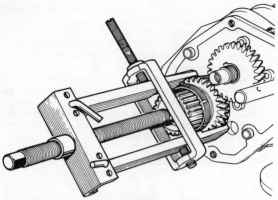

FIG 6:7   Removing fourth-speed synchro hub

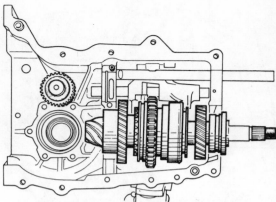

FIG 6:10   Withdrawing the secondary shaft

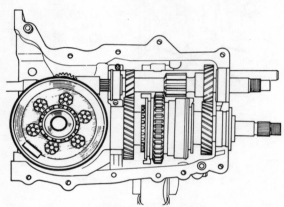

FIG 6:8   Withdrawing the differential assembly

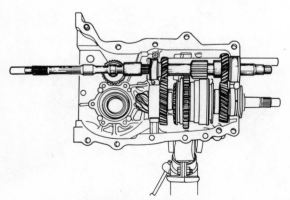

FIG 6:9   Withdrawing the primary shaft

14 Remove the gearbox front mounting (see **FIG 6:5**).
15 Unscrew and remove the sump to gearbox securing bolts (see **Chapter 1**) and those from the gearbox to cylinder block.
16 Using adequate support, withdraw the gearbox forward ensuring that the gearbox primary shaft does not catch the diaphragm spring of the clutch nor the weight of the gearbox be allowed to hang upon the shaft (even momentarily) while it is still in engagement with the splined hub of the friction disc.

1108 cc engines:

Disconnect the battery, support the front of the car on stands, remove the undertray and drain the gearbox.

Remove the two gearshift control rod assembly bolts and separate the two parts.

Select third gear, then lift off the rubber ring at the end of the selector lever on the gearbox, unhook the gearlever return spring and free the control rod from the selector lever and the crossmember.

Disconnect the gearbox earthing cable and free the starter cable from the clip on the steering box. Take out the two bolts from the flexible coupling on the steering column.

Remove the brake calipers without uncoupling the flexible hoses, then disconnect the steering arms at the adjustable end fittings and the upper ball joints. Refer to **Chapter 1**, **Section 1:3** and prepare the drive shafts for removal. Tilt the stub axles so as to free the drive shaft ends from the sun wheels, being careful not to damage the oil seals on the differential adjusting ring nut.

Mark the position of the steering box setting shims, remove the two securing bolts and lift off the steering box.

Disconnect the clutch cable from the operating lever.

Release the locknut and remove the water pump drive belt tensioner bolt. Remove the belt.

Take out three screws securing the camshaft pulley and remove the pulley and the pulley drive plate. Remove the exhaust pipe clamp. Take out the three securing bolts and withdraw the starter as far as possible.

Remove the gearbox front mounting pad and brackets. Disconnect the speedometer cable.

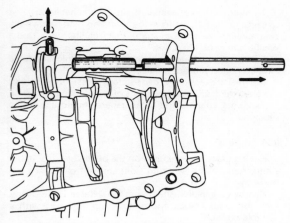

FIG 6:11 Fourth-speed selector rod removal

Remove the five nuts securing the clutch housing to the engine. Lift the front of the gearbox as far as possible. Remove the nuts securing the tubular crossmember, push in the front two bolts and swing the tube round to remove it.

Remove the five bolts securing the side reinforcements and the clutch coverplate.

Lower the front of the gearbox and remove it, taking care not to foul the clutch mechanism.

6:4 Dismantling the gearbox

It must be stressed that in view of the complexity of the operation and the number of special tools required, the complete stripping of the gearbox/transmission unit is not a suitable operation for the owner/driver. The following instructions will enable the home operator to dismantle the unit using such tools as should be available.

334 models:

Remove the gearlever and housing by taking out four bolts. Remove the rear plate (two bolts).

Using a screwdriver select fourth and reverse gears. Unscrew the starter dog and then remove the front cover (eight bolts).

Unlock and unscrew the fourth-speed gear and synchro hub nut (see **FIG 6:6**). Select neutral and push out the pin securing the fourth-speed fork. Mark the position of the sliding gear relative to the hub (these two parts are matched). Remove the fourth-speed sliding gear and fork.

Using a suitable extractor, pull out the synchro hub and fourth-speed gear, noting the friction washer (see **FIG 6:7**).

Remove the fourth-speed gearwheel from the primary shaft. Fit a thrust pad to protect the end of the shaft.

Remove the six Allen headed screws securing the intermediate plate and lift it off. Remove the eleven retaining bolts and separate the two half housings.

It is now possible to lift out the differential, the primary shaft and the secondary shaft, also the speedometer drive pinion (see **FIGS 6:8, 6:9** and **6:10**).

Remove the locking spring plunger from the fourth-speed selector rod and place them on one side (see **FIG 6:11**).

Push out the pin holding the first and reverse, and second and third-speed selector rods. Pull out the selector rod until it is in line with the first and reverse-speed fork (see **FIG 6:12**). Remove the selector rod guide sleeve and the selector rod and forks assembly.

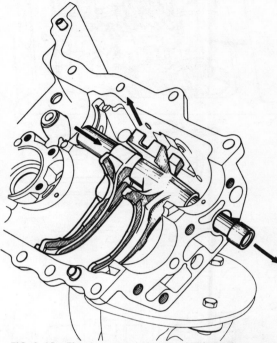

FIG 6:12 First/reverse and second/third selector rod removal

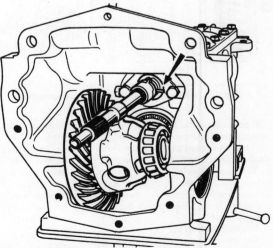

FIG 6:13 Removing clutch shaft and differential, 1108 cc models

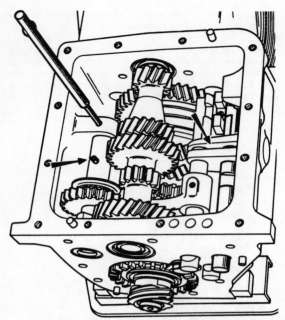

FIG 6:14 Removing reverse gear shaft

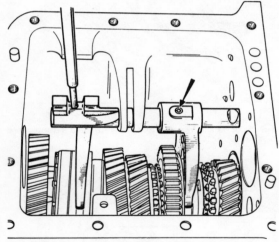

FIG 6:15 Removing the selector fork rollpins

If necessary, the forks may now be removed from the selector rods, but do not lose the balls and springs.

A rollpin is used to secure the clutch shaft to the primary shaft and must be tapped out with a drift to separate them.

The gearwheels on the secondary shaft can be removed for inspection, but note that the second and third-speed hub cannot be separated and the whole assembly must be replaced if any one of the following parts is worn:

Synchro hub or spring
Second-speed gear or moving cone
Final drive bearing or drive pinion
Crownwheel

To remove the reverse shaft cluster it is necessary first to drift out the rollpins from the shaft and then remove the two circlips when the shaft, gear cluster and thrust washers may be lifted out.

Further dismantling is not recommended unless suitable extractors and presses are available.

Clean and examine all parts before reassembly, renewing any which are showing signs of wear or damage. New seals, joints, rollpins and lockwashers should always be renewed.

354 models:

Having placed the gearbox on the bench or in a suitable stand, remove the securing bolts and lift off the clutch housing.

Remove the lockwashers from the differential adjusting ring nuts then unlock and remove the ring nuts with a suitable wrench.

Knock out the retaining spring and rollpin and withdraw the clutch shaft. Remove the differential assembly (see **FIG 6:13**).

Take out the securing bolts and remove the top cover. Then remove the springs, the first/second gear spring plunger and the selector fork shaft locking balls.

Remove the securing bolts and lift off the front cover. Remove the primary shaft adjusting shims. Take out two bolts and remove the retaining plate for the primary shaft rear bearing.

Refer to **FIG 6:14** and knock out the two pins holding the reverse gear pinion shaft. Remove the reverse gear selector shaft and the locking disc between the selector shafts.

Select second gear and with a suitable spanner unscrew the speedometer drive bolt and remove the rubber washer. Select neutral and push the final drive pinion towards the differential and remove the taper roller bearings. Take out the final drive pinion.

Push the primary shaft towards the differential to free the rear bearing cage. Lift out the primary shaft and also the reverse gear and shaft.

Punch out the first/second and third/fourth selector fork pins as shown in **FIG 6:15** and remove the selector forks and shafts.

Remove the lockplate for the secondary shaft bearing adjusting nut and unscrew the nut. Remove the fourth-speed gear thrust washer and push out the primary shaft front bearing cage.

Lift the gear and synchro cluster out of the gearbox casing.

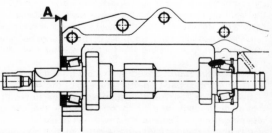

FIG 6:16 Primary shaft end play. The last shim should project .004 inch (.1 mm) beyond the gasket face of the casing at **A**

6:5 Reassembling the gearbox

334 models:

As mentioned earlier, dismantling of the differential assembly is not normally a job to be undertaken at home so rebuilding will commence with the installation of the primary shaft.

Fit the bearings on the shaft and the positioning washer. Fit the shaft into the righthand half housing. Fit the right-hand half housing and secure it in place by several bolts. Use the shims removed during dismantling with the thinnest of the shims on the bearing side.

The primary shaft should have an end play of .001 to .005 inch (.02 to .12 mm) and the last shim fitted should project by .004 inch (.10 mm) above the gasket face of the housing as shown in **FIG 6:16**. If this dimension is not obtainable, add or remove shims as necessary. Shims are available in seven different thicknesses from .004 to .118 inch (.10 to 3.0 mm).

When the correct adjustment has been obtained, remove the righthand half housing and the primary shaft. Fit the clutch shaft to the primary shaft and fit the key.

Assemble the secondary shaft by first fitting the spring onto the second and third sliding gear, with the larger end of the spring towards the selector fork groove and the locking end (3 in **FIG 6:17**) in the slot.

Fit the synchro sleeve on to the second/third sliding gear (largest end towards the selector fork groove) and fit the other locking end of the spring 4 into the hole in the sleeve.

Turn the sleeve clockwise until the two ends of the spring are opposite to one another as shown, then slide the synchro sleeve onto the sliding gear teeth.

Hold the assembly in this position and slide the synchro sleeve outer cage over the assembly. The outer cage will have to be pressed onto and crimped to the sliding gear-wheel and a bench press will be necessary for this (see **FIG 6:18**).

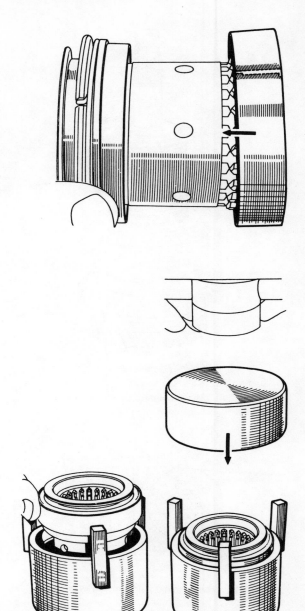

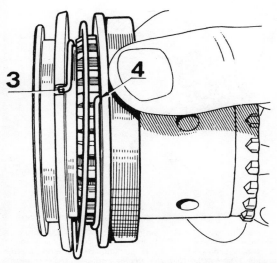

FIG 6:17   Second/third gear and synchro hub assembly

FIG 6:18   Crimping the second/third synchronizer outer cage

Fit onto the sliding gear the six balls and the first-speed gearwheel with the selector fork groove towards the final drive pinion. Fit the assembly on to the hub and then fit the third-speed gear and its ring and the double taper roller bearing as shown in **FIG 6:19**.

Fit the selector forks onto their shaft, not forgetting the locking balls. Fit the selector shaft and fork assembly into

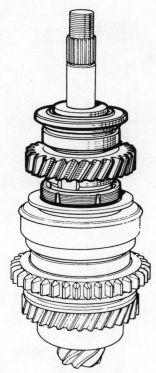

FIG 6:19   The secondary shaft assembled

Smear the joint faces with compound and fit the right-hand half housing, fit but do not tighten the bolts.

Fit the primary shaft shims with the thinnest on the bearing side. Fit the intermediate plate and gasket with a smear of jointing compound. Fit the screws in position and tighten to 15 lb ft noting that the two 7 mm screws are at the top.

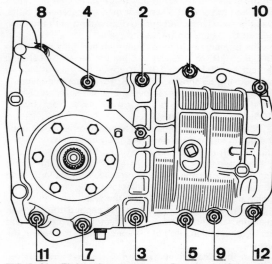

FIG 6:21   Tightening sequence for the half housing securing nuts

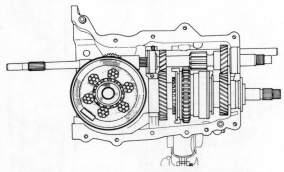

FIG 6:20   The lefthand half housing assembled

the case. Fit the shaft guide sleeve, then push the shaft in as far as possible and lock it with the rollpin. Secure the pin with its plug and sealing compound.

Fit the fourth-speed selector shaft also the ball, spring and plunger.

Fit the reverse gear cluster, observing that the relieved sides of the thrust washer are towards the gears. Push in the shaft and lock it with a flush fitting rollpin. Fit the two circlips.

Refer to **FIG 6:20**. Fit the following into the lefthand half housing: speedometer drive pinion, primary shaft, the secondary shaft with the hole in the roller bearing outer track ring opposite the lip in the housing and the differential.

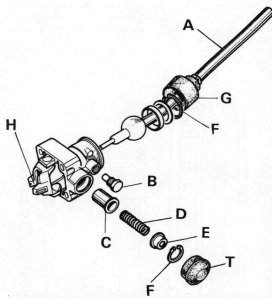

FIG 6:22   Components of the gear selector lever

Key to Fig 6:22   A Lever and washers   **B** Locking bolt
C Damper guide   **D** Spring   **E** Cup   **F** Circlips
G Rubber bellows   **H** Locking latch with two plastic
guides. (The smaller spigot on the lock opposite the damper)
T Cap

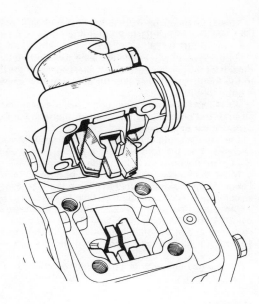

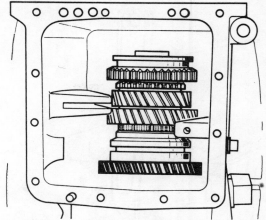

FIG 6:24 Showing gears assembled in the casing before fitting the final drive pinion

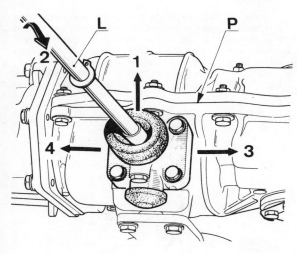

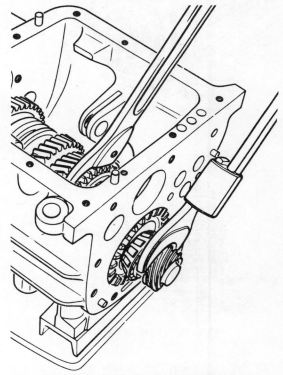

FIG 6:25 Fitting the speedometer worm

Assemble the two half housings and tighten the bolts to a torque of 15 to 20 lb ft in the order shown in **FIG 6:21**.

Fit the fourth-speed gearwheel onto the primary shaft, using a threaded rod, spacer and nut.

Onto the secondary shaft fit the fourth-speed friction sleeve together with the fourth-speed gear and ring, then the synchro hub using a bronze drift.

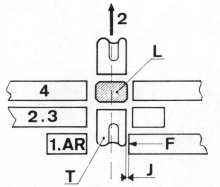

FIG 6:23 Gearchange mechanism assembly

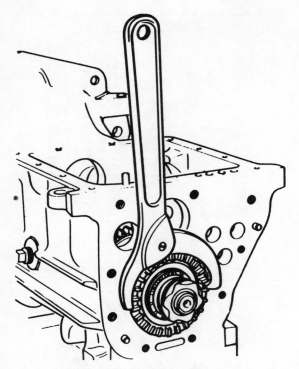

FIG 6:26 Bearing adjustment

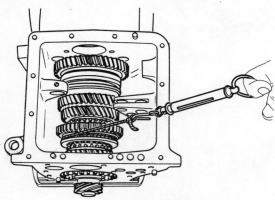

FIG 6:27 Checking the preload

Fit the fourth-speed sliding gear and selector fork together, with the mark on the gear opposite to that on the hub as made earlier. Pin the selector fork to its shaft.

Select fourth gear and reverse then tighten the fourth-speed gear and the synchro hub with tabwashers and nuts to 40 lb ft and 55 lb ft respectively. Lock the nuts.

Fit the front cover, using jointing compound on the gasket and tighten the screws to 15 lb ft for the smaller screws and 20 lb ft for the longer ones.

Refit the starter dog and select neutral.

Fit the clutch end plate and the cover using a little jointing compound on the gasket.

The components of the gear selector lever and locking latch are shown in **FIG 6:22** and it is fitted as follows, referring to **FIG 6:23**.

Fit the lever in place with the lever locking bolt to the outside of the gearbox and the smallest spigot of the latch in the fourth-speed gear selector fork. Partially screw up the four securing bolts.

As the lever housing mounting holes are oval and the selector rod notches are not aligned, the following procedure must be adopted:

Push the housing in the direction of arrow 1. Move the gearlever **L** to the fourth-speed position (arrow 2) and tighten up the housing bolts a little further.

Move the housing in the direction of arrow 3 until the flange of the locking latch **T** contacts the face **F** of the selector fork notch projecting out the farthest.

Move the housing in the opposite direction (arrow 4) by .004 to .012 inch (.10 to .30mm) to secure the clearance at **J** and then fully tighten the housing bolts to 15 lb ft, making sure that the latch flanges can move freely.

Fill the gearbox with oil after refitting in the car.

354 models:

Refer to **FIG 6:24** and fit: first-speed gear and its ring, first/second gear synchro hub, second-speed gear and its ring and intermediate sleeve, third-speed gear and ring, third/fourth synchro hub with the groove on the sliding gear facing towards the fourth-speed gear.

Fit the final drive pinion so that its splines mate with those on the first/second and third/fourth-speed synchro hubs.

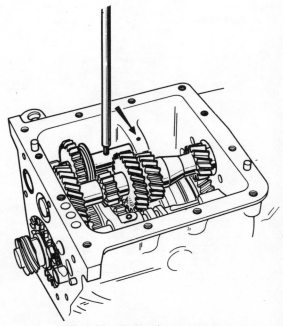

FIG 6:28 Fitting the reverse gear

Fit the fourth-speed gear and ring, then the two needle roller cages and the fourth-speed gear sleeve. Fit the thrust washer with the larger diameter towards the gear and screw on the bearing adjusting ring nut as far as it will go.

Fit the taper roller bearing on the final drive pinion. Screw on the speedometer worm and then lock the secondary shaft by means of the third/fourth-speed sliding gear (see **FIG 6:25**).

Using a suitable spanner screw on the speedometer worm to draw the bearing into position.

Unscrew the worm, fit the spring washer and refit the worm tightening it to 75 to 80 lb ft and lock.

Adjusting the bearings:

First unscrew the adjusting ring nut as shown in **FIG 6:26** until the outer track ring touches the rollers.

Old bearings should have no end play, so continue to unscrew the ring nut until all end play has been eliminated and then lock the ring by means of the locking plate.

New bearings must be fitted with a preloading and the secondary shaft should turn with an applied torque of $3\frac{1}{2}$ to 14 oz ft. Unscrew the ring nut until a slight resistance is felt when turning the shaft.

Wrap a length of string round the third/fourth sliding gear groove and pull the string by means of a spring balance as shown in **FIG 6:27**. The load required to turn the shaft continuously should be between 1 and $3\frac{1}{2}$ pounds. Adjust the ring nut accordingly and lock it with the lockplate.

Reassembling the selector forks:

Fit the first/second-speed selector fork in position then slide the selector shaft in and pin the fork using a rollpin $1\frac{3}{8}$ inch (35 mm) long with the slot parallel to the shaft.

Fit the third/fourth-speed selector fork then slide in the shaft and pin it with a 1 inch long (25 mm) pin, again with the slot parallel to the shaft.

Primary shaft:

Place the primary shaft in position with the fourth-speed gear resting in the casing, then use a length of tube to fit the bearing on the clutch shaft end.

Fit the reverse gear and shaft with the groove facing towards the differential.

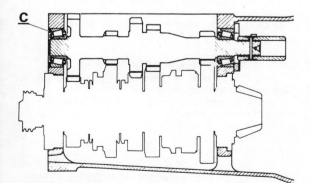

FIG 6:29 Adjusting the primary shaft bearings, showing position of shim at **C**. End play is .001 to .005 inch

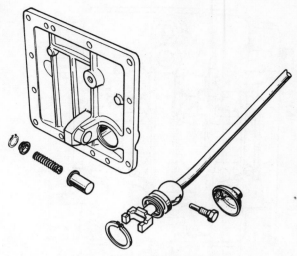

6:30 Assembling the top cover

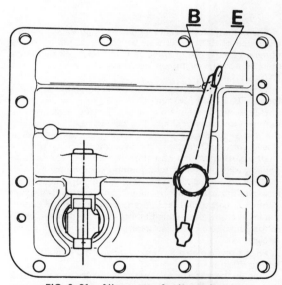

FIG 6:31 Alignment of selector lever

Pin the shaft as shown in **FIG 6:28** with a rollpin $1\frac{3}{8}$ inch (35 mm) long.

Fit the pinion stop pin ($1\frac{3}{8}$ inch) in position, seeing that it protrudes by the same amount on each side of the shaft.

Fit the primary shaft rear bearing cage, this is a sliding fit in the case. Fit the track ring retaining plate and the lockplate, tightening the bolts and locking with the lockplate tabs.

Slide the primary shaft front bearing into position and fit the outer track ring with the help of a tube, until it is flush with the case.

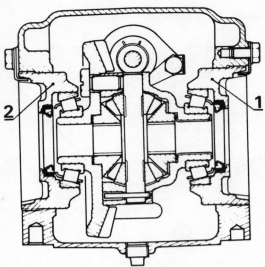

FIG 6:32 Adjusting the backlash

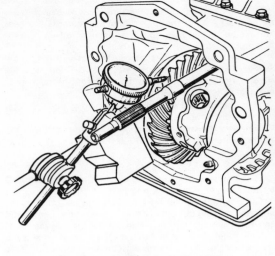

FIG 6:33 Measuring the backlash

The primary shaft bearings must be fitted to give an end clearance of .001 to .005 inch (.02 to .12mm). This is obtained by the use of shims at **C** in **FIG 6:29** for which there is a range of fifteen between .004 and .044 inch (.10 to 1.1mm).

When fitted the final shim should be proud of the gasket face by .012 inch (.30mm).

Before fitting the front cover, fit the locking disc between the selector shafts, the locking balls, springs and the first/second gear plunger. Fit the speedometer gear sleeve with its O-ring and the gearwheel. Fit the primary shaft adjusting shims and then the front cover with its paper gaskets smeared with jointing compound.

Refer to **FIG 6:30** when fitting the top cover. First lubricate the ball joint and then fit: the lever with the ball joint cage and spring washer and secure with the circlip, the lever stop screw (this fits into the notch in the ball), rubber dust cover, reverse gear plunger, spring, cup and circlip.

Fit the reverse gear selector in position and tighten the bolt to 20 lb ft.

Line up the selector lever with the reverse gearshaft and the end (**E** in **FIG 6:31**) of the selector opposite the boss **B** on the cover, smear the gasket with jointing compound and place in position. Then slide the reverse gear along so that it rests on the primary shaft fourth-speed gear.

See that neutral is selected, then place the cover so that the end of the gearlever slides into the selector fork notches. Fit the ends of the reverse gear selector lever into the notch on the selector shaft and the groove in the gear. Secure the top cover.

Fitting the differential:

Fit the differential into the housing and fit the clutch shaft with the rollpin hole in line with the hole on the primary shaft. Insert the pin and fit the retaining spring (see **FIG 6:13**).

Smear the threads on the differential adjusting ring nuts with jointing compound and adjust the backlash as follows:

Refer to **FIG 6:32** and note that the correct backlash is obtained by unscrewing ring nut 1 on the differential housing side and screwing up the nut 2 on the crownwheel side by the same amount.

Mount a clock gauge as shown in **FIG 6:33** and measure the backlash at the teeth of the crownwheel. It should be between .005 and .010 inch (.12 to .25mm).

If the measurement is excessive unscrew ring nut 1 and screw up ring nut 2 by the same amount. If the backlash is insufficient unscrew ring 2 and then screw up ring 1.

When the correct backlash has been obtained lock the ring nuts with the lockplates.

To fit the clutch housing, the use of tool BVi.488 will be helpful in fitting the oil seal to the housing.

Apply a smear of compound to the joint gasket and place the tube in position to spread the lip of the oil seal inside the withdrawal pad guide. Fit the clutch housing by sliding the tool along the clutch shaft.

Remove the tool and fit and tighten the housing securing bolts, noting that the shortest is at the top on the camshaft side. Fill the gearbox after fitting in the car.

6:6 Reinstalling the gearbox in the car

This is a reversal of the removal procedure paying attention to the following points:

Lightly lubricate the end of the clutch shaft and the ends of the drive shafts.

845cc models:

After inserting the rollpins in the holes in the drive shaft and sun wheel, seal the holes at each end of the pin.

Check the clutch free play, $\frac{1}{8}$ to $\frac{5}{32}$ inch (3 to 4mm) at the end of the fork.

1108 cc models:

Take care when fitting the drive shafts not to foul the differential adjusting ring nut oil seals.

Check the position of the drive shafts in relation to the gearbox as illustrated in **FIG 1 : 36**.

Adjust the clutch free play, $\frac{13}{64}$ inch (5mm) at the end of the lever.

Fill up with the correct grade of oil, EP.80.

6 : 7 The gearshift mechanism

Early 845 cc models:

To remove the gearlever control on these models it is necessary first to take out the rollpin at the top of the gearlever in the gearbox and then remove the bracket fixing bolts on the top of the radiator.

Remove the two assembly bolts on the shaft and separate the two parts.

If the rod has been loose in the bushes they should be renewed. To do this for the bush on the instrument panel side, the bracket must first be removed by taking out four retaining bolts.

Reverse these operations when refitting.

1108 cc and later 845 cc models:

First remove the rubber ring on the end of the gear selector lever and then the two bolts at the junction piece above the cylinder head.

Select third gear and separate the two portions of the control rod.

1108 cc models are now fitted with 'Grip-Ring' rings 'A' on the gearshift control tube (see **FIG 6 : 34**) to limit travel when selecting third gear.

Special pliers, Tool No. BV1.523, can be obtained to remove or refit these rings. With third gear selected the distance 'B' should be $1\frac{3}{32}$ to $1\frac{1}{4}$ inch (28 to 32 mm).

6 : 8 Fault diagnosis

(a) Jumping out of gear

1 Worn or damaged selector fork
2 Worn or damaged selector rod grooves
3 Loose or damaged detent spring

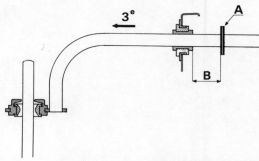

FIG 6 : 34 'Grip-Ring' fitting on gearshift control shaft

4 Bent selector arm
5 Loose or damaged selector arm
6 Worn coupling dogs

(b) Noisy transmission

1 Insufficient oil
2 Excessive differential end float
3 Worn or damaged bearings
4 Worn or damaged gear teeth

(c) Difficulty in engaging gear

1 Check 1 to 6 in (a)
2 Worn synchromesh
3 Incorrectly adjusted clutch

(d) Oil leaks

1 Damaged joint washers
2 Worn or damaged oil seals
3 Gearbox end plates loose or distorted
4 Distorted half housings

(e) Excessive backlash

1 Worn gears, bearings or bearing housings
2 Worn planet gear internal splines
3 Worn transmission shaft couplings
4 Loose or broken wheel studs

NOTES

CHAPTER 7

FRONT SUSPENSION, TRANSMISSION SHAFTS AND HUBS

7:1 Description

The front suspension is by means of torsion bars damped by double-acting hydraulic dampers mounted between the lower wishbone and the sidemember. Bump stops are fitted.

Drive from the combined gearbox/transmission unit is by two half-axles which comprise exposed solid or tubular transmission shafts connected at their inner ends to the gearbox/transmission unit by either Bendix-Weiss joints (tubular shafts) spider joints (solid shafts) and at their hub ends by BED universal joints. An anti-roll bar is fitted. The wheel bearings run on double ballraces.

A sectional diagram of the lefthand side of the suspension on 845cc models is shown in FIG 7:1.

The layout on 1108cc cars, which are fitted with disc brakes, is a little different and will be dealt with separately towards the end of this chapter in **Section 7:10**.

7:2 Maintenance

This is minimal and the occasional checking of the securing nuts on component parts is all that is required. There is no lubrication requirement.

7:3 Removing and replacing the front hubs

(a) Dismantling:

A sectional view of the front hub is shown in **FIG 7:2**. To remove, carry out the following procedure.

1 Release the handbrake and slacken the shoe adjusting cams.
2 Jack up the car securely and remove the road wheel.
3 The hub nut and washer should be removed but the brake drum and three retaining screws should remain in position. In order to remove the hub nut and washer the drum must be held still, this may be accomplished by applying the brakes or using a suitably drilled bar over two wheel studs.
4 Push out the drive shaft rollpins at the gearbox end and fit the retaining clips as described in **Section 1:3**.
5 Disconnect the steering arm ball joint and the two suspension arm ball joints with the aid of a suitable extractor or wedges and support the brake drum on a block.
6 Replace the nut on the upper suspension arm ball joint to hold in place the hub (drum assembly).

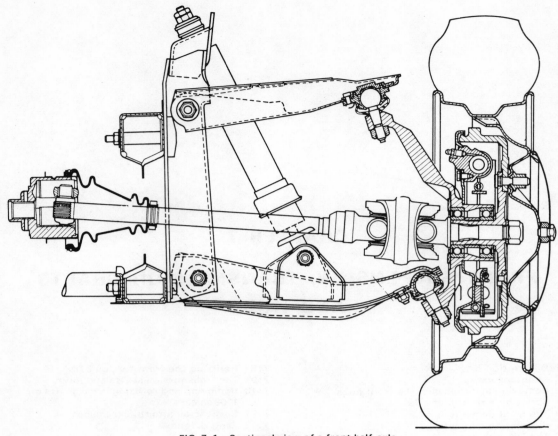

FIG 7:1   Sectional view of a front half-axle

7 Disconnect the drive shaft from the stub axle, using a suitable puller or by using tool T.Av.235 obtainable from your dealer (see **FIG 7:3**).

8 Without removing the drive shaft from the differential planet wheel, reset it on the tie-rod.

9 Remove the brake drum by withdrawing the three securing screws (see **FIG 7:4**) and screwing in two 6 mm x 100 pitch screws into the tapped holes provided (see **FIG 7:5**) then unscrew the two securing screws from the brake backplate to enable service tool T.Av.450 to be fitted into place and pull out the hub as shown in **FIG 7:6**.

10 Should bearing renewal be required, the front hub outer bearing may now be extracted by first removing the distance piece and using a suitable bearing extractor.

11 The inner bearing may be removed by unscrewing the four nuts from the bearing retaining plate (see **FIG 7:7**).

12 Remove the bearing backplate from the stub axle, place it to one side taking care not to strain the flexible brake hose.

13 Disconnect the two ball joints holding the stub axle, and place the stub axle to one side.

14 Place a tube $2\frac{3}{4}$ inch (70 mm) in diameter on the inner bearing of the stub axle, and push out the bearing with the aid of a press.

(b) Reassembling:

(i) The outer bearing:

Slightly grease the outside of the bearing and using a tube $1\frac{9}{32}$ inch (32 mm) in diameter, press in the new bearing (sealed end of the bearing towards brake drum).

(ii) The inner bearing:

1 Lightly grease the outside of the bearing and using a tube $2\frac{5}{16}$ inch (58 mm) in diameter, press in the new bearing (with the sealed end to the outside).

2 Fit the stub axle to the ball joint by screwing on the upper ball joint nut but do not tighten it.

3 Fit the brake backplate and the bearing retaining plate, smeared with recommended jointing compound.

When refitting, lightly grease the bearings, and put $\frac{1}{2}$ oz. (15 g) high melting point grease in the annular space between the two bearings.

(iii) The hub:

This is essentially a reversal of the dismantling procedure but tighten the upper ball joint to 25 lb ft, the lower ball joint to 35 lb ft and the steering arm ball joint to 15 lb ft torque.

The front hub retaining nut should be tightened to 90 lb ft torque. Remember to remove the drive shaft retaining clip and always use a new roll-pin. The ends of the roll-pin must be sealed with a recommended sealer. Adjust the front brakes on completion of the operation.

7:4 Servicing a front half-axle
(a) Dismantling:

1 Jack up the car and place axle stands or chocks under the frame at the front end.
2 Remove the road wheel.
3 To remove the upper suspension arm, unscrew the upper suspension arm ball joint nut and extract the ball joint, then remove the hinge pin as shown in **FIG 7:8**.
4 To remove the lower suspension arm, remove the upper suspension arm ball joint and the steering arm ball joint, withdraw the drive shaft. Now refit the upper suspension arm ball joint temporarily to the stub axle and undo the lower suspension arm ball joint.
5 Remove the torsion bar as described in the subsequent operations 8 to 15 and unscrew the lower suspension arm hinge pin nut. Unscrew the tie rod and disconnect the anti-roll bar as described in **Section 7:8**
6 Disconnect the damper at its lower connection and withdraw the lower suspension arm hinge pin (see **FIG 7:9**).
7 Lift out the lower suspension arm from the front axle support bracket as shown in **FIG 7:10**.

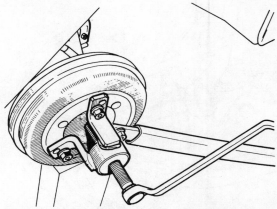

FIG 7:3   Disconnecting the drive shaft from the stub axle

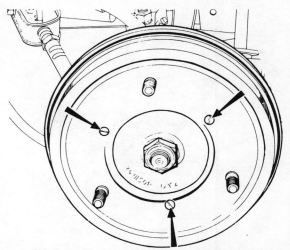

FIG 7:4   The front brake drum retaining screws

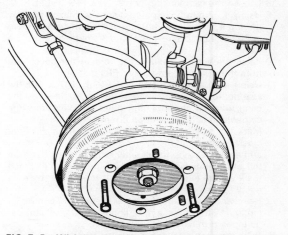

FIG 7:5   Withdrawing a front brake drum with pull-off screws

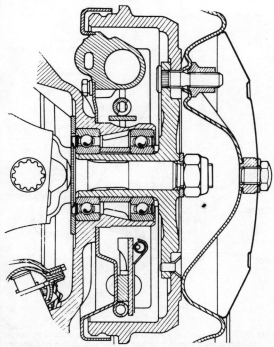

FIG 7:2   Sectional view of a front hub assembly

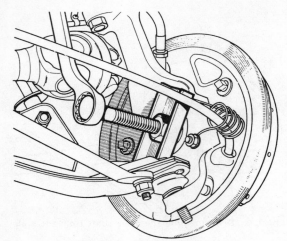

FIG 7:6 Extracting a front hub

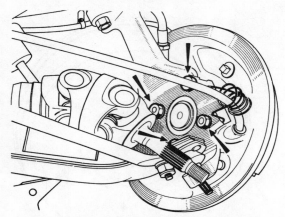

FIG 7:7 Front hub bearing retaining plate nuts

8 Loosen the cam locking bolt **A** (see **FIG 7:11**).

9 Using a 22 mm box spanner, set the cam to zero by turning it towards the outside of the vehicle as shown in **FIG 7:12** and screw an 8 mm diameter bolt into the cam.

10 Raise the vehicle, remove the torsion bar coverplate from the side concerned (see **FIG 7:13**).

11 Using service tool Sus.311 (see **FIG 7:14**) pull on the spanner to remove the load of the anchor lever on the cam, unscrew the retaining bolts and withdraw the cam which is fitted with an 8 mm bolt.

Mark the position of the adjusting lever on the floor crossmember, and the position of the bar on the lower arm anchor sleeve. Check after removing the bar from the arm if the mark made is in line with the punch mark on the end of the bar, or, if it is offset, by how many splines and in what direction.

12 Remove the nut from the lower suspension arm hinge pin and with a bronze drift, knock out the torsion bar by tapping the end of the hinge pin.

13 Push the anchor lever towards the front of the car (A) in **FIG 7:15**.

14 Slide the torsion bar to the rear of the vehicle to free it from the lower suspension arm and the anti-roll bar (B) in **FIG 7:15**.

15 Tip the bar and pull it out (C) in **FIG 7:15**.

(b) Checking for wear and distortion and servicing

Component parts will now have been sufficiently dismantled to check the necessity of renewing the bearings

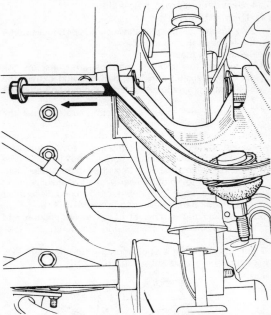

FIG 7:8 Removing a front upper suspension arm hinge pin

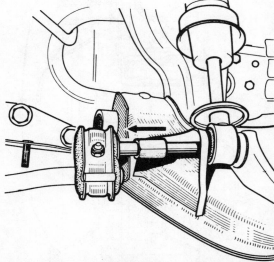

FIG 7:9 Removing a front lower suspension arm hinge pin together with anti-roll bar bearing and lower damper connection

and suspension arm rubber bushes. Renewal of these items is best left to a service station having the appropriate equipment as is checking for distortion in the component parts. Should the suspension ball joints require renewing then proceed as follows:

Upper suspension ball joint:

1 Drill out the ball joint attachment rivets.
2 Fit the new joint using the bolts supplied with it and **ensure that the round heads are on the dust cover side.**

Lower suspension ball joint:

Carry out the operations as for the upper joints. The upper ball joint nut should be tightened to a torque of 25 lb ft. The lower ball joint nut should be tightened to 35 lb ft.

The operations described under the foregoing **Section (b)** may be carried out without complete dismantling of the front suspension, hubs and drive shafts.

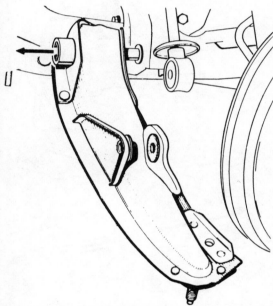

FIG 7:10   Lifting out the lower suspension arm

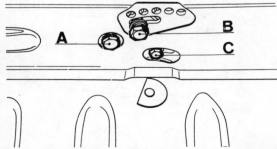

FIG 7:11   Front torsion bar locating bolts (vehicle interior)

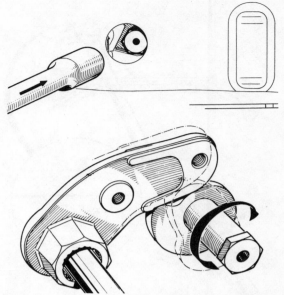

FIG 7:12   Setting a front torsion bar anchor lever cam to zero

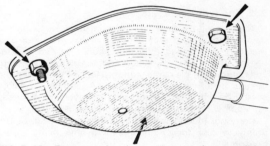

FIG 7:13   Front torsion bar end coverplate retaining bolts

(c) Reassembling:

This is largely a reversal of the dismantling procedure but the following details must be noted.
1 Smear the upper suspension arm inner hinge pin with grease.
2 Tighten the upper suspension arm nut to 25 lb ft torque with the equivalent of two people loading the car on its suspension.
3 Tighten the lower suspension arm hinge pin to 25 lb ft torque with the suspension compressed as detailed in the preceding operation.
4 Tighten the stub axle nut to 85 lb ft torque.
5 Smear the front damper bottom mounting pin with grease before fitting, also the ends of the anti-roll bar as described in **Section 7:7**.
6 Refit the torsion bars as described in **Section 7:8**.
7 Grease the drive shaft splines before engaging the shaft with the differential sun wheels.

After dismantling and reassembling a full check of the steering geometry, particularly tracking should be carried out as described in **Section 7:6** and **Section 9:6**.

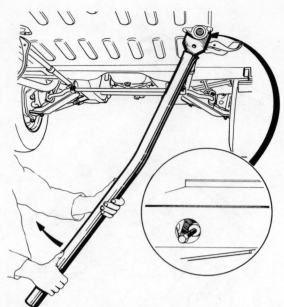

FIG 7:14 Using service tool Sus.311 to remove the torque loading from a front torsion bar anchor lever

7:5 The front dampers

No provision is made for topping up or servicing the dampers and if deterioration in cornering or ride indicates that they are at fault then they should be removed for testing. This is a simple matter and consists of extending and contracting the damper about 10 or 12 times with the damper held in a vertical position. A definite resistance should be felt in both directions of movement. If this is not apparent then the damper should be renewed.

Carry out this operation on new dampers also, before fitting, in case they require priming after being stored horizontally.

Removal and refitting:

1 Jack up the front of the car and remove the road wheel.
2 Jack up the lower suspension arm to free it from the torsion bar load.
3 Remove the two upper damper anchorage nuts.
4 Remove the anti-roll bar.
5 Remove the lower pivot pin (see **FIG 7:9**) and remove the damper, making a careful note of the stack of rubber bushes and cup washers for correct replacement at the top end, and compensating washers at the bottom end if fitted.

Refitting is a reversal of removal, but grease the lower mounting pivot pin and never secure the upper mounting with the damper fully extended, always raise the lower suspension arm so that the damper is only in the half extended position. Tighten the lower mounting nut to 25 lb ft torque.

7:6 Suspension geometry

The term 'steering geometry' refers to the layout of the steering mechanism and any of its dimensions, linear or angular, which contribute to the required behaviour of the steering system. The steering system is always designed to comply with the specification of the front suspension, in order that the best possible steering behaviour is obtained under all conditions.

Departure from any steering/suspension dimensions may result in unsatisfactory steering and/or abnormal wear of tyres, steering and suspension components.

Poor steering and tyre wear are often caused by unbalance of the tyres themselves.

The three angles to be considered are:

Camber which is the angle of slope from the vertical when viewed from the front of the car. Positive camber is the amount in degrees that the front wheels are tilted outwards at the top from the vertical. Correct settings are given in **Technical Data**.

Castor is the angle between the steering axis and a vertical line when viewed from the side of the car. It is considered positive when the steering axis is inclined rearward.

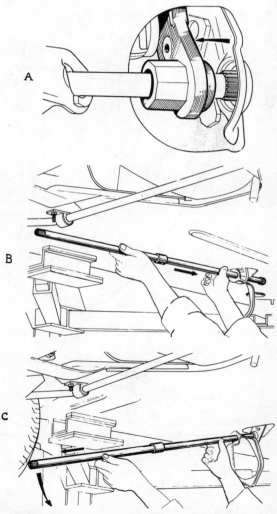

FIG 7:15 The removal sequence for a front torsion bar

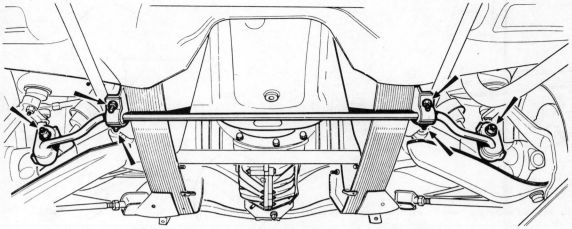

FIG 7:16 Attachment points for the anti-roll bar and bearings

Steering axis inclination is the angle when viewed from the front of the car between the vertical and an imaginary line drawn between the upper and lower ball joint centres. It is about this line that the wheel pivots as it is turned for control of vehicle direction.

While it is possible to check the camber angle of the front wheels using a plumb line against a fixed line marked on a board held edge on to the top and bottom wheel rims it is to be recommended that all suspension and steering angles be measured at a service station having the sophisticated up-to-date equipment required for precise and accurate measurement.

Always have such a check carried out immediately after severe kerbing or minor frontal impact.

Before any checks are undertaken, the front wheel toe-out should be checked as described in **Chapter 9, Section 9:9**. Always have the wheels in the straight-ahead position, and the car standing on level ground with tyres correctly inflated.

7:7 The anti-roll bar

Removing:

1 Unscrew the two nuts holding the crimped bearings of the anti-roll bar onto the shouldered studs (see **FIG 7:16**).
2 Unscrew the four bearing fixing nuts.
3 Remove the two bearings and anti-roll bar.

Refitting:

1 Set the front axle as described in **Section 7:11**.
2 Smear the ends of the anti-roll bar with grease before refitting.
3 Tighten the nuts to 25 lb ft torque.

7:8 Refitting the front torsion bars

Removal has already been described in **Section 7:4** but the refitting and attendant operations and adjustments are most important. The lefthand torsion bar may be identified by its dab of yellow paint and two triangular symbols, the righthand torsion bar by a dab of red paint and three triangular symbols. Later models

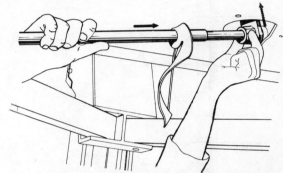

FIG 7:17 Refitting a front torsion bar

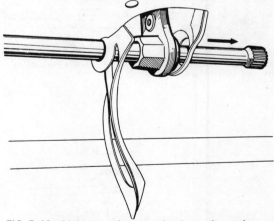

FIG 7:18 Lining up a front torsion bar to its anchorage point

may have a white/red and a white/yellow mark respectively. Also the number of splines differ at each end of the bar.

The end that goes into the suspension arm has 20 splines and the anchorage end has 21 splines.

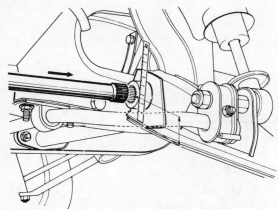

FIG 7:19 Entering a front torsion bar into its splined collar

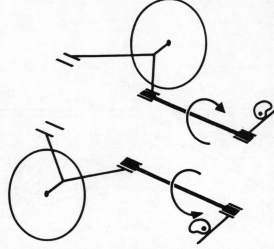

FIG 7:22 Diagram indicating direction of rotation of front torsion bars to raise or lower the car

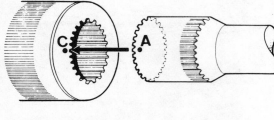

FIG 7:20 Offsetting the splines of a front torsion bar prior to assembly to its splined collar

For key see text

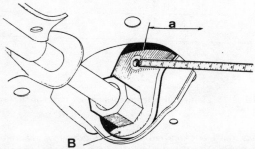

FIG 7:21 Initial positioning of a front torsion bar anchor lever

Key to Fig 7:21   a=measurement between edge of anchor lever hole to edge of anchorage bracket   B=anchor lever

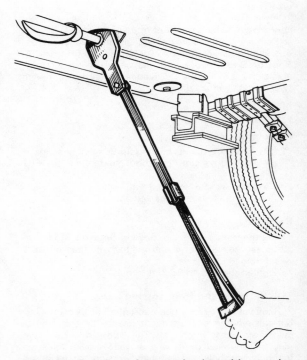

FIG 7:23 Twisting a front torsion bar with a service tool to allow the anchor lever cam to be fitted

(a) Refitting:

1 Smear the ends of the bar with molybdenum disulphide grease. Fit the anchor lever to the bar making sure that it is the right way round (see **FIG 7:17**).

2 Offer up the anchor lever to its housing.

3 Push the torsion bar towards the rear of the vehicle to enable it to be lined up to its front anchorage point (see **FIG 7:18**).

4 If the car is not already marked on the lower suspension arm splined collar, measure a distance of $1\frac{3}{32}$ inch (27.2 mm) between the inner face of the lower suspension arm and dot punch the face of the female splined collar as shown in **FIG 7:19**.

5 Then starting at point A offset the torsion bar 5 splines with reference to point C on the lower suspension arm, measured in the direction of movement of the torsion bar as shown in **FIG 7:20**.

6 See **FIG 7:21** and fit anchor lever B in order to obtain a measurement of about $1\frac{3}{4}$ inch (45 mm) measured from the edge of the hole in the anchor lever to the edge of the anchorage bracket (distance a).

This measurement is given purely as a guide. A difference of only one spline will give too great an offset of the anchor lever.

7 Adjust as required in the following manner:

To raise the vehicle, turn the bar in the opposite direction to the torsion. To lower the vehicle, turn the bar in the direction of the torsion (as shown by the arrows in **FIG 7:22**).

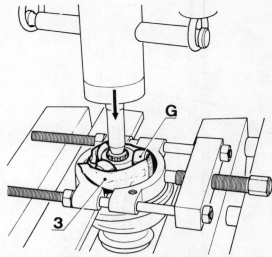

7:26 Extracting the spider from a splined drive shaft

Key to Fig 7:26
3 Temporary securing tape   **G** Needle roller cages

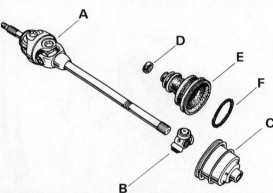

FIG 7:24 Exploded view of a transmission (drive) shaft fitted with a spider joint

Key to Fig 7:24   **A** Shaft complete with 'BED' outer joint
B Spider   **C** Tulip   **D** Bellows securing clip
E Rubber bellows   **F** Spring clip

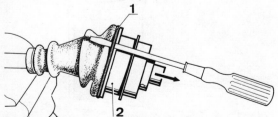

FIG 7:25 Removing the tulip from the spider of a drive shaft joint

Key to Fig 7:25   1 Bellows retaining spring clip   2 The tulip

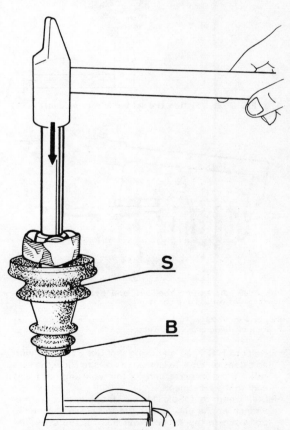

FIG 7:27 Fitting the collar (B) and bellows (S) to a drive shaft

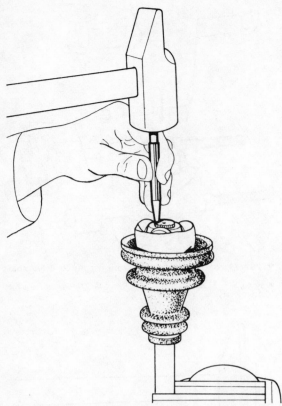

FIG 7:28   Fitting the spider to a drive shaft

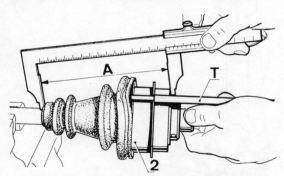

FIG 7:29   Arranging the 'set' and overall length of a spider joint on a drive shaft

Key to Fig 7:29   **A** 6 inch (153.4 mm)
T Joint retaining clip   2 Tulip

8 Refer to **FIG 7:23** and using tool Sus.311 fitted with an extension tube, twist the bar so as to allow the cam to be fitted in place and fix the adjusting lever and cam to the crossmember.
9 Still using tool Sus.311 but fitted with a torque wrench at the end, check the torque setting at the point where the anchor lever lifts off the cam. The cam being set to the zero position. With the wheel hanging free, this torque is approximately 160 lb ft.

10 Lower the car onto its wheels and road test it.
11 Check the underbody height as fully explained in **Section 8 : 5**.
   After any alteration to underbody height adjust the brake limiter.

7:9 The transmission shafts and joints

   Early 845 cc cars fitted with the BV.334 gearbox may be found fitted with a cast 'BED' joint, followed by a protected cast 'TE' joint at the wheel end and a Weiss joint or a spider G.162 joint at the gearbox end. A six ball joint may also be found at the wheel end with a Weiss joint at the gearbox end. Later cars with this gearbox have a spider GE.76 at the wheel end and a spider G.162 or G.169 at the gearbox end. Mixing is allowed but a spider GE.76 coupling must not be used on cars prior to Chassis No. 244979.
   On cars fitted with the BV.354 gearbox a cast 'BED' followed by a protected cast 'TE' joint at the wheel end

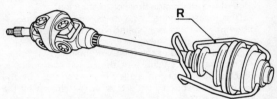

FIG 7:30   A spider type joint temporary retaining clip in position on a drive shaft

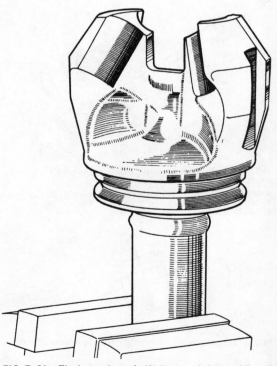

FIG 7:31   The lower jaw of a Weiss type joint positioned ready for assembly

will be found with a spider G.162 with end fitting at the gearbox end or a spider GE.76 at the wheel end with a spider G.162 or G.169 with end fittings at the gearbox end. Mixing is allowed but a spider GE.76 coupling must not be fitted to 1108 cc vehicles prior to Chassis No. 2042, because of unmodified lever suspension arms.

(a) Servicing shafts with spider G.162 joints (see FIG 7:24):

Before carrying out any repair to the drive shaft joint at the gearbox end, make sure that the condition of 'BED' joint at the wheel end is satisfactory.

The latter is not repairable and must never be dismantled. If necessary, therefore, a complete Service Exchange drive shaft must be obtained.

Repair kits are available to service the spider joints and rubber seals but they do vary between the year and the model. It is therefore essential to quote the model, chassis and year when ordering replacement kits. Each kit is supplied with a cachet of grease and in some instances a booklet of brief instructions on relevant points.

Renewal of the rubber bellows:

1 Hold the drive shaft in a vice fitted with soft jaws.
2 Remove the retaining spring 1 holding the bellows on the tulip 2.
3 Now hold the drive shaft vertically in the vice and remove the tulip 2 from the spider, as shown in **FIG 7:25**. On a coupling fitted with a retaining plate, bend up the three segments with a pair of pliers. On couplings with an extended nose, retain the thrust cap and spring.

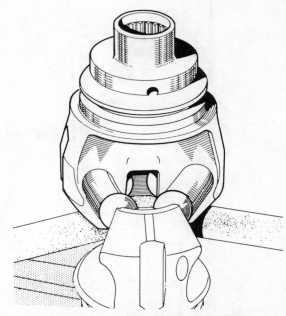

FIG 7:33   Pressing the top and bottom jaws of a Weiss type joint together with the temporary rubber assembly tube in position

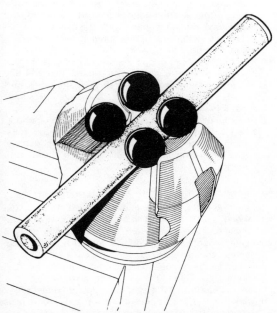

FIG 7:32   Preparing to assemble the top and bottom jaws of a Weiss type joint with the balls and temporary rubber tubing in position

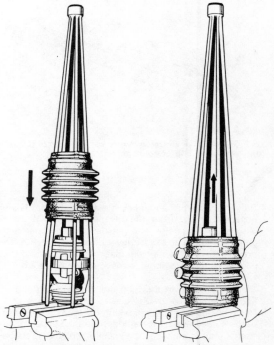

FIG 7:34   Sliding bellows over a Weiss joint by using guide strips

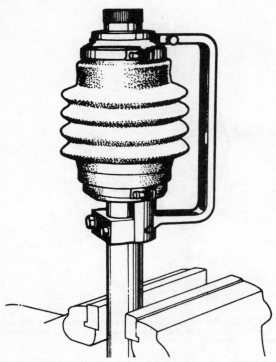

FIG 7:35 Service tool in position prior to refilling a Weiss type joint with lubricant

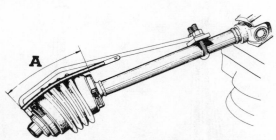

FIG 7:36 A drive shaft correctly set for refitting with a joint retaining clip in position

Key to Fig 7:36   A is 5½ inch (140 mm)

4 Refer to **FIG 7:26** and make sure that the cages G are never separated from their respective needle roller assemblies. The cages and needle rollers are matched on manufacture and must never be interfered with. To prevent this stick a piece of masking tape 3 round the cages. With a clean cloth remove all the grease round the spider.

5 Clean the inside of the tulip but thinning or diluting liquid must not be used to clean any of these parts.

6 Using a suitable press and taking the load on the body of the spider, extract the spider from the splined drive shaft, after removing the circlip on drive shafts fitted with a spider GE.76 coupling at the wheel end (see **FIG 7:26**).

The three crimping points on the spline and the drive shaft will disappear. Do not therefore, try and remove them earlier.

7 Remove the old bellows and the collar from the drive shaft.

8 Fit the collar B on the drive shaft (see **FIG 7:27**).

9 Fit the new bellows S carefully aligning it in position in relation to the grooves on the drive shaft.

10 Using collar B fix the end of the bellows.

11 Using a bronze drift fit the spider onto the drive shaft splines. The spider may be fitted either way round (see **FIG 7:28**). On shafts with a spider GE.76 coupling refit the retaining circlip.

12 Centre pop the drive shaft splines, on shafts with 'BED' coupling, on couplings with an extended nose, centralise the spring and cap on the spider, onto the spider at 3 points 120 deg. apart using a centre or pin punch similar to the original crimping on the spider hub.

13 Before refitting the tulip check the condition of the tulip bearing faces, the oil seal in the gearbox and the splines.

14 Remove the masking tape from the cages.

15 Place half the special lubricant supplied with the repair kit in the bellows and the other half in the tulip.

16 Fit the tulip on the spider and slide the bellows over the tulip. On a coupling with a retaining plate carefully tap the plate into its original position.

17 Slip a smooth bar T between the bellows and the tulip 2 to allow air to pass (see **FIG 7:29**).

   Before finally fitting the bellows retaining spring squeeze out some of the air in the bellows.

18 Refer to **FIG 7:29** and lengthen or shorten the spider joint in order to obtain a reading A=6 inches (153.4 mm) measurement taken from the bellows to the machined face of the largest diameter on the tulip. When in this position remove the rod T and slip over the bellows retaining spring onto the bellows.

   Do not stretch the spring more than is necessary when slipping it into place.

19 Refer to **FIG 7:30** and fit the retaining clip R in place in order to avoid collapse of the joint. You will find this tool in the boxes of new drive shafts when purchased from your dealer, or alternatively a simple substitute may be made up.

20 Renewal of the tulip or spider may of course be undertaken during the foregoing dismantling and reassembling procedure. A close check for wear or damage will indicate the necessity of renewing these components.

(b) Servicing shafts with Weiss type joints:

Ensure that the condition of the 'BED' joint at the wheel end is satisfactory. The latter is not repairable and in the event of it being worn or unserviceable then a complete factory exchange drive shaft must be obtained.

1 Remove the joint bellows securing clips.

2 Cut away the old bellows and empty out the oil.

3 Thoroughly clean the transmission joint.

4 Pull the top jaw of the joint in an upward direction.

5 Mark the relative positions of the top and bottom jaws regarding their exact mating positions.

6 Retain the four balls and scrupulously clean all component parts.

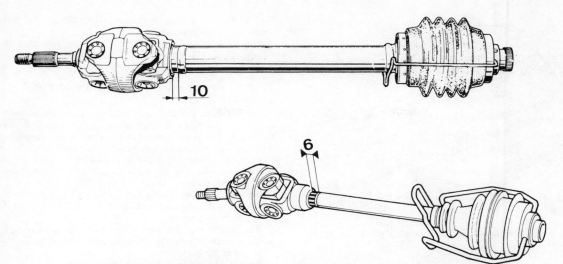

FIG 7:37 Essential measurements to ensure correct installation of drive shafts

Key to Fig 7:37   6 is $\frac{1}{4}$ inch (6 mm)   10 is .4 inch (10 mm)

7 Position the bottom jaw of the joint on a vice as shown in **FIG 7:31**.

8 Fit a rubber tube across the bottom jaw and lay the four balls against the tube as shown in **FIG 7:32**.

9 Lay the top jaw over the 4 balls and with a tap of the hand drive on the top jaw and then withdraw the rubber tube (see **FIG 7:33**).

10 Using a combination of metal strips slide a set of new bellows over the joint as shown in **FIG 7:34**.

11 Fit and tighten the bottom clip.

12 For a drive shaft of 30 mm in diameter use service tool T.Av.53 and for a drive shaft of 35 mm in diameter use tool T.Av.65. In both cases the half collar of the tool should be well pushed out against the bottom face of the lower jaw. The other end fitting in the recess for the upper jaw rollpin. Tighten up the tool in this position (see **FIG 7:35**).

13 From the container, pour the oil supplied with the repair kit into the bellows. To help the escape of air lift up the lip of the bellows.

14 Slide over and tighten the top clip. Remove tool T.Av.53 or tool T.Av.65.

The use of these specialized service tools is not essential if the original bellows positioning was marked prior to dismantling.

15 Bend the drive shaft slightly to assume its normal mounting position (overall length of joint A (see **FIG 7:36**) $5\frac{1}{2}$ inches (140 mm) and fit over the shaft retaining tool described in **Chapter 1** or the new tool supplied with new drive shafts.

It is possible to fit one drive shaft of either type to the same vehicle.

Where a drive shaft with a Weiss joint is fitted, check that the welded seam between the tube and the BED joint is about 10 mm from the flange of the BED joint.

Where a drive shaft is fitted with a 'Spider' joint check that where the splines enter the BED joint they

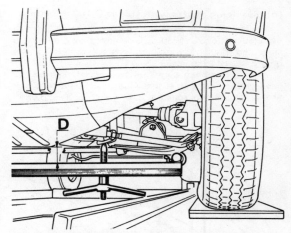

FIG 7:38 Compress front suspension to obtain measurement at **D**=2 inches (50 mm)

are visible along a length of approximately $\frac{1}{4}$ inch (6 mm).

Both the foregoing measurements are indicated in **FIG 7:37**.

(c) Servicing shafts with spider GE.76 couplings:

This spider is serviced in a similar manner to the spider G.162 except that the bell-shaped axle is retained by a three-pronged plate. Lift each prong as shown in **FIG 7:39**, but do not twist the ends. Retain the thrust ball and spring.

The bellows and clip are fitted in a similar manner to that shown in **FIG 7:34**.

To fit the three-pronged retaining plate, slide the roller cages towards the centre, position the plate so

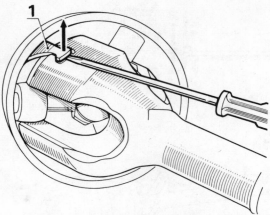

FIG 7:39 Lifting prong of retaining plate on GE.76 coupling

that each prong bisects an angle made by the spider. Make sure that each prong is correctly located in its slot, and that the coupling is quite free when operated by hand.

(d) Servicing shafts with spider G.169 coupling:

A metal cover is used on this coupling which must be removed for servicing, it is removed by cutting two slots and pulling away with pliers (see **FIG 7:40**) otherwise servicing is similar.

When assembling align the two raised pips on the cover with a cut-out in the yoke (see **FIG 7:41**) and fit the components together. Using a press as shown in

FIG 7:42 to hold the components together, crimp the cover all the way round.

The dimension 'A' (see **FIG 7:29**) for this type is $6\frac{3}{8}$ inch (162 ± 1 mm).

7:10 Removing and refitting drive shafts on 1108cc cars

First remove the stub axle nut and washer and then dismount the brake caliper without disconnecting the flexible hose. Using a suitable extractor, disconnect the steering arm and upper suspension arm ball joints.

Push the drive shaft out of the hub/disc assembly then withdraw it from the transmission sun wheel taking care not to damage the oil seal.

To refit the shaft, slide the end into the sun wheel checking its location according to **FIG 1:36**, then fit it to the stub axle carrier.

Reconnect the steering and upper suspension ball joints and refit the stub axle washer and nut, tightening to a torque of 90 lb ft.

Refit the brake caliper. Check the gearbox oil level.

7:11 Suspension arm rubber bushes

The following procedure should be used if it is necessary to tighten the rubber bushes on the suspension arm (see **FIG 7:38**).

By means of tool T.Av.238.02 or similar, compress the front suspension to obtain a measurement at **D** of 2 inches (50mm), and while in this position tighten the mounting pins on:

The upper and lower suspension arm hinge points.

The damper, steering arm and the tie rod at the chassis end.

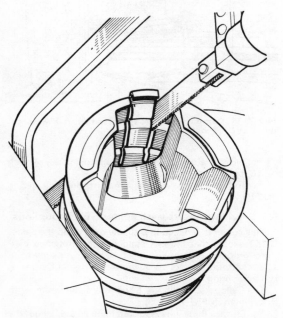

FIG 7:40 Cutting metal cover on G.169 coupling

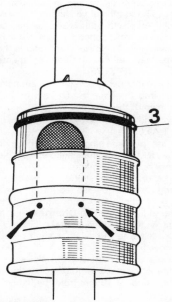

FIG 7:41 Aligning raised pips with cut-out on G.169 coupling

7:12 Fault diagnosis

(a) Wheel wobble

1 Worn hub bearings
2 Broken or weak torsion bars
3 Uneven tyre wear
4 Worn suspension linkage
5 Loose wheel fixings

(b) Bottoming of suspension

1 Check 2 in (a)
2 Dampers not working

(c) Heavy steering

1 Corroded or seized upper or lower swivels
2 Wong suspension geometry

(d) Excessive tyre wear

1 Check 4 in (a); 2 in (b) and 2 in (c)

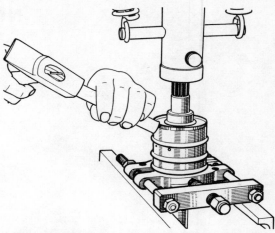

FIG 7:42 Crimping metal cover on G.169 coupling

(e) Rattles

1 Check 2 in (a)
2 Rubber suspension bushes worn
3 Damper connections loose
4 Suspension arm mountings loose or worn
5 Damper rubber bushes worn through

(f) Excessive rolling

1 Check 2 in (a) and 2 in (b)

(g) Vibration

1 Drive shafts bent or out of balance
2 Worn or damaged drive shaft couplings

NOTES

CHAPTER 8

REAR SUSPENSION AND HUBS

8:1 Description and construction

The rear suspension is independent on both wheels by means of torsion bars, double-acting hydraulic dampers and rubber override pads. The track measures 49 inches (1.244 m).

The wheelbase differs from side to side. The lefthand side measures $94\frac{1}{2}$ inches whilst the righthand side measures $96\frac{7}{16}$ inches. A sectional view of one side of the rear suspension is given in **FIG 8:1**.

8:2 Checking the rear axle alignment and suspension

Should abnormal tyre wear occur then the rear wheel toe-in should be checked. Although it is preferable to leave this operation to a service station which has modern measuring equipment, it is quite simple to make suitable gauges for use on both front and rear wheels. A track gauge may be made from tubing, suitably cranked to clear the gearbox and transmission unit (so that it may also be used on the front wheels) having one fixed end and one adjustable end (nut and bolt).

Measure the distance between the two inner wheel rims at the rear. Roll the road wheels through 180 deg. and measure the distance between the inner wheel rims at the front. The latter measurement should be less by $\frac{5}{32}$

inch (4 mm) which is the correct toe-in. If incorrect, adjust by moving the half-axles on their securing holes after loosening the retaining bolts. Having established the total toe-in now refer to **FIG 8:2** and make up a gauge which may be much less complex than the one illustrated. A pointer (preferably metal) with a clearly defined rule will be adequate if an assistant is available. Ensure that the pointer locates on the rear road wheel rims rather than on the tyre walls to avoid distortions.

The pointer should be at hub height and pointing towards the front of the vehicle. Measure distance A between the end of the pointer and the sidemember with the rule. Take a second measurement after just turning the road wheel through 180 deg. Repeat the operation on the other rear wheel. If the measurements differ then the toe-in is not equally distributed and further adjustment of the half-axles must be made, and the distribution again checked.

It will be apparent that correct rear axle alignment will require a certain amount of trial and error adjustment until both the total toe-in ($\frac{5}{32}$ inch) and the distributed toe-in ($\frac{5}{64}$ inch each half axle) measurements are correct.

The camber of the rear wheels should be checked occasionally. This may be done by making a simple board to engage the top and bottom outer wheel rim edges. The board should have a cut-out to clear the hub cap and should be held on to the rim. Draw a vertical line on the board parallel with the contacting edge and by a bob weight suspended from a pin placed at the uppermost point of the vertical line the camber can be measured. Correct camber should be 0 to 1 deg. 30 min. positive.

All adjustments and checking should be carried out with the car on level ground and tyres at correct pressure.

Should the rear axle camber measurements be outside the tolerance given then a full check should be carried out by a service station as it may mean one of the following conditions, assuming that the hub bearings are correctly adjusted and the wheel is not buckled.

Suspension arm twisted.

Stub axle and suspension arm hinge pin not parallel. Special gauges will be needed to carry out these checks.

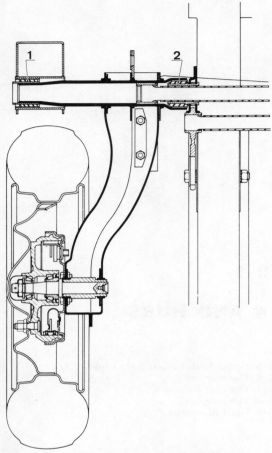

FIG 8:1 Sectional view of a rear half-axle 1 and 2 are rubber bushes

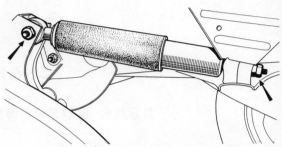

FIG 8:3 Rear damper attachment points

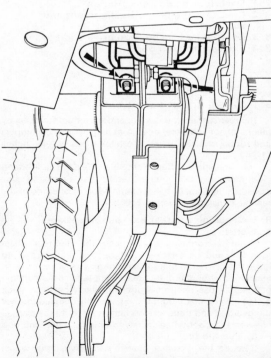

FIG 8:4 The brake pressure limiter cover exposing the two securing screws located between the limiter spring and rear suspension arm

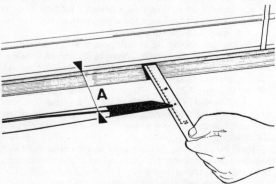

FIG 8:2 Gauge for measuring rear wheel toe-in distribution

Key to Fig 8:2   For key see Text

8:3 Overhauling suspension arms and bushes

(a) Removing and replacing a rear suspension arm:

1 Place the vehicle on stands and remove the road wheel. Disconnect the damper as shown in **FIG 8:3** and refer to damper removal procedure later on in this Chapter.

2 Remove the brake hose from the suspension arm mounting lug and plug the fluid line.

3 Release the adjusting cam on the torsion bar and set at zero.

4 Remove the torsion bar as described in the next Section.

5 Remove the shield from the brake pressure limiter, as well as the two securing screws between the limiter spring and rear suspension arm (see **FIG 8:4**).

6 Unscrew the 3 screws securing the torsion bar inner bearing to the rear chassis member (see **FIG 8:5**).

7 Remove the 3 bolts (see **FIG 8:6**) which secure the outer torsion bar bearing to the rear side member, withdraw the rear half-axle.

It is very important not to switch round the torsion bars.

The righthand torsion bar is marked with a touch of blue paint and three triangular symbols and the lefthand one by a touch of white paint and two triangular symbols. This may be applicable only to early models, see **Section 8:4** for markings on later models.

(b) Refitting:

1 Place the bearings in position on the sidemembers after having smeared the bolts with grease. Secure the bearings to a tightening torque of 25 lb ft.

2 Reconnect the brake hoses placing them on their supports without their being under tension and then twist them slightly by moving the end fittings through 2 notches in an anticlockwise direction (viewed from rear of the vehicle).

For the righthand hose, offset the end fitting by 2 notches in a clockwise direction.

3 Secure the damper in place (pivot pin tightening torque 35 lb ft). Tighten the suspension arm hinge pin to 35 lb ft with the car loaded with the equivalent of two passengers.

4 Smear the ends of the torsion bar with grease and slide it into position.

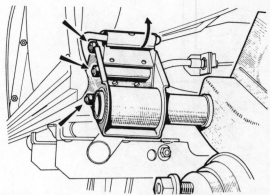

FIG 8:6 A rear torsion bar outer bearing and securing bolts

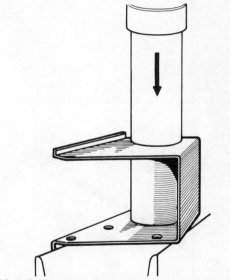

FIG 8:7 Pressing in a rear suspension arm outer bearing

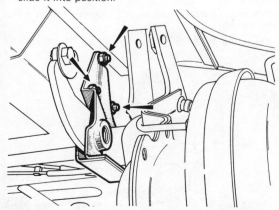

FIG 8:5 A rear torsion bar inner bearing and securing bolts

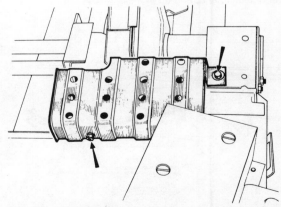

FIG 8:8 The brake pressure limiter cover and securing bolts

FIG 8:9 Setting a rear torsion bar adjusting cam to zero

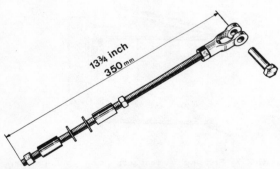

FIG 8:10 Diagram of service tool used as substitute for rear damper during torsion bar removal

13¾ inch
350 mm

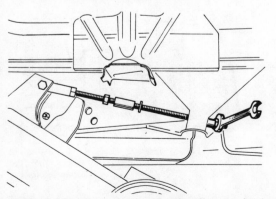

FIG 8:11 Service tool adjustment to allow torsion bar anchor lever to be lifted from adjusting cam

5 Bleed the brakes as described in **Chapter 10** and fit the road wheel.
6 Adjust the underbody height as described later in this Chapter.
7 Carry out alignment checks as described in the previous Section and adjust if required.
8 The rear suspension arms are fitted with outer bearings pressed into position.

Their removal requires the use of a press (see **FIG 8:7**).

9 Refer to **FIG 8:1** and the replacement rubber bush 2 is supplied already fitted to the inner bearing of the rear suspension arm.

Fitting is carried out using a press, taking care to locate it correctly, relative to the rear suspension arm.

10 The rubber bush 1 is pressed on the outer bearing until the end face of the bush is flush with the edge of the bearing.

It is not considered within the scope of the home mechanic to renew these bushes (operation 9 and 10) due to the presses and gauging equipment required and it is recommended that renewal be left to a service station having the appropriate equipment.

8:4 The rear torsion bars

(a) Removal:

1 Place the vehicle on stands.
2 Remove the road wheel.
3 Remove the cover and the two cover securing screws from the brake pressure limiter valve as shown in **FIG 8:8** if applicable.

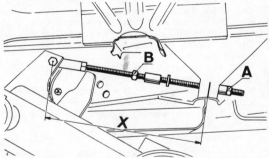

FIG 8:12 Service tool setting prior to fitting a rear torsion bar

Key to Fig 8:12   For key see text

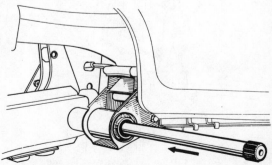

FIG 8:13 Fitting a rear torsion bar

4 Release the load on the torsion bar by setting the adjusting cam to zero (see **FIG 8 : 9**). A central securing bolt is used to retain the cam.

5 Remove the rear anti-roll bar, if applicable, and the damper as detailed later in this Chapter and in its place fit a screwed rod complete with clevis fork made up to the dimensions shown in **FIG 8 : 10**.

6 Screw up the nut to the point where the anchor lever lifts off the cam (see **FIG 8 : 11**).

7 Remove the torsion bar.

8 Note that there are 25 splines on the end of the bar that locates in the bearing and 24 splines on the end that locates in the lever arm. The righthand side is identified by three pyramid symbols and the lefthand side by two pyramid symbols on later models.

(b) Refitting:

1 Make sure that the anchor lever is in the correct position when replaced. Screw up nut A at the end of the bar in order to obtain the measurement X 11 inch (280 mm) for good roads or $10\frac{13}{16}$ inch (275 mm) for poor roads as shown in **FIG 8 : 12**.

2 When this position has been achieved, slide in the torsion bar through the bearing. When refitting, smear the splines of the torsion bar with molybdenum disulphide grease (see **FIG 8 : 13**).

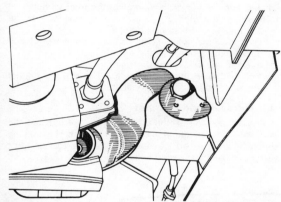

FIG 8 : 14 The correct position of a rear torsion bar anchor lever in relation to its adjusting cam when at zero setting

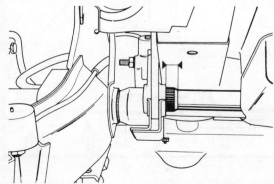

FIG 8 : 15 Initial stage of fitting a rear torsion bar showing exposed splines

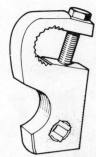

FIG 8 : 16 Detailed view of service tool Sus.392 for applying torque to torsion bars

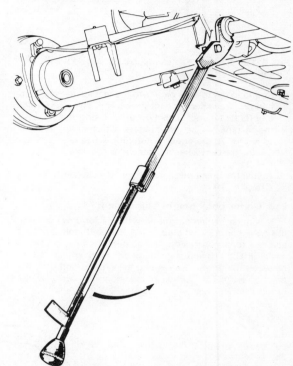

FIG 8 : 17 Applying torque to a rear torsion bar using service tool Sus.392

3 Set the anchor lever, this should come in contact with the cam when the cam is set to zero (see **FIG 8 : 14**).

4 When the anchor lever is correctly positioned, slide the torsion bar into the anchor lever leaving about $\frac{25}{64}$ inch (10 mm) of spline visible (see **FIG 8 : 15**).

In order to obtain the correct position of the anchor lever it may be necessary to offer up the torsion bar to the anchor lever several times, off-setting it each time by one or several splines.

5 Fit on service tool Sus.392 (**FIG 8 : 16**). Attach a torque wrench onto this tool and check that the anchor lever lifts off the cam (at zero) when the torque applied is 60 lb ft (see **FIG 8 : 17**).

6 Hold the torsion bar in position using clamp service tool Sus.25 Mark D (**FIG 8 : 18**), before applying this

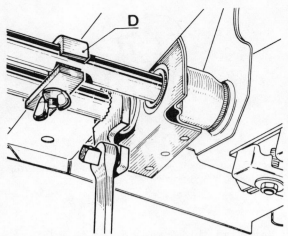

FIG 8:18 Torsion bar clamp fitted prior to applying torque

torque to the torsion bar. With the rear suspension arm hanging free check the torque setting. To do this, refer to **FIG 8:12** and unscrew nut A. Using nut B bring the distance piece into contact with the arm in order to neutralize the effect of the rubber bush.

7 Secure the cam when adjustment is correct and remove the clamp.

8 Adjust the brake pressure limiter valve, as described in **Chapter 10.**

8:5 Under body height adjustment

This must be carried out with the car on level ground, the tyres correctly inflated, a full fuel tank and the front and rear torsion bars adjusted as described previously.

See **FIG 8:19** and measure firstly the heights H_1 or H_4 between the wheel centres and the ground and then the heights H_2 or H_5 between the sidemembers and the ground (in line with the wheels).

Find the difference by calculation $H_1 - H_2 = H_3$,
$H_5 - H_4 = H_6$
The dimensions H_3 or H_6 should be within the following values given in the table.

For the most suitable performance on all road conditions adjust the front and rear torsion bars to give nominal measurements as follows:

Road condition	Front H_3	Rear H_6
Good roads	$2\frac{7}{32} + \frac{25}{64}$ inch	$4\frac{7}{8} + \frac{25}{64}$ inch
	56 + 10 mm	123 + 10 mm
Bad roads	$2\frac{7}{32} + \frac{25}{64}$ inch	$5\frac{3}{8} + \frac{25}{64}$ inch
	56 + 10 mm	137 + 10 mm

The difference of body height between right and left-hand sides should not be greater than .4 inch (10 mm).

At the rear of the car the greater the difference, the higher the vehicle.

At the front of the car the greater the difference, the lower the vehicle.

After any underbody height adjustment, adjust the brake limiter.

8:6 The rear hubs

The rear wheel hub is mounted on taper roller bearings as shown in **FIG 8:20.**

(a) Removal:

1 Jack-up the vehicle and remove the road wheel.

2 Remove the grease cap using a service tool or the careful use of Stilson pipe grips.

3 Withdraw the splitpin and unscrew the hub nut and remove the thrust washer.

4 Slacken the brake adjusting cams.

5 Pull off the drum by using a suitable three legged extractor bolted to the wheel studs.

(b) The seals and bearings

Any trace of oil on the brake linings will indicate the necessity for immediate oil seal replacement. This may be simply accomplished by using a suitable tubular drift to remove the old and replace a new seal in the brake drum.

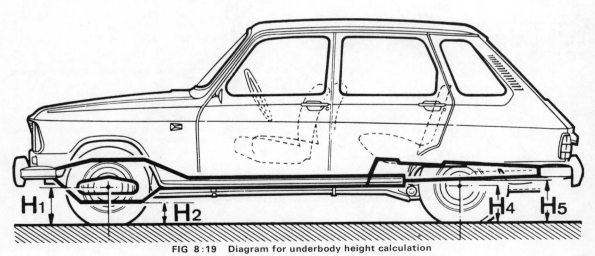

FIG 8:19 Diagram for underbody height calculation

Key to Fig 8:19   For key see text

Examine the bearings. If these require renewal, both the tracks and races must be withdrawn from the stub axle and brake drum by using suitable extractors. Check carefully the type and location of the roller bearings for exact renewal.

(c) Refitting and replacement:

1 Gently push on the bearing using a suitable sleeve 3 (see **FIG 8 : 21**) and the stub axle nut. Remove the nut, fit the stub axle washer and draw the bearing completely on.
2 Remove the sleeve and place a small amount of high melting point grease between the two bearings, then refit the drum.
3 Check the bearing end float as described later in this Section.
4 Fit the grease cap after filling it $\frac{3}{4}$ full of grease.
5 Adjust the brakes.

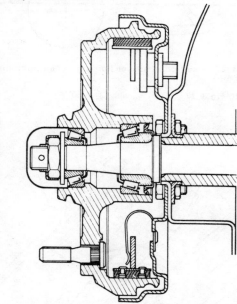

FIG 8 : 20   Sectional view of a rear hub, 845 cc

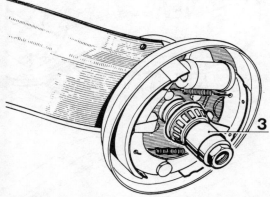

FIG 8 : 21   Pressing on a rear hub bearing using a distance piece 3 and a hub nut

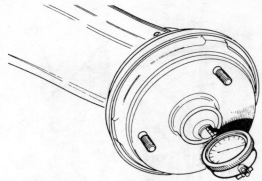

FIG 8 : 22   Checking the end float of a rear hub with a dial gauge

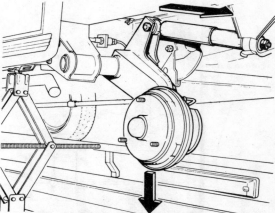

FIG 8 : 23   A rear suspension arm hanging free to fully compress the damper prior to its removal

(d) Checking the end float of rear hub bearings:

1 Tighten the stub axle securing nut to a torque of 20 lb ft turning the brake drum at the same time.
2 Unscrew the stub axle nut by about $\frac{1}{6}$ of a turn.
3 Fit a suitable puller located under the wheel studs and free the drum by turning the tool spindle.
4 Remove the puller and fix a bracket with a clock gauge to one of the wheel studs (see **FIG 8 : 22**).
   Alternatively, feeler gauges may be used between a bar fixed to the wheel stud.
5 Screw up or unscrew the stub axle nut and check that the end float is between .001 and .002 inch (.01 and .05 mm).
6 Fit a new splitpin and push on the grease cup $\frac{3}{4}$ filled with grease.
7 Adjust the brakes.

8 : 7 The rear dampers

De Carbon type:

Removal:

1 Jack up the vehicle and remove the road wheel.
2 Allow the rear suspension arm to hang free (see **FIG 8 : 23**).

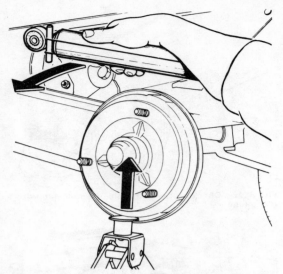

FIG 8:24 Jacking up a rear suspension arm in order to remove a damper

FIG 8:26 Arrangement of cup washers and rubber bushes, Allinquant type damper

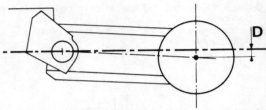

FIG 8:27 Position of suspension arm when tightening front pin

Key to Fig 8:27 $D = 1\frac{7}{32}$ inch (31 mm)

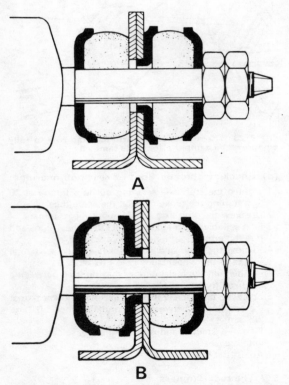

FIG 8:25 Rear damper lower connection inner cup alternative positioning

A Inner cup position for use on poor road surfaces or with 'special' vehicles.
B Inner cup position for use on good road surfaces with vehicles of standard specification.

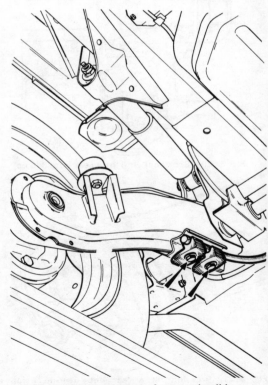

FIG 8:28 Attachment of rear anti-roll bar

3 With the damper now fully compressed, either fit a restraining cable and bar or if a new damper is to be fitted, the tool which is supplied with it. Withdraw the front retaining pin, and the rear nuts and fittings. Note the position of the cups and bushes for reassembly.
4 Raise the suspension arm with a jack as shown in **FIG 8:24** until the now restricted damper may be lifted away.

Refitting:

1 Fit the tool supplied with a new damper or restrict its travel with a restraining cable.
2 Grease the front fixing pin and connect both this and the rear securing nut. Remove the restraining tool or cable.

Tightening of the front fixing pin must be carried out with the car in the half loaded position to a torque of 40 lb ft.

On poor road conditions or with 'special version' vehicles, the inner cup washer must always be fitted on the side taking the greatest load A (see **FIG 8:25**).

On good road surfaces or with standard cars the inner cup washer is fitted on the other side of the bracket B (see **FIG 8:25**).

Allinquant type:

Remove in the same manner as the De Carbon type but there is no need to restrain the damper.

When refitting the damper arrange the rubber bushes and cup washers as shown in **FIG 8:26**.

Tighten the front retaining pin to a torque of 40 lb ft with the suspension arm in the position shown in **FIG 8:27**.

Testing rear dampers:

Testing of dampers can only be carried out by checking for lack of resistance or seizure. Either of these conditions will indicate the need for immediate renewal. Anything beyond a simple test is impossible for the home mechanic and such a test consists of extending and contracting the damper about 10 or 12 times with the damper held securely in a vertical position. A definite resistance should be felt in both directions of movement. If this is not apparent, renew the damper.

Carry out this operation on new dampers also, before fitting, in case they require priming after being stored horizontally.

8:8 Rear anti-roll bar

Removal and refitting:

1 Place the car over a pit.
2 Unscrew the two retaining bolts on each side, arrowed in **FIG 8:28**.
3 Remove the bar.

Refit in the reverse order.

8:9 Fault diagnosis

(a) Rattles

1 Rubber bushes in damper links worn through
2 Loose damper mountings
3 Broken torsion bar
4 Torsion bar bearing bolts loose
5 Suspension arm flexibloc bushes worn

(b) Wobble

1 Incorrect tracking
2 Worn hub bearings
3 Defective dampers
4 Worn flexibloc bushes
5 Loose wheel fixings
6 Uneven tyre wear

(c) Excessive tyre wear

1 Check 1 and 2 in (b)
2 Check 5 in (b)

(d) Bottoming of suspension

1 Check 3 in (a)
2 Check 3 in (b)

(e) Excessive rolling

1 Check 3 in (a) and 3 in (b)
2 Check 2 in (b)

NOTES

CHAPTER 9

STEERING GEAR

9:1 Operating principle and construction

The steering gear is of sealed rack and pinion type and sectional diagrams are given in **FIG 9:1**. Motion to the steering gear is provided by a two-spoked steering wheel operating through an exposed column to a flexible joint mounted at the top of the steering box. The steering column is supported at its upper end by a bush and the column is fitted with a bracket which holds the ignition/anti-theft switch (see **Chapter 3**).

Final motion to the road wheels is transmitted through two steering links connected between each end of the steering rack and a stub axle carrier arm.

No provision is made for overhaul of the rack and pinion and routine maintenance consists of periodically checking the security of the mounting bolts.

The assembly of the early 850 cc column differs from that of the 1108 cc column and both are explained separately in the ensuing sections. However, from Oct. 1971, vehicle No. 340486, the 850 cc has been brought more in line with the assembly of the 1108 cc, by the introduction of a universal joint. The servicing of the later column is described in **Section 9:7**.

9:2 Removing, dismantling and servicing the steering gear

(a) Removal and dismantling:

1 Unhook the handbrake return spring (see **FIG 9:3**) and remove the bolts B from the steering rack end fittings (arrowed in **FIG 9:2**).
2 Remove the two flexible coupling nuts from the side nearer the steering wheel (arrowed in **FIG 9:3**).
3 Remove the radiator stay, also the gear control rod bearing, unscrew nuts A and C (see **FIG 9:2**). Pull out the clip from the positive cable holder.
4 Disconnect the radiator from the steering box (see **FIG 9:4**).
5 Remove the two steering box securing bolts and lift the steering box away, retaining the setting shims carefully for exact replacement.
6 Remove the steering column/facia bottom cover from the flasher/lighting control.
7 Bend back the locking washer and unscrew the two steering column securing nuts A and the bolts B on the bulkhead plate (see **FIG 9:5**).
   Take care to retain shims C during removal of nuts A.

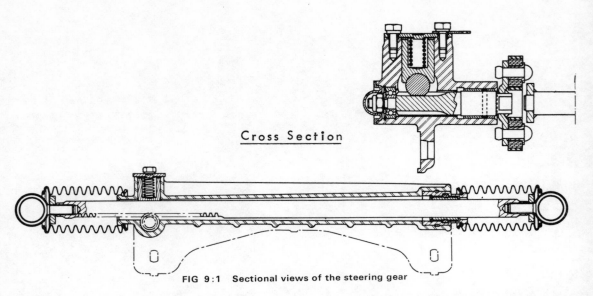

Cross Section

FIG 9 : 1 Sectional views of the steering gear

8 Remove the pin from the combined clutch and brake pedal shaft (see **FIG 9 : 6**) and remove the two return springs.

9 Push out the shaft and remove the splitpin and shaft D from the clutch pedal in order to slacken the clutch cable.

10 Undo the master cylinder fixing nuts, the cover and clutch cable inside the engine compartment as shown in **FIG 9 : 7**.

11 Pull the column complete with wheel in an upward direction but take care not to damage the sealing rubber grommet on the engine bulkhead.

12 Prise the steering wheel boss away, or on later cars take off the embellisher by removing the two screws underneath, and remove the steering wheel securing

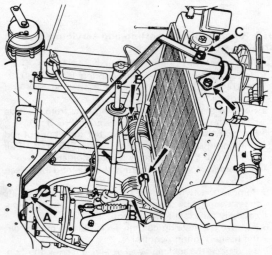

FIG 9 : 2 Steering gear disconnection points

Key to Fig 9 : 2
B Rack-end fitting nuts bush securing nuts
A Radiator stay nuts
C Radiator stay and gear control

nut now exposed. With a suitable puller remove the steering wheel. The Renault Tool No. DIR.21 is available.

The steering components are now fully dismantled and servicing is restricted to the following operation. Any wear or defects in the steering box will necessitate a factory exchange unit being obtained as the box is not repairable.

(b) Servicing the steering column top bush:

1 Withdraw the column from the steering column tube.
2 Remove the circlip which locates the top support bush (see **FIG 9 : 8**).
3 Using a tube $1\frac{3}{16}$ inch (30 mm) in diameter push out the bush having first lubricated the inside of the steering column tube (see **FIG 9 : 9**).
4 Fit a new circlip and lubricate the inside of the steering column tube.
5 From the lower end of the tube push up a new bush until it impinges upon the circlip.

9 : 3 Reassembly and refitting

Refitting is largely a reversal of the dismantling procedure but certain tools will be required.

1 Fit the steering column to the steering column tube.
2 Carefully push the steering column through the rubber bulkhead.
3 Screw on the two column tube securing nuts and use new tabwashers (see **FIG 9 : 5**). Replace the original shims in their exact location.
4 Screw in the bulkhead plate bolts.
5 Position the steering box, replace the retained shims in their original locations and fit the radiator connecting bolts and the two steering box securing bolts.

Where a new steering box has been fitted it may require adjustment with shims of varying thicknesses or quantities but the gauging will require special equipment and this should be left to a service station having the appropriate equipment.

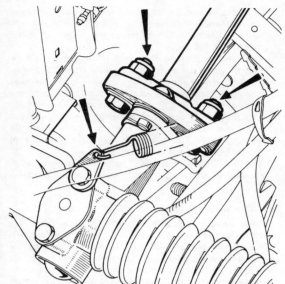

FIG 9:3 Handbrake lever return spring and the steering column flexible joint bolts

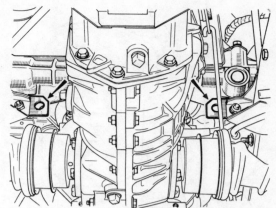

FIG 9:4 The steering box to radiator mounting points and setting shims

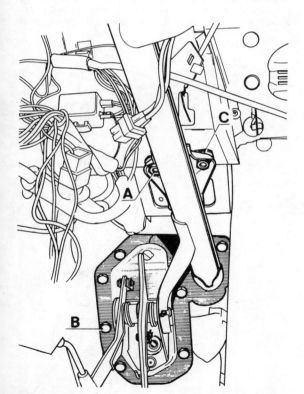

FIG 9:5 The steering column to bulkhead support plate and column bracket

Key to Fig 9:5
B Support bracket shims

A Support bracket nuts
C Support plate bolts

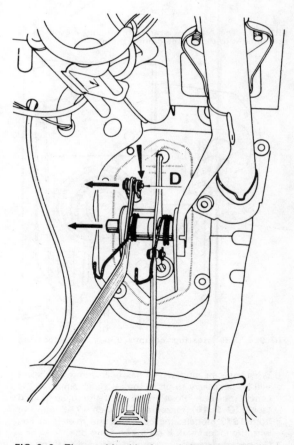

FIG 9:6 The combined brake and clutch pedal shaft. D is clutch pedal swivel pin

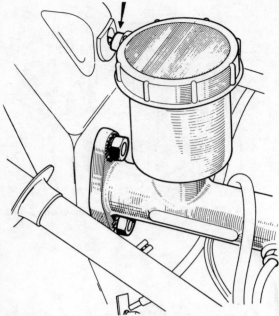

FIG 9:7 The brake master cylinder and clutch cable attachment in the engine compartment

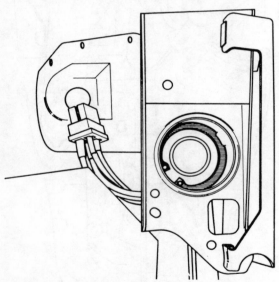

FIG 9:8 The steering column upper bush locating circlip

6 Where the steering wheel has been removed then it will be necessary to place the rack and pinion in the central position. Position the end fitting so that A (see **FIG 9:10**) measures $2\frac{13}{16}$ inch (71.5 mm) or from **1973** models, the centre of the rivet is in line with the index mark B on the steering box.

7 Connect the steering column flexible joint (nuts on the steering wheel side) as shown in **FIG 9:3**.

8 Making sure that the steering column is not moved the steering wheel may be fitted onto the splines so that two spokes are horizontal but in the lower half of the steering wheel circle.

9 Replace the steering rack end fittings, making sure that the steering arms are correctly positioned with the link pin horizontal, before tightening the steering box nuts. The simplest way of ensuring this is to use service tool DIR.209 shown fitted in position in **FIG 9:11**. A piece of sheet mild steel suitably cut will be a suitable substitute to ensure that the steering arms are level before final tightening of the rack end fittings is carried out.

10 The front wheel track will require checking and if necessary, adjusting as fully described in **Section 9:5**.

9:4 The steering links

These are attached to the rack end fittings of the steering box. The steering links themselves are non-adjustable, all adjustment being made to the rack-end fittings for correct front-wheel alignment. The steering link ball joints are sealed and no provision is made for dismantling, adjustment or lubrication. In the event of play developing due to wear, the complete link should be renewed. Check the condition of the rubber ball joint gaiters regularly and renew immediately if damaged or deteriorated to prevent the ingress of dirt or water. Always keep the ball joints absolutely in the centre of their plane of travel which in

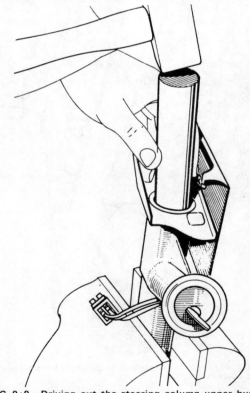

FIG 9:9 Driving out the steering column upper bush from the column outer tube

turn means that the adjustable rack-end fittings must be very carefully locked in position (see **FIG 9:11**). The ball joint nuts should be tightened to 25 lb ft.

9:5 Adjusting the front wheel track

The correct front wheel toe-out is between 0 and $\frac{1}{8}$ inch (0 to 3 mm) on early models. For 1973 the limits are 0 to $\frac{3}{16}$ inch (0 to 5 mm).

Preliminary checks:

Indications of incorrect tracking are evident if there is undue or uneven front tyre wear or road holding is not up to standard.

Before carrying out the front axle geometry checks, the points listed below should be checked.

Tyre pressures
Static and dynamic balance of wheel/tyre assemblies
Wear of tyre treads
Check any play in:
The front suspension and steering arm ball joints
The front hub bearings
The suspension arms
The drive shafts
Check the condition of:
The suspension rubber bushes
The efficiency of the dampers
The torque setting of the torsion bars
The under body height as fully described in **Chapter 8**.
The points at which the half-axles are secured to the sidemembers for security of retaining nuts.
Ensure that the car is standing on level ground and centralize the steering as described in the previous Section.

(a) Checking the total toe-out:

Although it is preferable to leave this operation to a service station which has modern measuring equipment it is quite simple to make suitable gauges to check both total and distributed toe-out.

A gauge to measure total toe-out may be made from tubing, suitably cranked to clear the gearbox/transmission unit, having one fixed end and one adjustable end (nut and bolt).

1 Measure the distance between the two inner wheel rims at hub height at the front. Move the wheel through

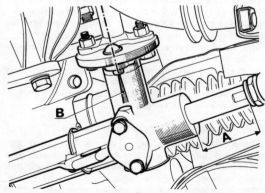

FIG 9:10 Steering centre position

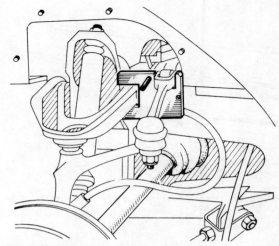

FIG 9:11 Service tool in position on steering link prior to locking end rack fittings

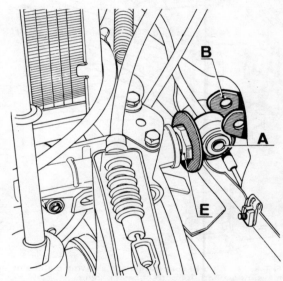

FIG 9:12 Steering rack end fitting and steering link

Key to Fig 9:12   **A** Rack-end fitting bush
B Steering link fork   **E** Rack-end fitting locknut

180 deg. (half a turn) and measure the distance between the inner wheel rims at hub height at the rear. The latter measurement should be less by between 0 and $\frac{1}{8}$ inch (0 to 3 mm), or 0-5 mm on 1973 cars.
2 If the toe-out is incorrect, loosen the steering rack end fitting (A) locknuts E (see **FIG 9:12**) and disconnect the steering arms (B).
3 Screw the end fittings in or out equally, temporarily connect the steering links to them and carry out the measuring operation 1 again. Repeat until the toe-out figure is within the correct tolerance.

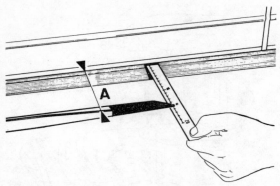

FIG 9:13 Front wheel toe-out distribution gauge. A is half total toe-out

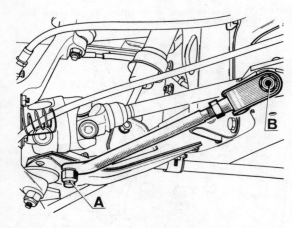

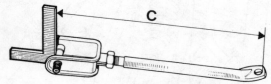

FIG 9:14 A tie-bar in position and showing method of measuring length for correct castor angle

Key to Fig 9:14   A Securing bolt   B Securing bolt
C Correct measurment of 11$\frac{11}{16}$ inch (296.5 mm)

Each half turn of the rack end equals approximately .059 inch (1.5 mm) of toe-in or toe-out. To decrease the toe-out, screw in the rack end. To increase the toe-out, unscrew the rack end.

(b) Checking the toe-out distribution:

To check the distribution of the toe-out between each front wheel make up a gauge similar to, but it may be much less complex than, the one shown in **FIG 9:13**. A pointer preferably metal with a clearly defined rule will be adequate if an assistant is available. Ensure that the pointer locates on the wheel rims rather than the tyre walls to avoid distortion. The pointer should be at hub height and pointing towards the rear of the car. Measure distance A between the end of the pointer and the side-member with the rule. Take a second measurement after first turning the road wheel through 180 deg. (half a turn). Repeat the operation on the opposite front wheel.

If the measurements differ than the toe-out is not equally distributed and should be adjusted as follows:

1 Disconnect the steering links and screw in or out the rack-end fittings by amounts to correct the unequal distribution but to maintain the correct total toe-out.

2 Temporarily reconnect the steering links and check and adjust (if necessary) the total toe-out.

3 When the adjustments are correct, tighten the rack-end fitting locknuts, ensuring that the steering links are in the centre of their planes.

The following points are emphasized when adjusting front wheel toe-out.

It is toe-out (wider distance at front of wheel than rear).

The car should be half-laden for correct adjustment.

Always keep the steering in the central position during operations.

9:6 Steering effects on tyre life
Inflation pressures:

There is an average loss of 13 per cent mileage for every 10 per cent reduction in inflation pressure below the recommended figure.

Severe and persistent under-inflation produces unmistakable evidence on the tread. It also causes structural failure due to excessive friction and temperature within the casing.

Pressures higher than those recommended reduce tread life by concentrating the load on a small tread area. Excessive pressures overstrain the casing cords, cause rapid wear and make the tyres more susceptible to impact fractures and cuts.

Effect of temperature:

Air expands with heating and tyre pressures increase as the tyres warm up. Pressures increase more in hot weather than in cold and as a result of high speed. Pressures in warm tyres should not be reduced to standard pressure readings recommended for cold tyres. Bleeding air from a warm tyre increases their deflections and causes the temperatures to climb still higher. The tyres will also become under-inflated when they cool.

The rate of tread wear may be twice as fast at 50 mile/hr as at 30 mile/hr.

High speed causes increased temperatures due to more deflections per minute and a faster rate of deflections and recovery. The resistance of the tread to abrasion decreases with increases in tyre temperature.

Camber, castor and kingpin inclination:

These angles normally require no attention unless they have been disturbed by a severe impact or abnormal wear in front hub bearings. It is always advisable to check them if steering irregularities develop.

Wheel camber, usually combined with road camber causes a wheel to try to turn in the direction of lean, due

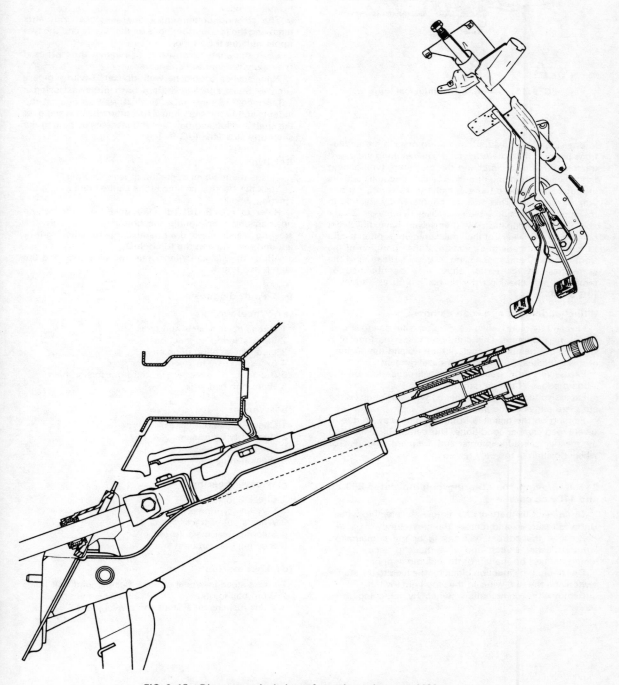

FIG 9:15   Diagrammatical view of steering column on 1108cc cars

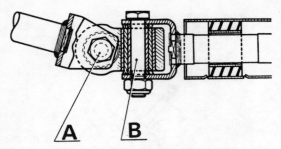

FIG 9:16 Securing the universal joint

to one side of the tread attempting to make more revolutions per mile than the other side. The resulting increased tread shuffle on the road and the off-centre tyre loading tend to cause rapid and one-sided wear. Unequal cambers introduce unbalanced forces which try to steer the car one way or the other. This must be countered by steering in the opposite direction which increases tread wear. Castor and kingpin inclination by themselves have no direct bearing on tyre wear but their measurement is often useful for providing a general indication of the condition of the front geometry and suspension. A good indication of the correctness of the castor angle may be obtained by removing and checking the tie-bar length as shown in FIG 9:14.

Wheel alignment and road camber:

Fins and feathers on the tread surface are due to severe wheel misalignment. This condition takes the form of a sharp fin on the edge of each pattern rib and the position of this indicates the direction of misalignment.

Excessive toe-in (rear wheels) will cause fins on the inboard edges of the pattern ribs.

Excessive toe-out (front wheels) will cause fins on the outboard edges of the pattern ribs.

Finning on the nearside front tyre only may be due to severe road camber conditions. This cannot be eliminated by mechanical adjustments and frequent changes of wheel position is the only remedy.

9:7 Removing the steering column, later 850 cc and 1108 cc cars

Disconnect the battery and remove the steering wheel. Undo four screws and remove the glove tray.

Remove the bottom half casing of the combination lighting/flasher switch and also the clip securing the wiring harness on the left of the column support.

Disconnect the junction block for the feed to the starter switch and the two wires to the stop light switch.

Remove the combination switch by removing three screws.

Take out the splitpin and clevis pin from the master cylinder pushrod.

Remove the top pin on the universal joint and extract the splitpin and clevis from the clutch cable and push the sleeve out of its stop. Remove the two nuts securing the master cylinder.

The steering column may now be taken out after removing the four bottom bolts on the scuttle and the two upper nuts on the support.

Push the shaft downwards to remove the bushes if they are worn and to be renewed.

New bushes should be well lubricated with a grease such as Spargraph and the top bush fitted first using a 1.378 inch (35 mm) tube. Push it well up against the indents and fit the snap ring. The bottom bush is slid over the shaft and located between the recesses by pulling the shaft upwards (see FIG 9:15).

Refitting:

This is the removal operation in reverse order.

Lock the steering column at the centre point and fit the steering wheel.

Refer to FIG 9:16. Turn the steering to the central position and then tighten the bottom bolt **A**. Turn the steering wheel one and a quarter turns to either right or left and then tighten the top bolt **B**.

Adjust the master cylinder pushrod clearance and the clutch free travel.

9:8 Fault diagnosis

(a) Wheel wobble

1 Unbalanced wheels and tyres
2 Slack steering connections
3 Incorrect steering geometry
4 Excessive play in steering gear
5 Broken or incorrectly adjusted front torsion bars
6 Worn hub bearings

(b) Wander

1 Check 2, 3 and 4 in (a)
2 Uneven tyre pressures
3 Uneven tyre wear
4 Weak dampers

(c) Heavy steering

1 Check 3 in (a)
2 Very low tyre pressures
3 Wheels out of track
4 Steering gear maladjusted
5 Steering column bent

(d) Lost motion

1 Loose steering wheel or worn flexible joint bolt holes
2 Worn ball joints
3 Worn suspension system and swivel joints

CHAPTER 10

BRAKING SYSTEM

10:1 Description

The brakes on all four wheels are hydraulically operated through a foot pedal acting directly on the master cylinder. On 845cc models, drum brakes are fitted to all four wheels, while disc brakes are fitted on the front of 1108cc cars.

A pressure distribution valve is incorporated into the system to equalize the pressure between the wheels and to limit the braking pressure on the rear.

Early models are fitted with a single master cylinder, but later models have a tandem master cylinder.

Dual brake systems incorporate a pressure drop indicator to warn the driver of any malfunction in either of the systems, front or rear.

A later type of pressure drop indicator, incorporates a bypass to give full braking in the rear system if a fault develops in the front system.

A handbrake lever located below the facia operates the brakes on the front wheels in the case of the smaller car and on the rear wheels for the larger engined models.

Since many components are common to both systems, it will be convenient to describe the drum layout first and then the items in the disc/drum system which are different.

10:2 Routine maintenance and brake shoe adjustment

Always maintain the fluid reservoir at the correct level in the reservoir body. This is approximately $\frac{13}{16}$ inch from the top rim of the reservoir.

Always use hydraulic fluid of the recommended type and ensure it is clean, free from air bubbles having been stored in an airtight tin. Hydraulic fluid which is exposed to the air for any length of time will, apart from becoming dirty, absorb moisture and the fluid will subsequently corrode the internal parts and surfaces of the system.

Occasionally check the security of the fluid line retaining clips and tightness of the hoses. If they require tightening, never twist them but see **Section 4** for full details of flexible hose treatment.

The only other regular servicing requirement is brake adjustment.

(a) The front brakes:

1 Ensure that the handbrake is off and chock the rear wheels.
2 Raise the front of the car until the road wheels are free.

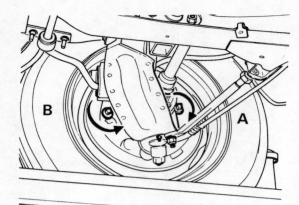

FIG 10:1 The front brake adjuster cams

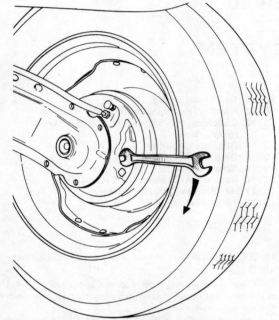

FIG 10:2 The rear brake adjuster cams (one only shown)

3 Adjust each of the shoe cam adjusters (see **FIG 10:1**) until the lining just rubs on the drum when the road wheel is turned. Adjust cam A first (leading shoe) followed by cam B (trailing shoe).
4 Apply the brake pedal sharply and recheck the adjustment by turning the road wheel.
5 Repeat the operations on the other front brake.
  Do not mistake transmission and shaft drag for binding brakes when adjusting the shoes.

(b) The rear brakes:

1 Ensure that the handbrake is on or front wheels chocked.
2 Jack up the rear of the car until the wheels are free.

3 Adjust each of the two cam adjusters (see **FIG 10:2**) until the lining just rubs on the drum when the road wheel is turned. Adjust the cam arrowed first.
4 Apply the brake pedal sharply and recheck the adjustment by turning the road wheel.
5 Repeat the operation on the other rear brake.

10:3 Removing, servicing and refitting the master cylinder

Before any operations are carried out to the hydraulic system, it cannot be emphasized too strongly that absolute cleanliness is essential. Prior to removing or dismantling component parts, always brush the exterior and unions with paraffin and wipe dry. Use only methylated spirit or clean hydraulic fluid for cleaning internal component parts and surfaces. Never allow grease or oil to contaminate the interior metal or rubber parts or surfaces.

(a) Removal:

1 Drain the reservoir(s).
2 Disconnect the pipelines at the master cylinder unions. On the tandem master cylinder unscrew the bolt securing the pressure drop indicator.
3 Remove the pushrod clevis pin at the brake pedal, tilt the pushrod downwards about 40 deg. and withdraw it from the cylinder.
4 Remove the two master cylinder unit securing nuts and withdraw the master cylinder.

(b) Dismantling single master cylinder:

1 Refer to **FIG 10:3** and unscrew and remove the master cylinder reservoir 9.
2 Unscrew the drain plug 8 and washer.
3 Detach the circlip 7 and the thrust washer 6.
4 The secondary cup 5 fitted to the piston 4 may now be withdrawn from the master cylinder housing. This may be achieved by applying a tyre pump to the drain plug orifice at the same time placing a finger over the reservoir port. Alternatively, gentle tapping on a block of wood may be sufficient to dislodge the piston from the cylinder.
5 The primary cup washer 3 followed by the return spring 2 and valve 1 and gasket should also be removed.

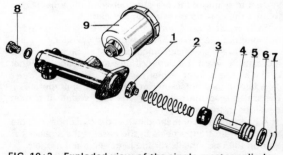

FIG 10:3 Exploded view of the single master cylinder

Key to Fig 10:3 1 Valve   2 Spring   3 Primary cup washer   4 Piston   5 Secondary cup   6 Thrust washer   7 Circlip   8 Drain plug   9 Reservoir

6 Carefully wash all component parts in either clean hydraulic brake fluid or methylated spirit. Closely examine the parts for scoring, scratching or wear. The latter will be indicated by bright surfaces or ovality in the internal bore of the master cylinder body. Renew any defective component parts.

7 Renew all rubber seals and gaskets. A suitable repair kit is available from your dealer, but ensure the seals are the correct size, particularly on the 850 cc model as the cylinder bore was reduced from .811 inch (20.6 mm) to .748 inch (19 mm) from vehicle No. 244979 (1971).

(c) Dismantling, tandem master cylinder:

1 Remove the reservoirs 6 (see **FIG 10:4**).
2 Push the pistons in about $\frac{3}{16}$ inch (5 mm) with a piece of wood, and unscrew the stop screw 1.
3 Remove the circlip 2.
4 Push out the piston assemblies 4 and 5 with air pressure.
  Primary and secondary piston assemblies cannot be dismantled, and if defective must be renewed as an assembly.
  Clean and inspect all parts in a similar manner to the single master cylinder.

(d) Reassembling and refitting:

1 Use only the fingers to manipulate the new seals into their grooves on single master cylinders and ensure that they are fitted with their contours and chamfers the correct way round, as shown in **FIG 10:3** (primary cup-flat face to piston).
2 Lubricate the component parts and the body interior with clean hydraulic fluid and fit the parts in the reverse order to dismantling.
3 Fit a new circlip 7 on single master cylinders.
4 Fit the master cylinder to the vehicle and tighten the retaining bolts. On tandem master cylinders refit the pressure drop indicator in its original position with a tilt of about 15 deg. to the vertical centre line of the master cylinder. The pressure drop indicator is not repairable and in case of any faulty operation must be renewed.

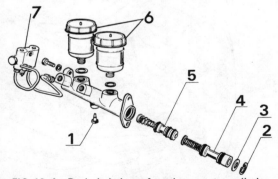

FIG 10:4   Exploded view of tandem master cylinder

Key to Fig 10:4   1 Stop screw   2 Circlip   3 Stop washer
4 Primary piston assembly   5 Secondary piston assembly
6 Reservoirs   7 Pressure drop indicator

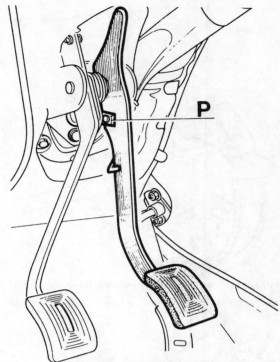

FIG 10:5   The footbrake pedal

Key to Fig 10:5   P is pushrod fork and clevis

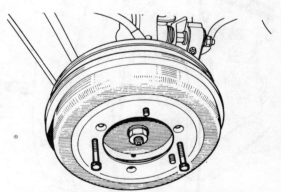

FIG 10:6   Brake drum withdrawal screws (front)

5 Connect the unions using only spanners of short length.
6 Adjust the free movement between the foot pedal operating rod and the master cylinder piston.
  This is carried out by slackening the locknut (see **FIG 10:5**) at the fork end P of the pushrod and turning the operating rod until the pedal shows a very slight free movement before the rod actuates the piston ($\frac{3}{16}$ inch, 5 mm at the pedal). Tighten the locknut.
7 Bleed the brakes as fully described in **Section 8.**

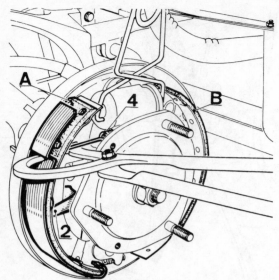

FIG 10:7 Front brake shoe removal (near side front)

Key to Fig 10:7   **A** Leading shoe   **B** Trailing shoe
2 Shoe to backplate retaining clips   4 Shoe return spring

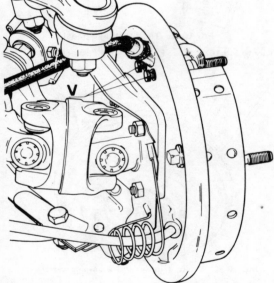

FIG 10:8 Front nearside wheel cylinder retaining bolts (V)

10:4 Dismantling the brakes

(a) Front:

1 Jack up the car, remove the road wheel and release the handbrake and ensure that it is fully off.
2 Release the shoes by slackening the cam adjusters to zero on the brake backplate.
3 Unscrew and remove the three drum securing screws. Mark the drum in relation to its hub.

4 Withdraw the drum by inserting two 6 mm x 100 pitch screws in the tapped holes provided, as shown in **FIG 10:6**.
5 Spring off the brake shoe retaining clips 2 (see **FIG 10:7**).
6 Using return spring pliers and a lining protector as shown in **FIG 10:7** and restraining the wheel cylinder with a clip, remove the top spring.
7 Remove the brake shoe A and the handbrake link.
8 Remove brake shoe B and disconnect the handbrake cable.
9 To remove the wheel cylinder unscrew and remove the two wheel cylinder bolts V (see **FIG 10:8**). Take out the wheel cylinder.

    Disconnect the flexible hose from its rigid coupling and pull out the clip (see **FIG 10:9**) then separate the hose from the wheel cylinder. Do not on any account twist the hose. Full details of flexible hose treatment are given in the next Section.
10 Plug the end of the rigid hose line with a rubber or plastic plug and do not press the brake pedal until reassembly is complete.

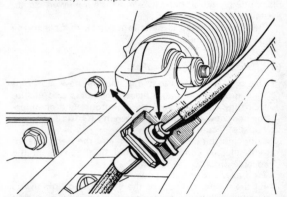

FIG 10:9 Flexible to rigid fluid line union (front brake)

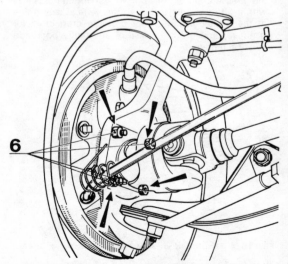

FIG 10:10 Front brake backplate removal
Key to Fig 10:10   6 retaining nuts

11 To remove the front brake backplate, withdraw the hub as fully described in **Chapter 7, Section 7:3** then disconnect the handbrake cable and remove the cable cover and the cable from the anchor plate. Unscrew the four nuts 6 (see **FIG 10:10**). Disconnect the joint between the rigid brake line and the hose on the support clip, free the hose clip and remove the backplate and unscrew the hose.

12 Plug the rigid fluid line.

13 Note that the 850 cc models, from vehicle Nos. 102746 to 329646, were fitted with a new type backplate assembly that is not interchangeable with later models; which underwent a further modification.

(b) Rear:

1 Jack up the car. remove the road wheel.

2 Withdraw the hub cap, splitpin and nut as fully described in **Chapter 8, Section 8:6.**

3 Slacken the brake cam adjusters to zero on the backplate and withdraw the drum also as detailed in **Section 8:6**.

4 Withdraw the shoe spring clips 3 (see **FIG 10:11**).

5 Carefully prise the upper brake shoe ends outwards together until they clear the wheel cylinder and pull the shoes forward.

6 Similarly the bottom ends may now be pulled apart to clear the pivot and the complete shoe assembly together with return springs 1 and 2 lifted away.

7 Carefully note the positioning of the shoe return springs with regard to the shoe hole positions and double and single coils. Make sketches if necessary for exact replacement.

8 Place a rubber band or piece of copper wire round the wheel cylinders to prevent the pistons dropping out. Do not press the brake pedal until reassembly is complete. (No further dismantling is required for brake shoe replacement.)

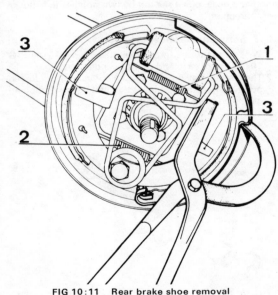

FIG 10:11   Rear brake shoe removal

Key to Fig 10:11   1 and 2 Shoe return spring   3 Brake shoe to backplate retaining clips

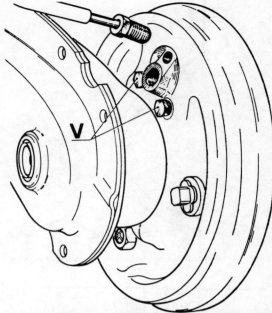

FIG 10:12   Rear wheel cylinder securing bolts and fluid line union

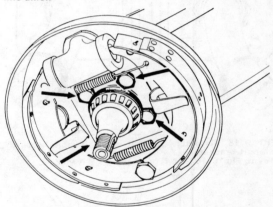

FIG 10:13   Rear brake backplate securing bolts

9 To remove the wheel cylinder, disconnect the rigid hydraulic brake line by unscrewing the union at the wheel cylinder (see **FIG 10:12**). Remove the two cylinder securing bolts V and withdraw the cylinder. Plug the fluid line with a suitable rubber or plastic plug.

10 To remove the brake backplate, withdraw the stub axle bearing and unscrew the four plate securing bolts shown in **FIG 10:13**.

10:5 The flexible brake hoses

It is of utmost importance that the flexible hoses should be regularly examined for perishing or chafing. Keep them free from oil or grease and when connecting components are to be removed, the following procedure should be followed to prevent twisting or damage.

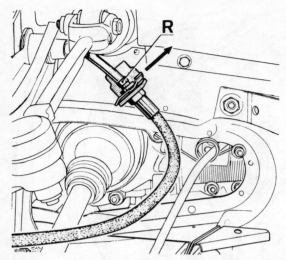

FIG 10:14 A front flexible hose union R is securing clip

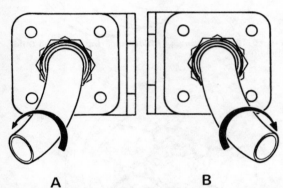

FIG 10:15 Assembly of front wheel flexible hoses to support brackets
Key to Fig 10:15   A is front right   B is front left

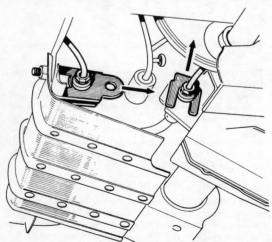

FIG 10:16 Rear brake flexible hose removal

(a) Dismantling the front flexible hoses:

1 Either drain the fluid reservoir or the rigid fluid line may be plugged after disconnecting the flexible hose.
2 Refer to **FIG 10:14** and unscrew the fixed union R.
3 Lift out the clip.
4 Remove the flexible hose from the support bracket.
5 Unscrew the hose from the wheel cylinder taking care not to twist the hose.

(b) Refitting a front flexible hose:

1 This operation should be carried out with the car jacked up and the road wheels hanging free. Screw the flexible hose into the wheel cylinder using only a spanner of short length. Use a new copper washer.
2 Offer up the hose to the support bracket and turn the end in the direction of the arrows shown in **FIG 10:15** a minimum of one notch and a maximum of two notches.
3 Bleed the brakes as described later in this Chapter.

(c) Rear flexible hose removal:

1 Drain the brake fluid reservoir unless it is intended to plug the ends of the rigid brake pipes upon disconnection.
2 Refer to **FIG 10:16** and disconnect the fixed unions.
3 Pull out the retaining clips in the direction of the arrows.

(d) Refitting a rear flexible hose:

Refitting is a reversal of removal procedure. On completion, bleed the brakes as detailed later in this Chapter.

Place it in front of its support without applying any tension or twist to it (see **FIG 10:16**). Then twist it gently by moving the nut through two notches in an anticlockwise direction (looking towards the front). For the righthand hose, offset the nut by two notches in a clockwise direction.

10:6 Servicing a wheel cylinder

1 Peel off the rubber protective dust covers 4 (see **FIG 10:17**) from each end of the cylinder housing.
2 The pistons may now be shaken out carefully or forced out by using a tyre pump at the fluid orifice or tapping gently on a piece of wood.

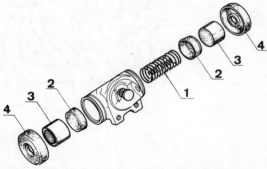

FIG 10:17 Exploded view of a brake wheel cylinder

Key to Fig 10:17   1 Spring   2 Seals   3 Pistons
4 Dust covers

3 Remove the clips and spring all as shown in **FIG 10:17**. Make sketches if necessary to ensure correct replacement.

4 Wash all component parts in clean brake fluid or methylated spirit.

5 Examine all interior housing and piston surfaces for scoring or wear and renew the cylinder as a complete assembly if necessary.

6 If component parts are unworn, renew all rubber seals and dust covers (obtainable in repair kit form).

7 Lubricate the cylinder interior with clean hydraulic fluid and fit the component parts in correct order.

The seals 2 must have their flat faces to the outside and the pistons 3 their flat faces to the inside.

8 Place a securing rubber band over the ends of the pistons to prevent them falling out of the cylinder during refitting to the brake backplate.

10:7 Reassembling the brakes

Refitting of wheel cylinders and backplates is a reversal of the dismantling instructions given in the previous Section.

Where these components have been dismantled it will be necessary to bleed the brakes as fully described in the following Section. Where dismantling has been limited to brake shoes then bleeding will not be required after the following reassembly procedure has been carried out.

The brake shoes should be renewed on a factory exchange basis. Do not attempt to reline them as the exchange ones will be correctly fitted and ground to contour. This cannot be achieved by the home mechanic.

(a) Front shoe replacement:

1 Position the two shoes in the same relative position on the bench as that occupied by the old shoes (shortest lining to the rear) when in position on their backplate and fit the lower return spring.

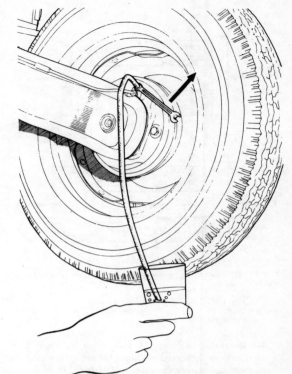

FIG 10:18   Bleeding the brakes

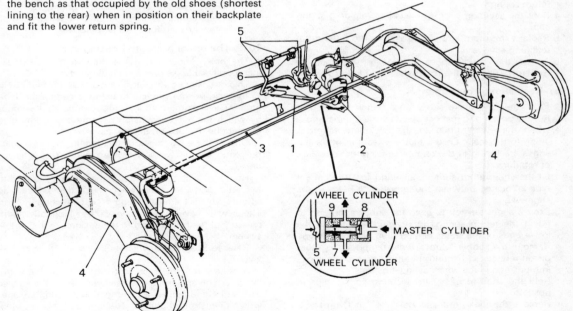

FIG 10:19   Rear brake and pressure limiting valve layout

Key to Fig 10:19   1 Control rod   2 Clamp   3 Anti-roll bar   4 Suspension arm   5 Spring linkage   6 Pivot   7 Piston   8 Valve head   9 Limiting valve body

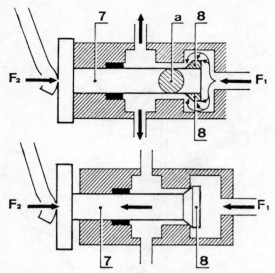

FIG 10:20 Sectional view of the brake pressure limiting valve

Key to Fig 10:20   a Piston (cross-section)   7 Piston
8 Valve head F_1 Master cylinder applied pressure
F_2 Load (mechanical)

2 Fit the lower section of the shoes to their cam position on the backplate. Remove the wheel cylinder temporary securing rubber band or wire and locate the upper ends of the shoes, on the piston ends.
3 Holding the shoes in position, fit the spacer and upper return spring.
4 Refit the securing shoe to backplate retaining spring clip.
5 Replace the drum and secure it with the three drum retaining screws.
6 Adjust the brake shoes previously described in **Section 10:2**, fit the road wheel and lower the car.

(b) Rear shoe replacement:

1 Place the new brake shoes on a bench in a similar relative position to that occupied by the original shoes when they were fitted to the backplate (shortest lining to the rear). Ensure that any leading or trailing edges are facing in the original and correct direction of rotation.
2 Fit the shoe return springs, ensuring that the correct type is located between the appropriate holes in the shoe web.
3 Exert a slight tension to keep the shoes apart and to retain the return springs in position and locate the lower ends of the shoes behind their backplate pivot.
4 Remove the rubber band or wire temporary cylinder piston retainer and spring the upper part of the shoes into position in the wheel cylinder pistons.
5 Refit the shoe to backplate securing spring clips in position.
6 Replace the brake drum as described in **Chapter 8** complete with nut, new splitpin and hub cap. Adjust the hub end float as detailed in **Chapter 8.**
7 Adjust the shoes as described in **Section 10:2**, fit the road wheel and remove the jack.

10:8 Bleeding the brakes

Whenever a component part of the hydraulic system (master cylinder, wheel cylinder, rigid or flexible hose) has been removed or dismantled, the following procedure must be carried out after subsequent refitting, to bleed the system of air. All bleeding operations should take place with the car standing on its wheels so that the brake pressure limiting valve takes up its normal position.

1 Check the level of hydraulic fluid in the reservoir and top up if necessary.
2 Brush the dirt from the bleed screws and remove the rubber bleed screw dust caps.
3 Pour some clean brake fluid into a jar and fix a bleed tube to the wheel cylinder bleed screw so that the other end of the tube will remain submerged below the level of fluid in the jar as shown in **FIG 10:18**.
4 Carry out the bleeding operations on the right rear wheel cylinder followed by left rear, left front and right front, in that order.
5 Using a spanner of short length, unscrew the bleed screw one quarter of a turn and depress the brake pedal slowly to the full extent of its travel. Repeat until no bubbles are seen coming from the end of the submerged bleeder tube. Always allow the pedal to return unassisted.
6 Tighten the bleed screw when the pedal is fully depressed at the end of a stroke. Do not overtighten.
7 Repeat the operation on the other wheels in the sequence given.
8 Adjust the brakes after bleeding is complete.
    Always keep the reservoir level topped up during bleeding.
    Always keep the bleed tube end below the fluid level in the jar.
    Always use new brake fluid for topping up, from a sealed container. Discard fluid drained from the system or used for bleed jar purposes.

10:9 The brake pressure limiting valve

The brake line carrying the fluid to the rear brakes incorporates a brake pressure limiting valve.

This is designed to limit the hydraulic pressure going to the rear wheel cylinders to below a certain maximum figure. This maximum figure is proportional to the amount by which the rear suspension is depressed at any given moment by the load on the rear axle.

One of the advantages of this limiting valve is that it prevents the rear wheels locking when the vehicle is unladen.

However, when the vehicle is more heavily loaded the hydraulic pressure at the rear wheel cylinders can reach a figure which is almost as high as that affecting the front. There will, nevertheless, always be a slightly higher pressure at the front owing to the design of the hydraulic system.

Refer to **FIG 10:19** which will indicate the rear brake layout.

A control rod 1 is secured to the anti-roll bar 3 by a clamp 2. The anti-roll bar is itself secured to the suspension arm 4 and applies an end load to a spring linkage 5 which pivots round point 6. The end load is proportional to the rear suspension travel.

Linkage 5 subjects piston 7 to a load which is proportional to the position of the suspension. Piston 7 slides in a body 9 and its head 8 acts as a valve core.

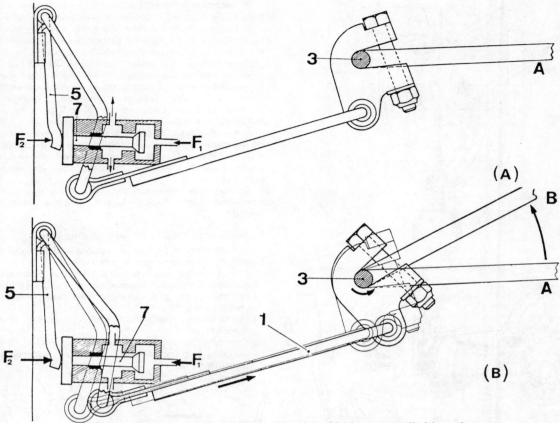

FIG 10:21   Diagrammatic sequence operation of brake pressure limiting valve

Key to Fig 10:21   A Car unloaded   **B** Car loaded

Operation:

For details of operation refer to **FIG 10:20**.

When the brakes are applied the cross-sectional area (a) of piston 7 is subjected to two opposing forces:

From one side the mechanical load F2, which is proportional to the position of the anti-roll bar and, therefore, to the load on the vehicle, and at the opposite end the resultant hydraulic load F1 caused by the pressure from the master cylinder.

In fact, the cross-sectional area (a) is subjected to the pressure load because head 8, which is the portion of piston 7 and which acts as a valve, has the hydraulic pressure F1 on both sides of it whereas cross-sectional (a) receives hydraulic pressure on only one side.

When the load caused by hydraulic pressure F1 is greater than the mechanical load F2 piston 7 moves in the direction shown by the arrow and causes head 8 on the piston, which acts as a valve, comes against its seat.

The rear system is then closed off and the hydraulic pressure in the rear wheel cylinders can no longer rise in proportion to the load that the driver applies to the brake pedal.

When the vehicle is empty (see **FIG 10:21** (A))— Anti-roll bar 3 is in position (A).

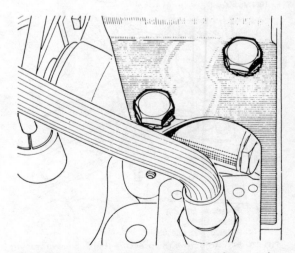

FIG 10:22   The brake pressure limiting valve securing bolts and protective cover

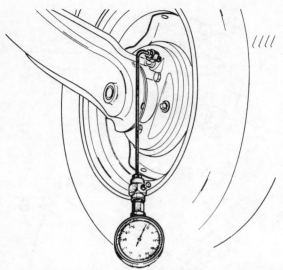

FIG 10:23 Checking the pressure limiting valve setting

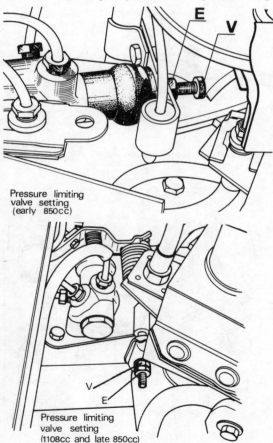

Pressure limiting valve setting (early 850cc)

Pressure limiting valve setting (1108cc and late 850cc)

FIG 10:24 Adjusting the pressure limiting valve setting

Key to Fig 10:24   E Locknut   V Adjuster screw

In this position the load applied by spring linkage 5 to piston 7, is adjusted to provide a minimum thrust of F2.

In this way, fluid can flow to the rear wheel cylinders up to a value of F1 which is sufficiently low to prevent the wheels locking when the brakes are applied.

When the vehicle is loaded (see **FIG 10:21** (B)).

As the load on the rear axle increases, the suspension moves down and the torsion bar 3 moves up towards position (B). This, through control rod 1 applies a torsional load to spring linkage 5 and, as a result, increases the mechanical load F2 acting on piston 7.

In this position B, when the brakes are applied, load F2 on the piston is higher and resultant force F1 must reach a higher value before the valve closes, thus permitting a higher hydraulic pressure to reach the rear wheel cylinders.

Consequently, the maximum pressure acting at the rear wheel cylinders will be higher when the vehicle is loaded.

Renewing the brake pressure limiting valve:

This component cannot be repaired and if faulty or leaking, then it must be renewed as a unit.

1 Drain the brake fluid reservoir as previously described.
2 Remove the protective cover shown in **FIG 10:22**.
3 Disconnect the pipe unions on the brake pressure limiting valve.
4 Unscrew the fixing bolts and remove the valve complete.
5 The new limiting valve will require setting and checking but first bleed the brakes as described in **Section 10:8**.

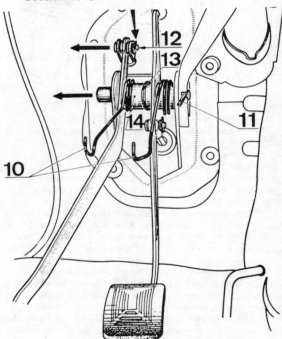

FIG 10:25 The foot-operated control pedals

Key to Fig 10:25   10 Return springs   11 Roll-pin
12 Clevis pin   13 Washer   14 Shaft

Checking and setting the brake pressure limiting valve:

This can only be carried out if a suitable pressure gauge is available, otherwise the operation must be left to a service station. The adjustment location differs between the early 850 cc models and the later ones. Since 1970 the limiter valve has been modified and a return spring has been incorporated to bring it in line with the 1108 cc models. The two types are shown in **FIG 10:24**.

1 Place the car on level ground and have the fuel tank full and the car weighted with the equivalent of one person.
2 Fit a 0 to 600 lb/sq in pressure gauge in place of a rear wheel bleed screw as shown in **FIG 10:23**.
3 Bleed the pressure gauge.
4 Check the cut-off pressure which should be as given in **Technical Data**.
5 Refer to **FIG 10:24** and unscrew the locknut E.
6 Turn screw V and check the pressure. If after this the pressure has not changed, rock the car.
7 Lock the locknut E.

10:10 The brake pedal

The brake and clutch pedals are removed simultaneously. Dismantling may be required for renewal of the pedals or shafts due to wear or when pedal withdrawal is required for steering column removal.

1 Refer to **FIG 10:25** and remove the two return springs 10 from both pedals.
2 Remove the two return springs 10 from the clutch pedal and brake pedal.
3 Pull out the roll-pin 11 from the pedal shaft 14.
4 Push out the shaft, retain the two springs and the washer 13.
5 To completely remove the clutch pedal, remove the splitpin and pin 12 from the clutch cable fork.

Refitting the pedals is a reversal of removal operations but remember to lubricate pin 14. Adjust the pedal free movement as previously described.

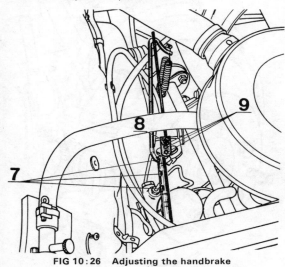

FIG 10:26 Adjusting the handbrake

Key to Fig 10:26   7 Adjustment holes (fine)   8 Pin
9 Adjustment holes (coarse)

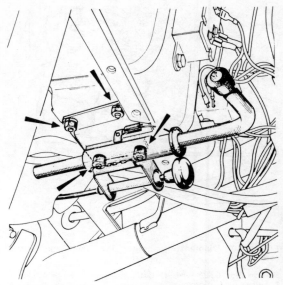

FIG 10:27   The handbrake control securing bolts

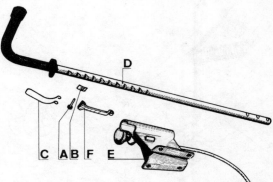

FIG 10:28 Exploded view of the handbrake control lever (early)

Key to Fig 10:28   **A** Pin   **B** Clip   **C** Spring   **D** Lever
E Bracket   **F** Ratchet

10:11 Handbrake adjustment and servicing

(a) Adjustment:

The handbrake should be adjusted only when stretch in the cable causes the hand lever to be moved an excessive distance before locking the wheels (correct full-on travel is 5 or 6 notches).

In the normal way, adjustment of the front wheel cam adjusters will automatically ensure adjustment of the handbrake.

1 Refer to **FIG 10:26** and release fully the handbrake.
2 To take up a small amount of play, make use of the holes 7 on the handbrake control lever and move the rod to the required position.
3 If this is insufficient, use the holes 9. Remove the pin 8, move the cable clamp up one hole.
4 Refit the pin and secure with a new splitpin.

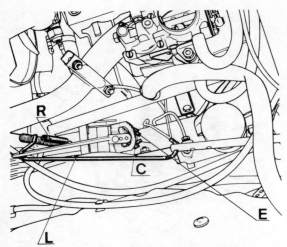

FIG 10:29 Dismantling points for handbrake cable renewal

Key to Fig 10:29   C Cable clamp   E Cable sleeve
L Lever   R Spring

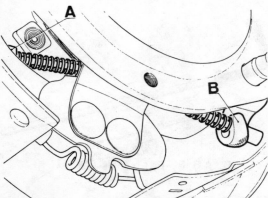

FIG 10:30 Handbrake cable shoe attachment (for Key see text)

(b) Servicing the handbrake control lever:

1 Release the handbrake fully and refer to **FIG 10:27**.
2 Unscrew the four bolts fixing the handbrake control under the facia.
3 Disconnect the bonnet opening control.
4 Disconnect the end of the handbrake control lever under the bonnet.
5 Remove the handbrake assembly and the bonnet opening control.
6 Refer to **FIG 10:28** and pull out clip B.
7 Remove pin A and spring C.
8 Retain ratchet F and pull out the control lever D from the bracket E.
9 Renew faulty parts and carry out refitting the control lever following, in reverse order, the removal operation.
10 Lightly lubricate the moving parts of the handbrake control.
11 Adjust the handbrake.

(c) Renewing a handbrake cable:

1 Refer to **FIG 10:29** and fully release the handbrake.
2 Unhook the spring R on lever L.
3 Pull out the clip with its washer and remove the lever from the handbrake control rod.
4 Disconnect the ends of the handbrake cable and retain the cable clamp C.
5 Withdraw the handbrake cable sleeve E from its stop.
6 Chock the vehicle, remove the wheel.
7 Pull off the brake drum as previously described and refer to **FIG 10:30**.
8 Unhook the handbrake cable at B.
9 Disconnect the handbrake cable sleeve from the backplate at A.
10 Remove the sleeve of the handbrake cable from the brake backplate.

Fitting a new cable entails carrying out the dismantling operations in reverse. Finally adjust the handbrake as previously described.

10:12 Checking for braking bias and uneven retardation

Probably the most common brake malfunction is braking bias—the pulling to one or other side when the footbrake is applied. Although a full check list of braking faults is given under **Fault Diagnosis, Section 10:10**, a more detailed description of checking and correction methods for braking bias is given here.

The car should decelerate uniformly from all speeds, whether the brakes are warm or cold. The brakes should release as soon as pressure is removed from the brake pedal.

If the vehicle pulls to one side when brakes are applied, carry out the checks described in the following list.

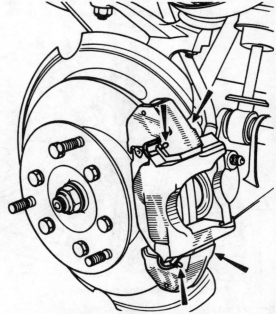

FIG 10:31 Removing the caliper

Check:

1 The tyre types, degree of wear and tyre inflation pressures on both axles.
2 The degree of wear and stiffness on the front axle components.
3 The brake anchor plate fastenings.
4 The clearance between the brake shoes and the drums.
5 The front axle geometry.
  The condition of the dampers.
  The condition of the suspension torsion bars.

When these components have been checked and any defects corrected, carry out a detailed check on the mechanical and hydraulic components which form the braking system.

If normal brake pressure can be felt on the brake pedal, check the following components to determine the cause of the vehicle pulling to one side.

1 Drums: for dirt, dust, eccentricity, ovality, scoring or cracks.
2 Linings: for grease, wear, differing grades, incorrect lead, poorly bonded or riveted to the shoe.
3 Shoe return springs: to ensure that they apply equal-load to the shoes on both the wheels on any given axle.
4 The condition of the brake shoe pivot points.
5 The wheel cylinders: to ensure that they are not seized.
6 The wheel cylinder cup washers: to ensure that they are not swollen.
7 The brake line unions: for leakage at the wheel cylinders.
8 The brake line cross-sectional areas of the pipes (to ensure that these are not crushed or blocked).

10:13 Disc brake pads

The thickness of the friction pads should be checked periodically by measuring with a rule. The minimum thickness is $\frac{9}{32}$ inch (7mm) and if the pads are under this size they should be renewed. Pads should always be changed in complete sets and no mixture of makes and grades be allowed.

Remove the four clips shown in **FIG 10:31** and then using a pin punch and a hammer, knock out the key on one side of the pad as shown in **FIG 10:32**. The key on the other side should slide out easily.

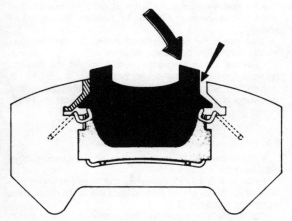

FIG 10:32   Removing a friction pad

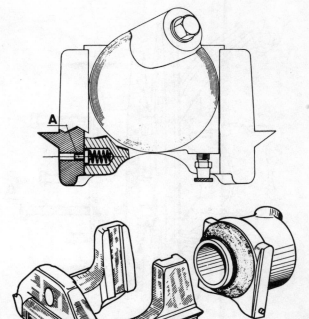

FIG 10:33   Removing the hydraulic cylinder

Remove the brake caliper and note that steps must now be taken to see that the brake pedal is not depressed. Remove the brake pads and the springs under the pads.

Before fitting the new pads, take off the rubber dust cover and clean it and the end of the piston with methylated spirit. A light application of a suitable grease may be used on the side of the piston where it slides in its bore.

Replace the dust cover and lever (as with a wooden block and a screwdriver) the piston inwards. Note that this may cause the fluid level in the reservoir to rise to the point of overflowing unless some is syphoned off.

Fit the springs under the pads and then the pads, making sure that they slide freely.

Slip one end of the caliper between the hairpin spring and the keyway on the caliper bracket, then fit the other end of the caliper by compressing both springs.

Insert the first key of the friction pad, which should slide in easily, and then lever the other key in with a screwdriver, pushing it fully home with a pin punch and a hammer. Fit four new hairpin springs.

10:14 Disc brake calipers

Remove the brake caliper from the caliper bracket. Take steps to catch any escaping fluid, then unscrew the metal pipe union on the flexible hose.

Lift out the clip holding the flexible hose on the support lug and free the caliper. Unscrew the hose from the caliper and examine it for wear or damage.

Remove the rubber dust cover and clean all the parts in methylated spirit. The square section rubber seal in the

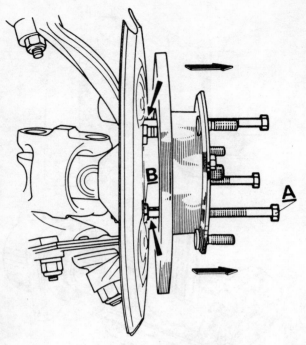

FIG 10:34   Removing a brake disc

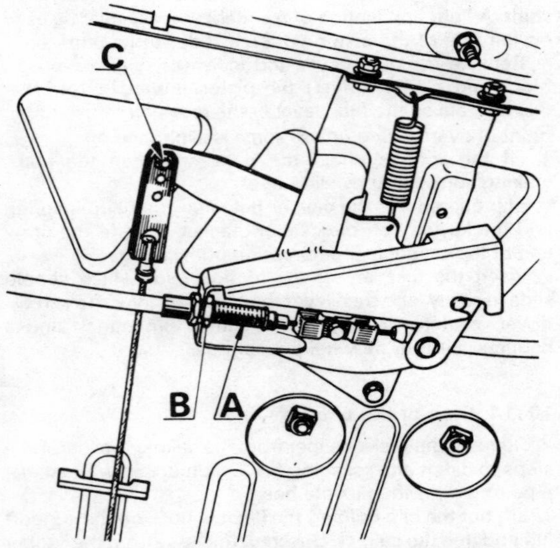

FIG 10:35   Handbrake adjustment 1108cc models

Key to Fig 10:35   **A** Adjusting sleeve   **B** Locknut
C Fork end

groove inside the bore should be carefully eased out and a new seal inserted.

The hydraulic cylinder is a sliding fit in the support as shown in **FIG 10:33** and is removed by pressing in the spring-loaded peg **A** and then sliding it out of the grooves. It may be necessary to spread the two arms on the cast cylinder support to enable this to be done.

Spreading the arms will also be necessary when refitting the cylinder, not forgetting to press in the peg and spring and ensuring that the peg engages with its hole in the support.

Prime the caliper before reconnecting the flexible hose and use a new copper washer.

10:15   Brake discs

To remove a disc it is first necessary to remove the caliper and the caliper bracket. This latter is done by taking out the two bolts securing the bracket to the deflector and two bolts securing it to the stub axle carrier.

Unscrew the three bolts securing the disc, then, while preventing the assembly from turning, unscrew the hub nut.

Refer to **FIG 10:34** and screw three bolts (ROV.482.01) into the hub, positioning the first bolt **A** over the head **B** of the deflector securing bolt as shown.

Check that the bolts are in direct contact with the stub axle carrier and then tighten them progressively in rotation to extract the hub/disc assembly.
Separate the hub from the disc.

Refit the disc to the hub, noting that special bolts are supplied for this purpose with Y3 stamped on the head.

Smear the bearing with L.C. grease, line up the hub/disc assembly and draw it into position using tool T.Av.409 or equivalent.

Refit the caliper bracket and the caliper.

10:16   Rear drum brakes, 1108cc models

These are very similar to the rear brakes described earlier, but require a slightly different procedure as they include the handbrake mechanism.

After removing the brake drum, clamp the brake cylinder and shoes as shown in **FIG 10:11**, then free the top return spring.

Disconnect the handbrake cable and remove the shoe steady springs by compressing them with a $\frac{5}{16}$ inch rod.

Ease the brake shoes out and take off the bottom return spring. Remove the handbrake lever.

Refitting is a reversal of the removal procedure, and adjusting is carried out as described in **Section 10:2**.

10:17   Handbrake, 1108cc models

The handbrake on these cars must be adjusted after adjusting the footbrake.

Refer to **FIG 10:35**. Screw up the threaded end fitting **A** until the brake linings just contact the brake drum, then tighten the locknut **B**

Check the lever travel and if necessary carry out a final adjustment by altering the position of the fork end **C**.

10:18 Fault diagnosis

(a) Spongy pedal

1 Leak in the system
2 Worn master cylinder
3 Leaking wheel cylinder
4 Air in the system
5 Gaps between shoes and underside of linings

(b) Excessive pedal movement

1 Check 1 and 4 in (a)
2 Excessive lining wear
3 Very low fluid level in supply reservoir
4 Too much free movement of pedal

(c) Brakes grab or pull to one side (also refer to Section 10:12)

1 Brake backplate loose
2 Scored, cracked or distorted drum
3 High spots on drum
4 Unbalanced shoe adjustment
5 Wet or oily linings
6 Front suspension loose
7 Rear suspension loose
8 Worn steering connections
9 Mixed linings of different grades
10 Uneven tyre pressures
11 Broken shoe return springs
12 Seized handbrake cables
13 Wheel cylinders seized
14 Incorrect or lack of chamfers on linings

NOTES

CHAPTER 11

ELECTRICAL EQUIPMENT

11:1 Description

The models covered by this manual have a 12-volt negative earth return system. The battery is charged by a belt-driven generator and current is controlled by a voltage regulator within the control box which also houses a cut-out. These control devices are not capable of adjustment and should be renewed as an assembly if faulty after carrying out the tests described later in this Chapter.

A wiring diagram is to be found in **Technical Data** which will enable wiring fault diagnosis to be easily carried out by reference to the cable coding key given.

Full servicing details are given in this Section for the electrical components fitted but in the event of major repairs having to be carried out then the cost of a factory reconditioned exchange unit should be considered in comparison with the cost of individual component renewal. These remarks apply particularly in the case of the major electrical units such as the starter motor and the generator. A plan of the wiring harness is shown in **FIG 11:1**.

11:2 The battery

This is of 12-volt 30 amp/hr rating 6 cell type. With a battery of conventional design, the electrolyte level should be maintained at just above the tops of the separators.

Never use a naked light to inspect the interior of a battery.

Keep the outside of the battery casing clean, the terminal connections tight and lightly covered with petroleum jelly.

If the battery is subjected to long periods of discharge without suitable opportunities for recharging, a low state of charge can be expected. A defect in the charging system can also result in a discharged battery.

Checking the specific gravity of the electrolyte is a simple method of assessing the state of charge of a battery.

A hydrometer is an instrument used to determine the specific gravity of a liquid. The specific gravity of the acid contained within a battery varies according to the condition of the battery and also with temperature. Therefore, the state of battery charge can be assessed by specific gravity readings.

Hydrometer readings taken after topping up are unreliable. The battery should be given a gassing charge to thoroughly mix the acid and water, before taking a hydrometer reading.

There should be little variation in the specific gravity readings between one cell and another of a battery in reasonably good condition.

The following chart gives comparative readings:

	Actual hydrometer readings at temperature of:						
Conditions of cells	5°C (41°F)	10°C (50°F)	15°C (60°F)	20°C (68°F)	25°C (77°F)	30°C (86°F)	35°C (95°F)
Fully charged	1.287	1.284	1.280	1.277	1.273	1.270	1.266
Half charged	1.207	1.204	1.200	1.197	1.193	1.190	1.186
Fully discharged	1.117	1.114	1.110	1.107	1.103	1.100	1.096

It is unlikely that the addition of acid to a battery will ever be needed unless there has been a loss by spillage. In this event, always mix the electrolyte away from the vehicle in a non-corrosive vessel. **Always add sulphuric acid to distilled water, never the reverse.** The specific gravity for such electrolyte mixture should be 1.260 at a temperature of 60°F (15°C).

Always give a periodic charge to a battery which is not being used and preferably remove it from the vehicle if it is to be off the road for some time.

Never spill acid or electrolyte on body cellulose.

Battery condition diagnosis may be made from the following chart:

Specific gravity readings

Readings uniform within the range of 1.230 to 1.260

Readings uniform and within the range 1.180 to 1.220

One cell about .030 or more lower than remainder

Readings irregular and more than one cell about .050 or more lower than remainder

Readings very low (about 1.100 or below)

11:3 The generator—routine maintenance

The only regular maintenance required is to:

1 Inject a few drops of oil to the rear bearing oil hole fitted to certain models.

2 Maintain the correct tension of the fan belt as described in **Chapter 4** and with reference to **FIG 4 : 3**.

3 Keep the generator mounting bolts tight, also the electrical terminal nuts.

Battery condition

Healthy and in a reasonably charged condition. No action required.

Healthy but battery half-discharged. Use mains charger.

(a) May be failing cell, or
(b) Cell out of step.
Condition (b) may possibly be rectified by extended charge.

Battery at end of life.

Battery in deeply sulphated condition—usually beyond recovery but may respond to an extended mains charge.

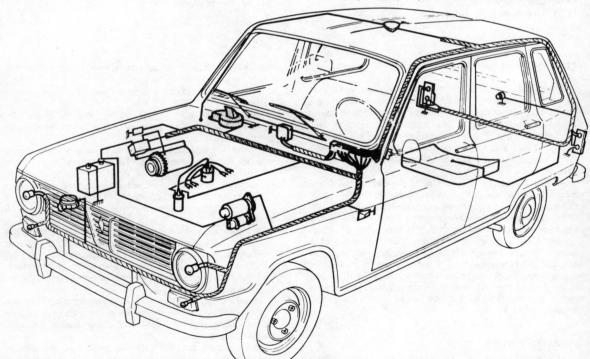

FIG 11 :1   The wiring harness location and layout

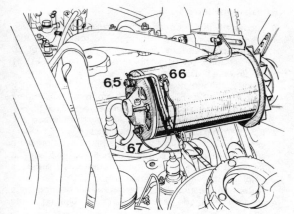

FIG 11:2   The generator terminals

Key to Fig 11:2   65 Positive   66 Field   67 Earth

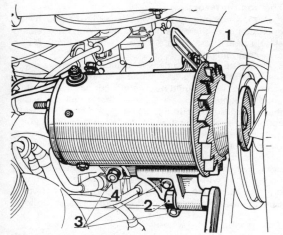

FIG 11:3   The generator fixing and adjustment bolts

Key to Fig 11:3   1 Sliding strap bolt   2 Water pump belt tensioner bolt   3 Tensioner securing bolts   4 Generator securing bolt

Testing the generator in the vehicle:

1 Check driving belt tension and electrical connections to the generator.
2 Remove the connectors from the generator terminals marked 65 (positive) and 66 (field) as shown in **FIG 11:2** and link both with a jumper lead.
3 Observing correct polarity, connect a 0-20 volts moving coil voltmeter or pilot bulb between the 66 terminal and the earthing point 67 on the yoke.
4 Start the engine and gradually increase its speed to 1000 rev/min during which the meter reading should rise rapidly and steadily but should not be allowed to reach 20 volts. Dismantle the generator for examination if the reading is low, slow to rise and fluctuates violently, or if the commutator sparks excessively.
5 If the generator is in good order, remove the jumper lead and restore the original connections. If faulty, carry out the operations detailed in the next section.

11:4 Servicing the generator

The generator may be one of two types, a Ducellier model 7-346 or a Paris-Rhone model G.10c.35. Both types give an output of 22 amps.

(a) Removal:

1 Refer to **FIG 11:3** and remove bolt 1 from the slotted strap.
2 Disconnect the three electrical leads.
3 Loosen nut 2 on the water pump belt tensioner.
4 Remove the three bolts 3 which secure the tensioner.
5 Remove bolt 4 and withdraw the generator.

On 1108cc engines, the generator has a special method of mounting, being held by a bracket in the form of a strap.

The removal procedure is similar to that just described, but if the bracket is removed together with the strap care must be taken to see that the locating dowel is correctly replaced in its hole in the generator body.

(b) Testing the generator:
Testing the field coils:

Before removing the field coils (see **FIG 11:4**) check the resistance and insulation of the coils by using an ohmmeter connected between the field terminal and the yoke.

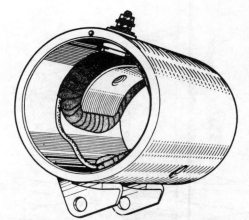

FIG 11:4   The generator field coil location

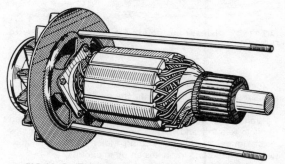

FIG 11:5   The generator with body withdrawn

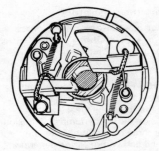

FIG 11:6   The generator brushes in position

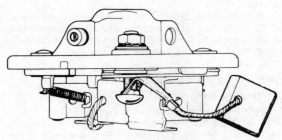

FIG 11:7   The generator brushes and lead terminals

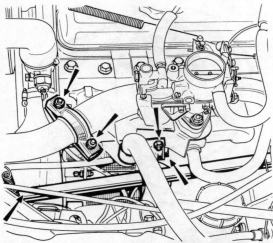

FIG 11:8   Dismantling points for components prior to removing the starter motor

A reading of 6 ohms is correct; less indicates faulty insulation and an 'infinity' indicates an open circuit.

If an ohmmeter is not available, connect in series a 12-volt 'direct current' supply and an ammeter between the field terminal and yoke. The reading should be 2 amps approximately; a higher reading indicates faulty insulation; a zero reading indicates an open circuit.

If a fault is indicated, renew the field coils.

(c) Dismantling:

1 Loosen the pulley but do not remove it.
2 Remove the nuts from the two tie rods at the rear bearing plate end and remove the rear bearing plate.
3 Remove the body from the armature (see **FIG 11:5**) holding the brushes in position (see **FIG 11:6**).
4 Remove the pulley and take out the front bearing.
5 Remove the brushes by lifting them from their holders and unscrewing the terminal screws (see **FIG 11:7**).
6 The field coils may be removed by dismantling the field terminal and removing the pole screws. These are very difficult to remove without a bench type pressure screwdriver and it is suggested that field coil tests be first carried out before this operation, in order to establish the need for dismantling.

If the front bearing plate bearing or rear bearing plate bush are damaged, renew the entire bearing plate assembly.

(d) Overhauling and checking the component parts:

The commutator:

Burned commutator segments may be caused by an open circuit in the armature windings. Armature testing should be left to a service station or by substitution of a new component.

Undercutting of segment insulation is rarely required but if the insulation is level with the surface of the copper segments then it should be carefully cut back. To do this, grind a suitable hacksaw blade so that it will not widen the groove during cutting. Using gentle back and forth action cut each lamination of insulation below the commutator surface level until they are all .020 inch undercut. Finally clean with a petrol-moistened cloth.

The commutator should be smooth and free from pits or burned spots. Slight burning may be rectified by carefully polishing with a strip of fine glasspaper while rotating the armature. **Do not use emerypaper for this operation.** Finally clean with a petrol-moistened cloth.

The brushes:

Check that the brushes move freely in their holders by holding back the tension springs and pulling gently on the flexible connectors. If a brush is inclined to stick, remove it from its holder and clean its sides with a petrol-moistened cloth.

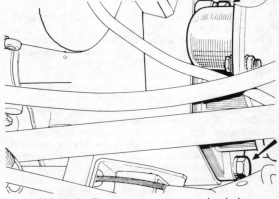

FIG 11:9   The starter motor securing bolts

Replace the brushes in their original position or renew those which are less than the length given in **Technical Data**.

New carbon brushes must be ground to contour before fitting to the commutator. To do this, fit them in their sprung holders, wrap emerycloth around a dowel rod of a similar diameter to that of the commutator and rotate this between the brushes until the required curvature on their bearing surfaces is obtained.

(e) Reassembling and refitting:

These operations are essentially a reversal of removal and dismantling procedure but the following points should be noted.

1 When refitting the rear bearing plate, pull back the brushes with two strips so that they will fit correctly over the commutator.

2 After reassembling the generator should it be found to be de-energized, re-energize it by connecting it for a few seconds to the battery. The negative post(−) to the generator earth (ground), and the positive (+) post (see 65 in **FIG 11 : 2**) to the field terminal marked (EXC.) (see 66 in **FIG 11 : 2**).

3 Remember to adjust the belt tension as described in **Chapter 4** and shown in **FIG 4 : 3**.

11 : 5 Testing the starter motor

One of four types of starter motor may be fitted.

Ducellier type 6185 or 6187 or Paris-Rhone type D8E74 or D8E81. All are solenoid operated.

In the event of non-operation of the starter motor, carry out the following checks and tests before attempting to remove or dismantle the unit.

1 If unsatisfactory operation is experienced, first check that the battery connections are tight and that the battery itself is charged.

2 Check the cable connection to the starter for tightness and also the cables to and from the starter solenoid and the cables to the switch according to type.

3 Do not confuse a jammed starter drive with an inoperative motor. In the event of a distinct click being heard when the starter switch is operated but the starter motor will not rotate then the starter drive is jammed and should be freed. The car may be placed in gear and gently rocked backwards and forwards or

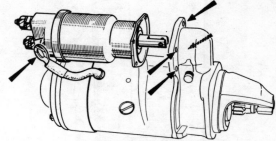

FIG 11 : 11   Withdrawing the starter solenoid, D8E74

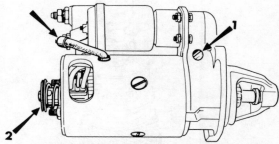

FIG 11 : 12   The starter motor showing **1** the armature stop fixing bolt and **2** the friction washers, D8E74

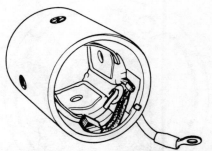

FIG 11 : 13   Soldering the starter motor brushes

the starting handle used, when the drive should disengage.

4 Assuming the conditions outlined to be normal, test the motor by first withdrawing the connector from the distributor LT terminal to prevent the engine from firing.

5 Connect a 0-20 volt meter between the starter terminal and earth, and operate the starter switch to crank the engine and note the reading. A minimum reading of 4.5 volts indicates satisfactory cable and switch connections. Slow cranking at this voltage indicates a fault in the motor.

6 With the engine cranking and the meter connected between the battery and the starter motor terminal, to measure the voltage drop, this should not exceed half voltage. A higher reading indicates excessive resistance in the starter circuit.

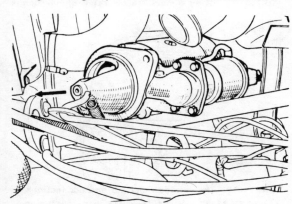

FIG 11 : 10   Withdrawing the starter motor

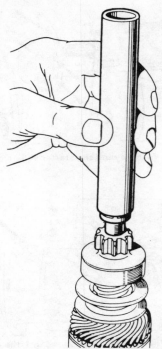

FIG 11:14 Removing the starter drive pinion flange

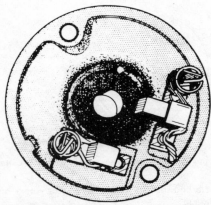

FIG 11:15 The starter motor cover bearing plate without positive brush ready for refitting

11:6 Removing and servicing the starter motor

(a) Removal:

845 cc engines:

1 Disconnect the battery.
2 Remove the air filter, the exhaust pipe clamp, the water hose clip and the steering column flexible joint, all as indicated in **FIG 11:8**. If necessary on later models remove the inlet and exhaust manifold.
3 Disconnect the starter cables.
4 Unscrew and remove the starter securing bolts shown in **FIG 11:9**.

1108 cc engines:

1 Disconnect the battery.
2 Remove the air filter, exhaust pipe clips pushing the pipe to one side, engine support arm and the clutch cable support lug.
3 Remove the steering column shaft, the insulating shield and the solenoid feed wire.
4 Take out the starter securing bolts and lift the starter out towards the front.

(b) Dismantling:

1 Disconnect the starter cable and the four solenoid securing bolts arrowed in **FIG 11:11**.
2 Lift the solenoid to disengage and draw out the solenoid with its fork.
3 Remove the coverband, D8E74 only.
4 Undo the armature stop fixing bolt 1 (see **FIG 11:12**).
5 Lift out the positive brush from the brush holder by way of the body aperture.
6 Remove the bearing pin from the solenoid pinion fork.
7 Remove the rear brush holder plate and remove the friction washers 2 (see **FIG 11:12**) from the armature shaft.

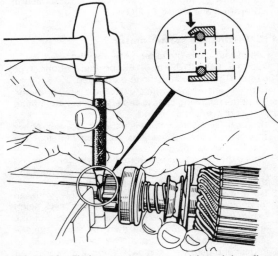

FIG 11:16 Fitting a new starter drive pinion flange

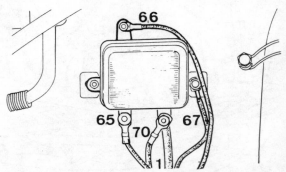

FIG 11:17 The voltage regulator and connections

Key to Fig 11:17   1 Main feed   65 Dynamo+
66 Dynamo field   67 Dynamo earth   70 Battery+

8 Renewal of brushes is carried out by unsoldering the worn ones and re-soldering the new as shown in **FIG 11 : 13.**

9 The starter pinion assembly may be removed by driving off the flange using a suitable tube (see **FIG 11 : 14**).

10 With the starter now completely dismantled, check for wear in the brushes and if they are less than the minimum lengths specified in **Technical Data,** they should be renewed. Ensure that they move freely in their holders. The armature should be cleaned with a petrol moistened cloth and if necessary the insulation between the segments of the commutator undercut to .020 inch in a similar manner to that described for the generator.

If a fault is suspected in the field coils, test them for continuity by connecting a battery and bulb between the starter terminal and each brush in turn.

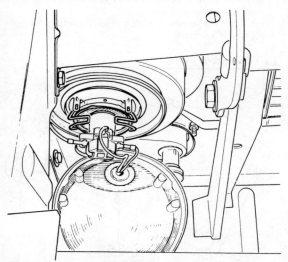

FIG 11 : 18   Renewing a headlamp bulb (typical)

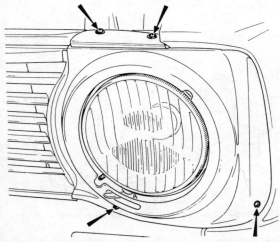

FIG 11 : 19   A headlamp rim securing screws (pre 1974)

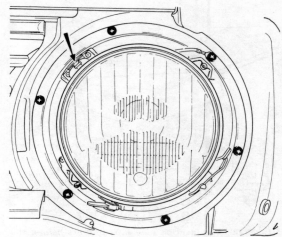

FIG 11 : 20   A headlamp unit securing screws (pre 1974)

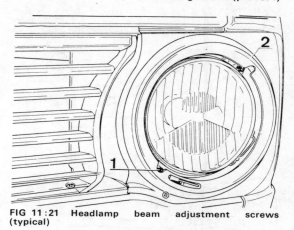

FIG 11 : 21   Headlamp beam adjustment screws (typical)

Use an ohmmeter test for insulation between the terminal and yoke, and between the brush boxes and end cover.

If a fault in the field coils is indicated, it may be advisable to renew the complete starter motor on an exchange basis.

(c) Reassembling :

This is largely a reversal of dismantling procedure but the end cover bearing plate will be fitted without of course the positive brush in position (see **FIG 11 : 15**).

Always use a new flange when refitting a starter pinion.

Cover the snap rings with the flange and turn the flange over in several places to trap the snap rings as shown in **FIG 11 : 16.**

With all starter drive gear, the component parts should be washed thoroughly in paraffin and very sparingly oiled with light oil after reassembly.

11 : 7 The voltage regulator and cut-out

The voltage regulator may be one of two types according to the make of generator fitted. It may be a Ducellier Type 8311A or a Paris-Rhone 57416.

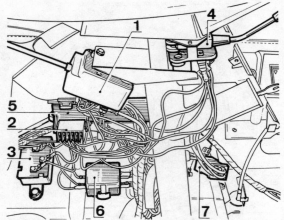

FIG 11 : 22 The location of electrical units behind the facia

Key to Fig 11 : 22   1 Lighting switch   2 Instrument panel junction box   3 Flasher unit   4 Flasher control   5 Instrument panel   6 Fuses   7 Neiman junction box

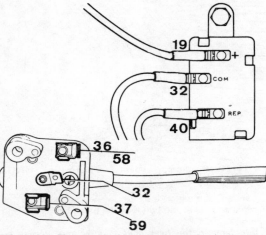

FIG 11 : 23 The terminal connections of the direction indicator flasher unit and switch

Key to Fig 11 : 23   19 Feed to flasher switch   32 Feed to flasher unit   40 Flasher pilot light   32 Feed to flasher unit   36 Front lefthand flasher unit   37 Front righthand flasher unit   58 Flasher rear lefthand   59 Flasher rear righthand

The component is of simple type and if it has been established that the dynamo is charging satisfactorily then withdraw the two securing screws from the regulator cover and with the engine running, rev the engine and watch for the opening or closure of the points. If they are not operating it may be due to stickiness. Clean them by rubbing the contact surfaces with fine 'wet' or 'dry' paper used dry and finally wipe them over with methylated spirit.

Should the points be welded together then the unit should be renewed as an assembly.

As well as controlling the charge from the generator to the battery, the cut-out portion of the unit ensures that

when the engine is switched off, the current will not drain back to earth via the generator. It is therefore essential that any fault be rectified immediately either by a service station having the necessary testing equipment or by substitution of a new unit. FIG 11 : 17 shows the regulator and leads identified.

11 : 8 The headlamps

The headlamps are of conventional type with a bulb and carrier fitted to the rear of the reflector by spring clips. Slightly unusual is the facility for adjustment provided by a load adjustment lever situated just below the head-lamp rim. Later models have a square pattern headlight but the bulb renewal and beam adjustment are very similar.

(a) Bulb renewal:

1 Open the bonnet (see FIG 11 : 18).
2 Pull out the nylon holder.
3 Lift the two retaining hooks. When refitting always replace the washer.

Left-hand side

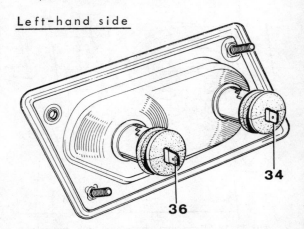

Right-hand side

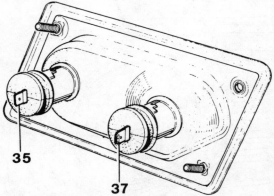

FIG 11 : 24 The front flasher and side lamp unit (pre 1974)

Key to Fig 11 : 24   34 Side light   36 Flasher   35 Side light   37 Flasher

(b) Dismantling:

1 Remove the screws arrowed (see **FIG 11:19**) and withdraw the headlamp rim.
2 Disconnect the leads to the bulb socket.
3 Remove the light unit by lifting the hook arrowed in **FIG 11:20** withdrawing the six mounting screws and pulling the unit forward.

Replacement is a reversal of the dismantling procedure, always adjust the headlamps afterwards as follows:

Adjusting:

Adjustment of the headlamps is preferably left to a service station having the appropriate optical beam setting equipment but the following guide will assist in cases where this cannot be done.

1 Ensure the car is square with a screen 25 ft from car.
2 Car to be normally loaded and on level ground.
3 Place the load adjustment lever in the 'normal' position.

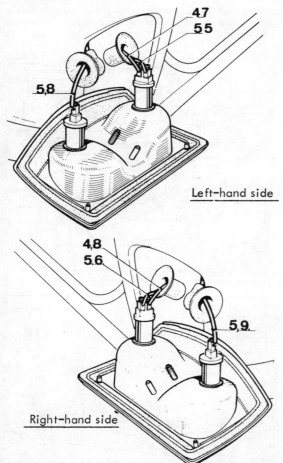

Left-hand side

Right-hand side

FIG 11:25 The rear flasher and rear lamp unit (pre 1974)

Key to Fig 11:25

58 Rear flasher	47 Stoplight	55 Rear light
59 Rear flasher	48 Stoplight	56 Rear light

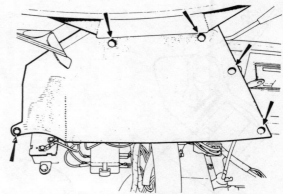

FIG 11:26 The facia bottom protective panel

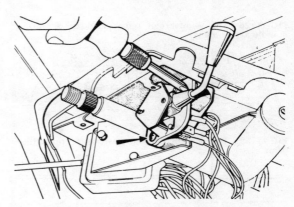

FIG 11:27 The flasher operating switch

4 Cover one headlamp, switch both to undipped setting (main beam).
5 Make two chalk crosses on the screen at the same height and centres as the headlamps and in direct line with them.
6 Remove the headlamps bezels. Adjust the beam by means of the two spring-loaded screws now exposed, shown in **FIG 11:21**. Screw 1 is for height adjustment. Screw 2 is for side adjustment.
7 Adjust each lamp until the brightest point is over the chalk mark and the oval light pattern is equalized on each side of it.

11:9 The direction indicators

These are of the flasher type and the operating unit is located behind the facia panel (see **FIG 11:22**). Both audible and visual indications are given of flasher actuation. Failure of the warning light to flash will indicate a fault in the system, such as failure of one of the indicator bulb filaments.

Flasher units cannot be dismantled. A defective unit must therefore be replaced, care being taken to reconnect as the original (see **FIG 11:23**).

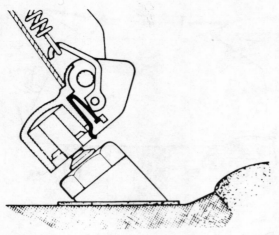

FIG 11 : 28 The windscreen wiper arm to operating spindle attachment

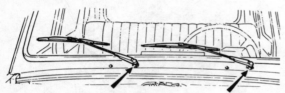

FIG 11 : 29 The correct parking position of the wiper arms

FIG 11 : 30 The wiper linkage mounting plate

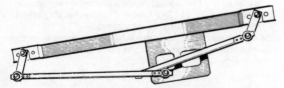

FIG 11 : 31 The wiper linkage

In the event of trouble occurring with a flashing light direction-indicator system, the following procedure should be followed:

1 Check the bulbs for broken filaments.
2 Refer to the vehicle wiring diagram and check all flasher circuit connections.
3 Switch on the ignition.

4 Check with a voltmeter that the flasher unit positive terminal is at 12 volts with respect to earth.
5 Connect together flasher unit terminals + and REP and operate the direction-indicator switch. If the indicator lamps now light, the flasher unit is defective and must be replaced.

Location of the front and rear flasher bulbs which are combined in the side and rear lamp clusters are indicated in **FIGS 11 : 24** and **11 : 25**.

Renewing a flasher operating switch:

Removal:

1 Disconnect the battery.
2 Remove the bottom protective panel (see **FIG 11 : 26**).
3 Remove the steering wheel as described in **Chapter 9**.
4 Raise the top part of the dashboard, disconnect the wires and unscrew the two securing screws as shown in **FIG 11 : 27**.

Refitting:

Carry out the removing operations in reverse, taking care to position the steering wheel correctly as described in **Chapter 9**. For refitting the wires, see **FIG 11 : 23**.

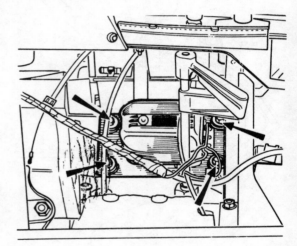

FIG 11 : 32 Disconnecting the wiper motor, early four bolt plate

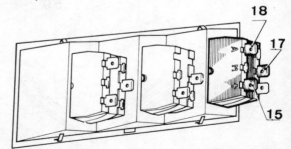

FIG 11 : 33 The windscreen wiper operating switch terminals

Key to Fig 11 : 33 15 Feed to switch   17 Feed to motor 18 Windscreen wiper park

11:10 The wiper mechanism and motor

(a) The wiper arms:

The wiper arms are secured to the splined spindles by means of a retaining spring as shown in **FIG 11:28**.

Removal is effected by swivelling the arm at right angles to its normal plane of travel and slightly lifting the tension coil spring hook to depress the securing spring and pulling off the blade assembly from the splined spindle.

Refitting is a reversal of removal but ensure the parking position is as shown in **FIG 11:29**.

Renew the rubber blade inserts every two years or earlier if they cease to wipe the screen satisfactorily.

(b) Mounting plate and linkage removal:

1 Disconnect (see **FIGS 11:30** and **11:31**) by pulling on the driving arm (mounting plate side) in order to separate it from the driving link (motor side).
2 Unscrew the top securing screws of the support plate.
3 Unscrew the bottom securing screws of the support plate.
4 Remove the plate by turning it towards the top.

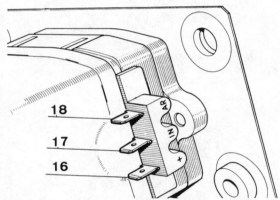

FIG 11:34 The windscreen wiper motor terminals

Key to Fig 11:34   16 Feed to motor direct   17 Feed to motor   18 Park windscreen wiper

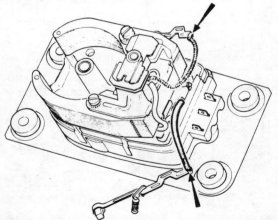

FIG 11:35 The windscreen wiper motor brush holders

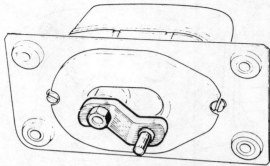

FIG 11:36 The wiper motor crank and support plate. Later support plates have three bolts

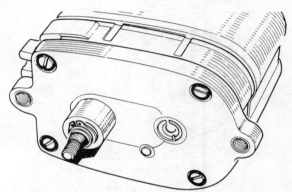

FIG 11:37 The shaft circlip and gear securing screws

(c) Motor removal:

1 Disconnect the battery.
2 Disconnect the 3 wires shown in **FIG 11:32**.
3 Unscrew the securing screws.
4 Pull on the motor to remove it.

Refitting:

Carry out the removing operations in reverse but ensure that the silentbloc are in the correct position.

Make sure that the driving link is secure.

(d) Servicing the motor:

The wiper operation is controlled by a facia mounted switch and if failure has occurred, first check the security of the connecting tags on the leads at the switch and motor terminals shown in **FIGS 11:33** and **11:34**.

1 Unscrew the cover retaining screw located on the motor side of the unit.
2 Check the condition of the carbon brushes, if worn unhook the coil spring and remove them by unsoldering the brush holders as shown in **FIG 11:35**.
3 Check the condition of the armature, if any of the wiring is broken or the commutator is scored, then it should be withdrawn by removing the shaft circlip shown in **FIG 11:37**. The armature should either be repaired by a competent auto electrician or a new one obtained.

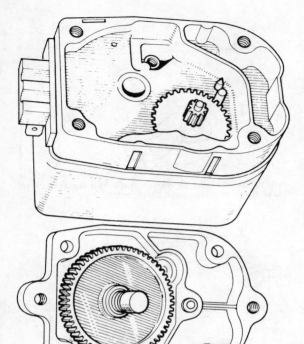

FIG 11:38   The wiper gears exposed

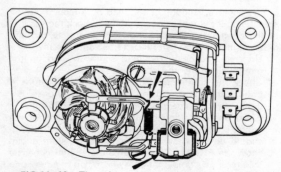

FIG 11:39   The wiper motor armature and shaft

FIG 11:40   The wiper motor correctly assembled

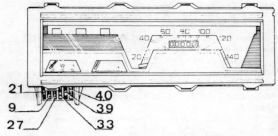

21
9
27
40
39
33

FIG 11:41   The instrument panel junction box

Key to Fig 11:41   21 Headlamp indicator lamp
9 Feed to oil pressure switch and water temperature transmitter
27 Feed to instrument panel   33 Instrument panel earth
39 Instrument panel light   40 Flasher indicator lamp

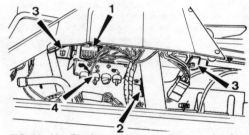

FIG 11:42   The instrument panel removal points
Key to Fig 11:42   1 Terminal block   2 Speedo cable
3 Retaining clips   4 Cables

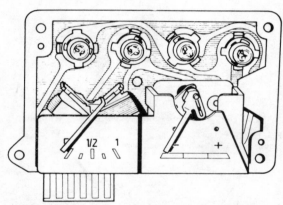

FIG 11:43   Instrument   panel   indicator   lamps   and
gauges

FIG 11:44   Fuel   and   temperature   gauge   sub panel
securing screws
Key to Fig 11:44   1 Earth wire terminal   2 Fuel gauge
cable terminal

4 Check the drive gear mechanism by first removing the cranked lever from its splined shaft and the two support plate screws (see **FIG 11 : 36**).

5 Withdraw the four cover screws shown in **FIG 11 : 37**.

6 Examine the gearwheels now exposed (see **FIG 11 : 38**) and also the spiral gearing cut on the end of the armature shaft (see **FIG 11 : 39**). Renew any badly badly worn components.

7 Reassembly is a reversal of dismantling procedure but observe the following points. Grease the gearwheels liberally during refitting. Resolder the new carbon brush holders in position, fit the coil spring and position the insulation piece all as shown in **FIG 11 : 40**.

11 : 11 Replacing a gauge or indicator bulb

1 Disconnect the battery.

2 Disconnect the junction box located beneath the instrument panel (see **FIG 11 : 41**).

3 Remove the speedometer drive cable from the speedometer head.

4 Pull on the two instrument panel securing clips and withdraw the panel from below, all as arrowed in **FIG 11 : 42.**

5 Indicator lamp bulbs may be renewed simply by turning the appropriate holder (see **FIG 11 : 43**) and pulling out.

6 To remove the water temperature or fuel gauges, unscrew the five securing screws shown in **FIG 11 : 44** and withdraw the gauge/gauge lamp assembly.

7 In order to remove the speedometer, it is necessary to lift the glass off first. To do this, lift up the securing tags (see **FIG 11 : 45**) and pull out the glass. Unscrew the two securing screws and remove the speedometer.

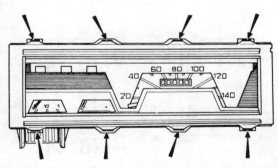
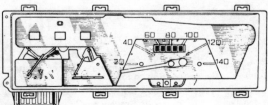

FIG 11 : 45 Instrument panel glass removal

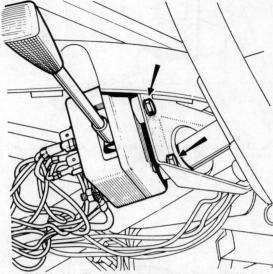

FIG 11 : 46 The lighting switch securing bolts

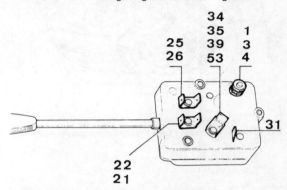

FIG 11 : 47 The lighting switch terminal connections

Key to Fig 11 : 47   1 Main feed   3 Feed to Neiman ignition switch   4 Main feed to fuses   21 Headlight indicator lamp   22 Main feed to headlight   25 Dipped beam lefthand side   26 Dipped beam righthand side   31 Horn   34 Front lefthand side light   35 Front righthand side light   39 Instrument panel light   53 Rear lights

11 : 12 Renewing the lighting switch

Should the lighting switch require removal for servicing or renewal, carry out the following operations:

1 Disconnect the battery.

2 Refer to **FIG 11 : 26** and remove the protective panel beneath the facia panel after withdrawing the securing screws.

3 Remove the switch retaining screws (arrowed in **FIG 11 : 46**) and withdraw the switch.

4 Detach the electrical connectors.

Replacement of the switch is a reversal of the dismantling procedure. The location of the connecting wires is given in **FIG 11 : 47**. Remember to reconnect the battery.

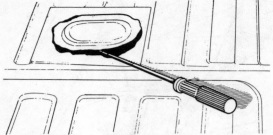

FIG 11:48 Lifting the fuel tank level transmitter unit recess cover

11:13 The fuel tank transmitter unit

Should a fault occur in the indication given by the fuel gauge located on the instrument panel, first check the security of the terminal connectors at both the gauge and the tank transmitter unit.

When checking for continuity between terminals with the wiring disconnected, do not shortcircuit the fuel gauge to earth. Having checked the wiring circuit after reference to the wiring diagram in **Technical Data** any fault must lie in the tank unit or gauge head. No servicing or repair is possible and either unit should be renewed. Removal instructions for the gauge are given in the

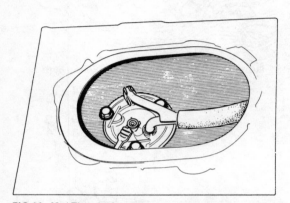

FIG 11:49 The fuel tank transmitter unit securing screws

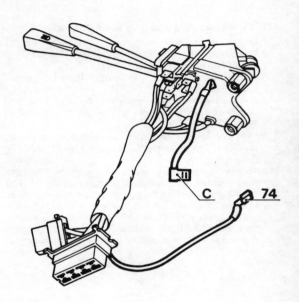

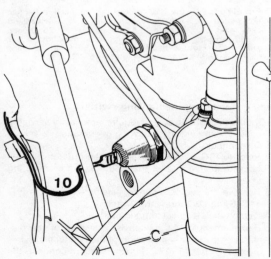

FIG 11:50 The oil pressure switch

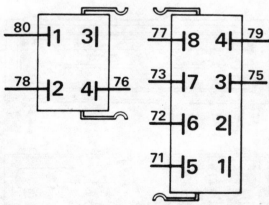

FIG 11:51 Combination lighting—flasher switch, showing cable connection to junction boxes

Key to Fig 11:51 71 Main beam 72 Dipped beam 73 Sidelights 75 Horns 76 Rear lights 77 Lefthand front flasher 78 Lefthand rear flasher 79 Righthand front flasher 80 Righthand rear flasher

previous **Section 11 : 11**. To remove the tank level transmitter unit carry out the following operations.

1 Lift up the rear seats.
2 Remove the boot carpet.
3 Using a screwdriver remove the cover as shown in **FIG 11 : 48**.
4 Unscrew the three securing screws shown in **FIG 11 : 49**.
5 Disconnect the wire and the fuel pipe and remove the unit.

When replacing, change the gasket, reseal the cover and secure it in place with two self-tapping screws.

11 : 14 The oil pressure indicator switch

Although this component rarely gives trouble, it is possible for it to either illuminate continuously or more likely not to illuminate at all. Always check the indicator lamp therefore when switching on the ignition prior to starting the engine.

Should the indicator lamp not come on when switching on the ignition, check the condition of the bulb and the security of the connecting tag to the switch itself. The switch is located below and forward of the fuel pump and is screwed into the side of the engine block (see **FIG 11 : 50**).

A faulty unit should be renewed immediately, do not use excessive force when screwing in the new switch.

Although the reason for the oil warning lamp illuminating when the engine is running should be immediately established and the condition rectified, if it is known that the engine is in good condition and filled with the correct grade of oil then the checking of the efficiency of the pressure switch, by substitution of a new one, should not be overlooked.

11 : 15 Combination lighting/flasher switch

On 1108 cc cars, a combination switch is used for the lighting and direction indicator circuits and is shown in **FIG 11 : 51**. The layout of the wiring is clearly shown and the table herewith gives the function and identification of each cable.

No.	Description	Colour
71	Feed to headlights	Blue
72	Feed to 'dipped beam'	Red
73	Horns	White
74	Feed to flasher change-over switch	Green
75	Feed to front sidelights	White
76	Feed to rear lights	White
77	Lefthand front flasher	Blue
78	Lefthand rear flasher	Blue
79	Righthand front flasher	Red
80	Righthand rear flasher	Red

11 : 16 The alternator

On certain late model cars an alternator may be fitted in place of the DC generator. This will be either Ducellier or Paris-Rhone, and in either case the manufacturers do not advise the dismantling of the instrument unless very adequate servicing equipment is available.

No maintenance is required beyond keeping the connections dry and clean and checking the tension of the driving belt as for the generator in the manner described in **Chapter 4, Section 4 : 2**.

When working on cars fitted with an alternator there are a number of precautions which must be observed:

It is most important that all electrical components be connected with the correct polarity as a wrong connection may cause irreparable damage.

Do not make or break any connections while the alternator is running and do not run the engine with the battery disconnected.

Always disconnect the battery before removing or installing the alternator or regulator.

Do not start the engine with a battery charger or booster still connected.

Always disconnect the alternator when carrying out any welding on the vehicle.

Testing :

In the event of a fault in the charging circuit it is possible to determine whether the alternator or the regulator is responsible as follows:

Connect an ammeter in series with the output (thick) cable, then disconnect the excitation cable at the alternator.

Using a separate wire connect the alternator EXC terminal to the battery positive.

Run the alternator very shortly at 3500 rev/min and check that the output is close to 22 amps. If this figure is not obtained the alternator is faulty. If it is then the regulator must be renewed.

11 : 17 Fault diagnosis

(a) Battery discharged

1 Terminals loose or dirty
2 Lighting circuit shorted
3 Generator not charging
4 Regulator or cut-out unit not operating
5 Battery internally defective

(b) Insufficient charging current

1 Loose or corroded battery terminals
2 Fan belt slipping

(c) Battery will not hold a charge

1 Low electrolyte level
2 Battery plates sulphated
3 Electrolyte leakage from cracked casing or top sealing compound
4 Plate separators ineffective

(d) Battery overcharged

1 Voltage regulator needs renewing

(e) Generator output low or nil

1 Fan belt broken or slipping
2 Regulator unit out of adjustment
3 Worn bearings, loose polepieces
4 Commutator worn, burned or shorted
5 Armature shaft bent or worn
6 Insulation proud between the commutator segments
7 Brushes sticking, springs weak or broken
8 Field coil wires shorted, broken or burned

(f) Starter motor lacks power or will not operate

1 Battery discharged, loose cable connections
2 Starter pinion jammed in mesh with flywheel gear
3 Starter switch or solenoid faulty
4 Brushes worn or sticking, leads detached or shorting
5 Commutator dirty or worn
6 Starter shaft bent
7 Engine abnormally stiff

(g) Starter motor runs but does not turn engine

1 Pinion sticking on screwed sleeve
2 Broken teeth on pinion or flywheel gears

(h) Noisy starter pinion when engine is running

1 Restraining spring weak or broken

(j) Starter motor inoperative

1 Check 1 and 4 in (f)
2 Armature or field coils faulty

(k) Starter motor rough or noisy

1 Mounting bolts loose
2 Damaged pinion or flywheel gear teeth
3 Main pinion spring broken

(l) Lamps inoperative or erratic

1 Battery low, bulbs burned out
2 Faulty earthing of lamps or battery
3 Lighting switch faulty, loose or broken wiring connections

(m) Wiper motor sluggish, taking high current

1 Faulty armature
2 Bearings out of alignment
3 Commutator dirty or shortcircuited
4 Cranks or spindles binding

(n) Fuel gauge does not register

1 No battery supply to gauge
2 Gauge casing not earthed
3 Cable between gauge and tank unit earthed

(o) Fuel gauge registers full

1 Cable between gauge and tank unit broken

CHAPTER 12

BODYWORK

12:1 Description and construction

The R6 body comprises two separate assemblies, the body proper and the floor section as shown in **FIG 12:1**.

Although it is unlikely that complete body shell renewal would be required, **FIG 12:2** shows the attachment points and the removal sequence is as follows:

Remove the undertray, front and rear dampers, the bonnet, the battery and battery tray 1, the earth wire 2, the air filter 3, the expansion chamber valve 4.

Disconnect the feed wires to the dynamo 5, the heater hoses 7 and 8, the feed wires to the coil 9 and to the oil pressure sender switch 10, the speedometer cable 11, the handbrake control lever 12, the brake pipes to the master cylinder, the exhaust pipe 13, the steering column flexible joint, the clutch cable 14, the temperature transmitter switch wire on the water pump, the wire to the starter solenoid, the choke cable 15, the accelerator cable 16, all as indicated in **FIG 12:3**.

As shown in **FIG 12:2** the body is fixed to the floor section by 21 bolts spread out round the outside of the body assembly (white arrows) and by 20 fixing bolts (black arrows) for those components bolted to the front sidemember and the front crossmember. (Engine undertrays removed).

Waterproof sealing strips are located between the body and floor section mating flanges and these will require heating in order to facilitate removal.

It must be emphasized that great care must be taken when using a blow torch and the fuel tank must first be removed.

12:2 Detachable components

A certain number of detachable panels is a feature of the bodywork as shown in **FIG 12:4**. This system is of great value in the event of minor damage when the affected panel can be removed and a new one of appropriate matching colour may be quickly substituted. This will normally show a saving over normal body repairs as applied to all-welded coachwork.

Bonnet renewal:

The front bonnet is opened by means of two swan neck hinges pivoting from the rear towards the front.

It is retained in the open position by a stay attached to the right cowl side.

1 Unscrew the four fixing screws 1 or the two screws 2 (see **FIG 12:5**) and lift the bonnet away.

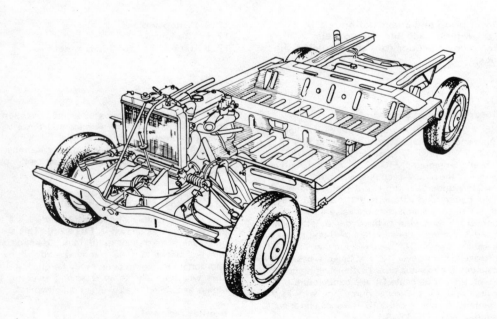

FIG 12:1   The body and floor section, separated

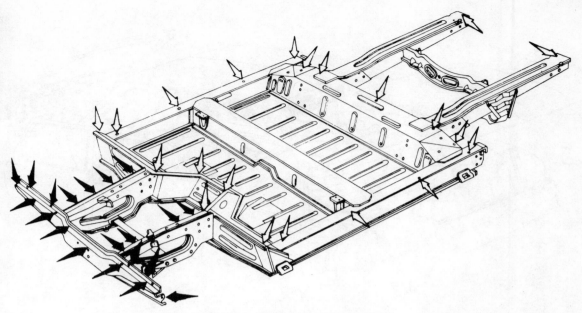

FIG 12:2   The body and floor section attachment points

2 When refitting an adjustment can be carried out if necessary by sliding the screw holes 1 on the swan neck hinges.

3 The rubber buffers are held in place by being clamped under the bridge pieces 4.

Front panel renewal:

1 Remove the engine undertrays, the front grille and headlights, the sidelights, wiring harness and the bonnet.

2 Remove the four screws 1 from the top (see **FIG 12:6**), the four screws 2 with captive nuts on the front crossmember.

3 Remove screw 3 at the joint between the front apron in the battery.

4 Remove screw 4 at the joint between the reinforcement and the two screws 5.

It is not necessary to remove the bumper blades or the wings in order to renew the front panel.

Radiator grille renewal:

1 Remove the two side mouldings (see **FIG 12:7**) fitted by four self-tapping screws 1.

2 Remove the retaining bar 2 fitted by four screws.

3 Remove the grille from its housing L pulling outwards and downwards.

To remove the clips 3, fit a small screwdriver between the clip and the grille and lever lightly in order to pull out the plastic clips from their housings.

Front wing renewal:

1 Remove the flasher repeater 1 (see **FIG 12:8**).

2 Remove the bottom sill moulding attached by clips and one screw at 2.

3 Remove the wing held by five screws 3 on the cowl side, by three screws on the front panel, three screws 5 on the front pillar, two screws 6 at the bottom of the body, one screw 7 at the end of the front crossmember and one screw 8 at the joint with the lower under panel.

Removal of the door and the bonnet is not necessary.

4 When fitting the new wing, check the condition of the captive nuts on the cowl side and the front pillar.

Before fitting the wing, place strips of suitable mastic on the wing mounting points on the scuttle, the cowl side and the front pillar to ensure a watertight joint. Fit the rubber spacers for the bonnet making sure that the clearance is correct.

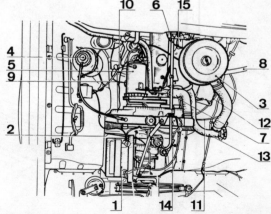

FIG 12:3   Components to be removed or disconnected prior to body removal (for Key see text)

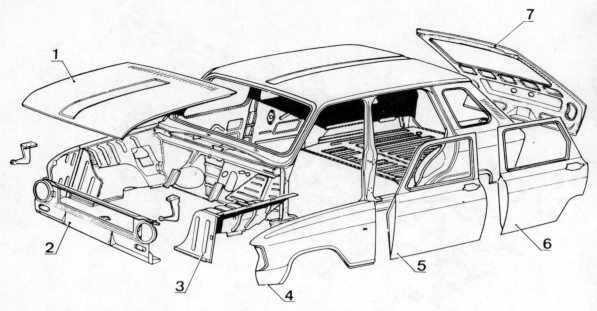

FIG 12:4   Detachable panels of the body

Key to Fig 12:4   1 Bonnet   2 Front panel   3 Cowl side   4 Front wing   5 Front door   6 Rear door   7 Tailgate

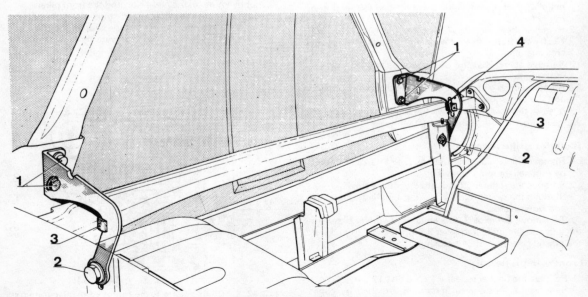

FIG 12:5   The bonnet hinges (for Key see text)

Cowl side renewal:

Having removed the damaged components (wing or front panel), remove the sound deadening material from the inside of the scuttle and disconnect the different mechanical units and electrical components fitted on the cowl side.

1 Remove the two screws 1 (see **FIG 12:9**) from the front crossmember.
2 Remove the four screws 2 from the inside on the side-member.
3 Remove the three screws 3 from the inside of the body at the joint between the cowl side and the scuttle.
4 Remove screw 4 at the joint with the heater cross-member.
5 Before replacing a cowl side, waterproof seal the scuttle with a strip of mastic.
6 Offer up and attach the cowl side, complete the water proofing by an application of mastic at the joint between the scuttle and the cowl side.
7 Leave to dry before painting.

Door renewal:

Either the front or rear passenger door may be removed or replaced by withdrawing the clips P which hold the hinge pin as shown in **FIG 12:10** and knocking out the pin with a suitable cranked driver.

Later doors have modified hinges and a door check at the bottom hinge. If it is necessary to fit a later type door to an early model, a $\frac{1}{16}$ inch (1.5 mm) thickness of metal will have to be removed from the top and bottom surfaces of the hinge.

Alternatively, the hinge fixing bolts (E or G) may be removed after withdrawing the interior trim as shown in **FIG 12:11** (front doors), **FIG 12:12** (rear doors).

Tailgate renewal:

To remove the tailgate, unscrew the four screws V fixing it to the tailgate frame (see **FIG 12:13**). .

When removing the counterbalance take great care as there will be a spring-load still in the arms.

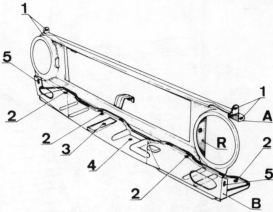

FIG 12:6 The front panel (for Key see text)

The lock assembly consists of a casing attached by two screws 1 and a push button with integral barrel 2 (see **FIG 12:14**).

Care must be taken when removing this push button because the collar 4 is fragile. Raise the collar slightly and using a piece of string draw in the three lugs 3 so that they lie in their grooves (see **FIG 12:15**). Pull out the pushbutton towards the rear.

Refitting the tailgate is a reversal of removal procedure. Insertion of the lock mechanism causes the three spring lugs 3 to move outwards (arrow), retaining the assembly in place under the outer door panel (see **FIG 12:16**).

12:3 Removing the door trim and servicing the lock

1 Remove the window winding handle by peeling back the flexible covering A shown in **FIG 12:17** in order to gain access to nut B.
2 Push back the lock tab, remove the nut and withdraw the winding handle.

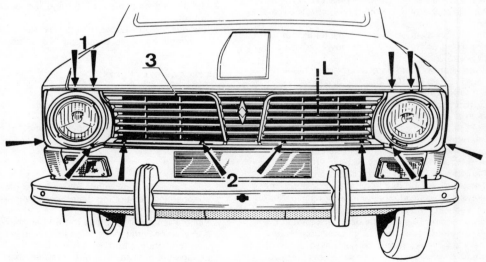

FIG 12:7 The radiator grille (for Key see text)

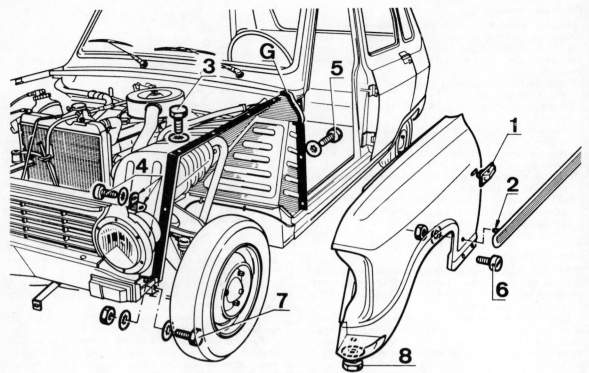

FIG 12:8   The front wing (for Key see text)

3 Remove the two screws C and withdraw the door pull.
4 Remove the door trim by inserting a piece of wood D between the trim and the door frame, then twist the wood to spring out the trim from the clips S (see **FIG 12:18**).
5 Unstick the seal panels.
6 Remove the three fixing screws F (see **FIG 12:19**). Wind the window down to within $5\frac{7}{8}$ inch (150 mm) of the seal.
    Disconnect the window winding mechanism at the bottom of the glass by means of the lower aperture in the door frame.
7 Pull out the window winding mechanism by moving it sideways as shown in **FIG 12:20**.
8 Remove the lock remote control gear by unscrewing the two fixing screws on the door frame H, drop the lever down to reach the handle retaining screw J (see **FIG 12:21**).
9 Undo the retaining clip of the remote control lever on the door frame and pull out the remote control lever.
10 Remove the two fixing screws K (see **FIG 12:22**). To pull out the lock, push the push button inside the door frame. Screw L holds the handle in position, the other screw is fitted inside the door outer panel.
    Faults or wear occurring in the window winding mechanism or remote control gear of the door lock should not be repaired or rectified as this is seldom satisfactory. Complete new assemblies should be purchased. Refitting the component parts is a reversal of the removal procedure. Grease the rotating mechanism and slides.

12:4 Window glass

Front and rear door glass removal.
    Assuming that the winding mechanism has previously been removed as described earlier then:
1 Remove the inside seal by inserting a screwdriver between the seal and the door frame (see **FIG 12:23**).
2 Lift out the door glass by turning it (pivoting at the bottom).
3 Remove the outside seal held by six clips.
    Refitting is a reversal of removal procedure.

The rear quarter lights:

Removal:
1 Remove the exterior bright trim by carefully prising it from the rubber channel.
2 Press on the inside of an upper corner of the glass in an outward direction.

Refitting:
1 Insert sealing compound between the glass and its channel and positioning the rubber channel round the glass.
2 Place a length of string in the rubber channel which is to engage with the frame, so that its ends are crossed over but hanging from the channel.
3 Engage the bottom edge of the rubber channel on the frame and by using gentle pressure on the glass and

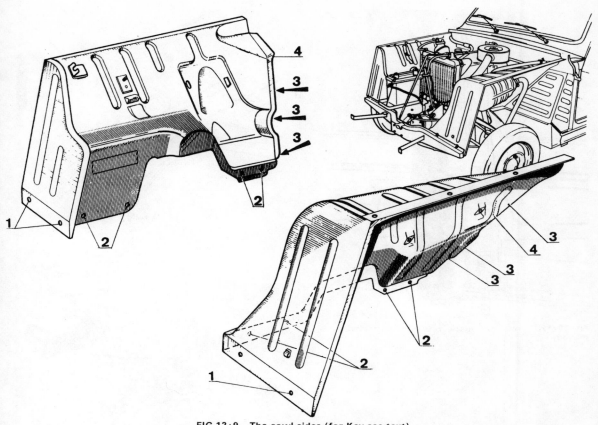

FIG 12:9   The cowl sides (for Key see text)

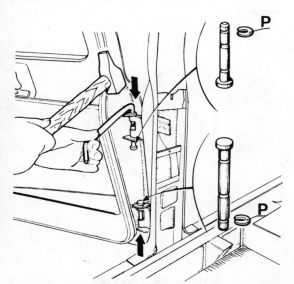

FIG 12:10   The door hinge pins. **P** is retaining clip

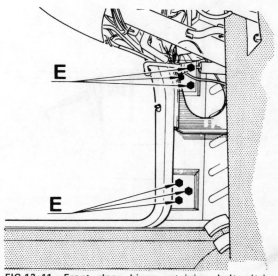

FIG 12:11   Front door hinge retaining bolts (trim removed)

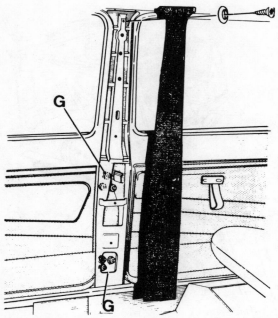

FIG 12:12 Rear door hinge retaining bolts (trim removed)

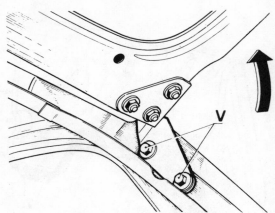

FIG 12:13 A tailgate hinge

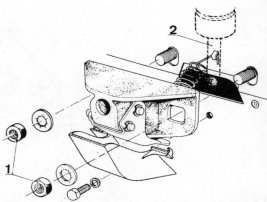

FIG 12:14 The tailgate lock (exploded view) (for Key see text)

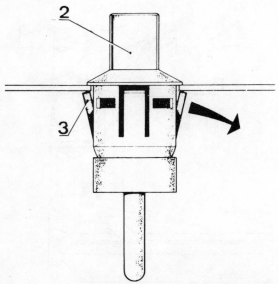

FIG 12:16 Method of inserting the tailgate lock push button

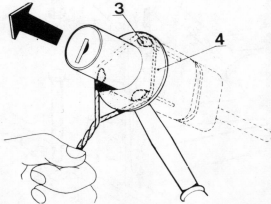

FIG 12:15 Removing the tailgate lock push button (for Key see text)

pulling the string outwards the channel lip will become engaged with the frame throughout its periphery.

4 Carefully insert the exterior trim. Do not cut the rubber during replacement.

Windscreen and rear window glass removal is best left to specialists due to the size of the glass and the necessity of completely waterproof sealing being required.

12:5 The heater

The heater operates with water heated by the engine cooling system which runs through the heater matrix and convection of hot air being assisted by an electric fan. The water or electrical component parts of the assembly may be removed independently of each other.

The sophisticated fresh air heating/ventilation system provides full width demisting to the windscreen and a balanced supply of fresh air at face level. A special feature is an automatic cut-out of the booster fan when the ram effect of the current of air reaches a certain level.

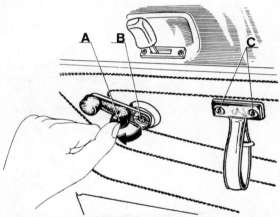

FIG 12:17 Removing a window winding handle and door pull (for Key see text)

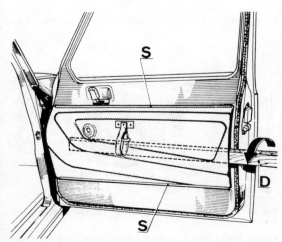

FIG 12:18 Removing the door trim (for Key see text)

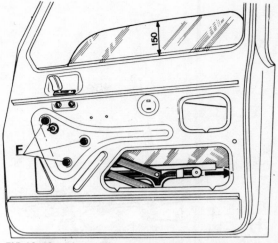

FIG 12:19 Dismantling the window winding mechanism (for Key see text)

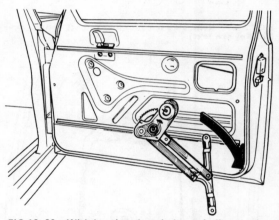

FIG 12:20 Withdrawing the window winding mechanism

(a) The heater body and motor

Removal and dismantling:

1 Disconnect the battery.
2 Disconnect the switches and remove the instrument panel as described in **Chapter 11**.
3 Remove the gear control rod as described in **Chapter 6** if necessary.
4 Remove the facia (see next **Section**).
5 Disconnect the feed wire as shown in **FIG 12:24**.
6 Remove the support bracket for the gear control rod (see **Chapter 6**) if necessary.
7 Remove the heater body by withdrawing the retaining screws arrowed in **FIG 12:25**.
8 Unscrew the securing screws from the two half-cases, and separate them (see **FIG 12:26**).
9 Remove the fan wheel (see **FIG 12:28**) and, if applicable, the bottom cover, and clamp ring.
10 Unscrew the three motor securing screws (see **FIG 12:27**) and lift out the motor.

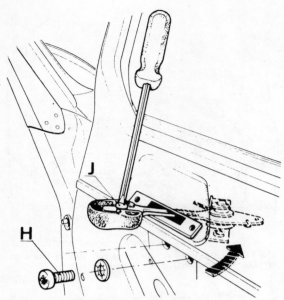

FIG 12:21 Removing the door lock remote control gear (for Key see text)

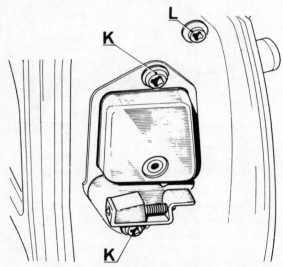

FIG 12:22 The door operating push button and catch securing screws (for Key see text)

Any defective components should be renewed. Refitting is a reversal of removal and dismantling procedure.

When refitting the motor, carefully position the silentblocs.

(b) The heater matrix:

Removal:

1 Drain the cooling system as necessary as described in **Chapter 4**, retaining the coolant for further use or clamp the hoses.

2 Remove the air filter and the bonnet locking mechanism.

3 Push down the wiring harness.

4 Disconnect the gear control rod if necessary and remove the cover and pull it out, all as arrowed in **FIG 12:29**.

5 Disconnect the heater hose (see **FIG 12:30**).

6 Unscrew the three securing screws from the cold air flap.

7 Undo the matrix from the front.

The heater matrix may be backflushed if it has not been warming up, to remove any clogging deposits. Should this not prove effective, than a factory exchange unit should be obtained. Refitting is a reversal of removal procedure, always remake the seal.

(c) The water flow control tap:

Removal:

1 Disconnect the two heater hoses (see **FIG 12:31**), after clamping them to prevent leakage.

2 Remove the heater control rod bracket (see **FIG 12:32**) early type only.

3 Unlock the tap securing nut.

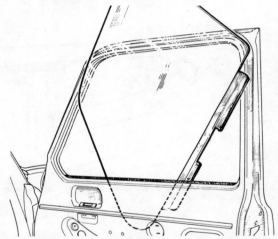

FIG 12:23 Method of removing a door window glass

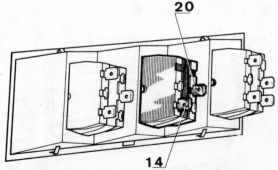

FIG 12:24 The instrument panel heater switch (rear view)

Key to Fig 12:24   14 Feed wire to motor   20 Feed wire to switch

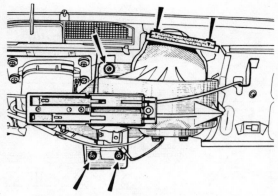

FIG 12:25   The heater body retaining screws

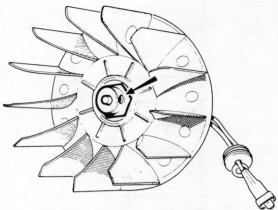

FIG 12:28   The heater fan wheel locknut

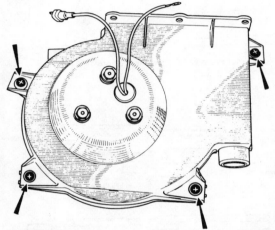

FIG 12:26   The heater half casing securing screws, early model

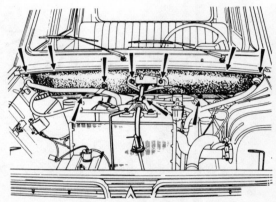

FIG 12:29   Removal points prior to heater matrix withdrawal

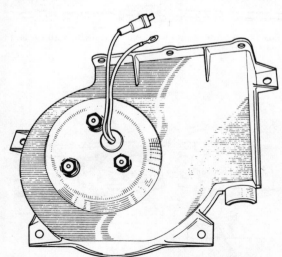

FIG 12:27   The heater motor securing bolts, early model

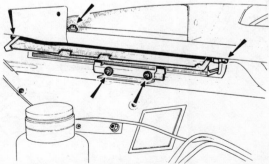

FIG 12:30   Disconnection points for heater matrix removal

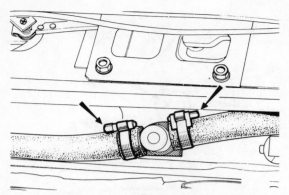

FIG 12:31 Heater hose connection to the water flow control tap

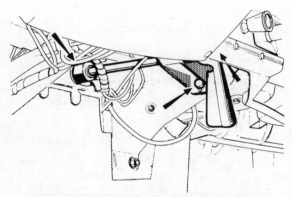

FIG 12:32 The heater tap control rod, early type

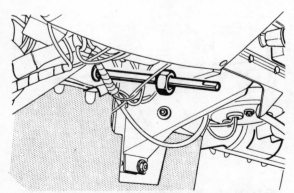

FIG 12:33 Withdrawing the heater tap control rod

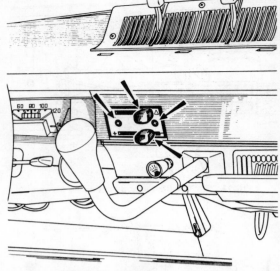

FIG 12:34 The heater control levers

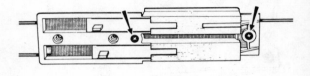

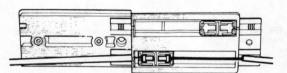

FIG 12:35 The heater operating control cables and method of attachment

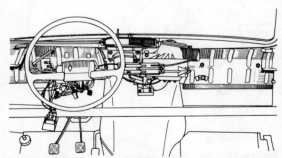

FIG 12:36 The air channeling securing screws

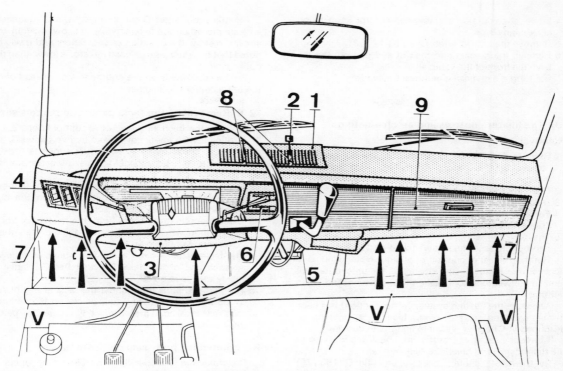

FIG 12:37   The facia and parcels shelf removal points

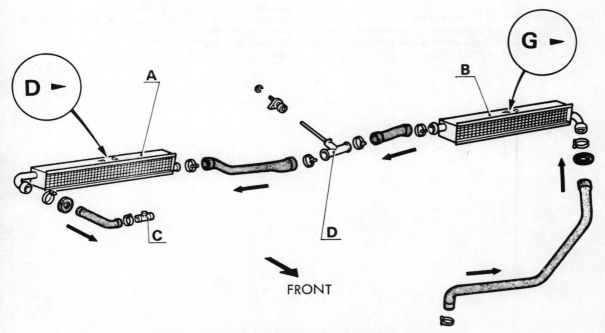

FIG 12:38   Showing the water circulation on R1181 engines

Key to Fig 12:38   A Righthand radiator   B Lefthand radiator   C Bleed screw   D Heater valve

RENAULT 6

4 Lower the rod and unscrew the control knob fixing screw early type.

5 Remove the control knob (see **FIG 12 : 33**).

6 Remove the bracket and the nut and pull out the tap from the front of the vehicle.

Refitting is a reversal of removal procedure.

(d) The heater controls and air channeling:

Removal:

1 Refer to **FIG 12 : 34** to remove the control gear and remove the two knobs by pulling them from their levers.

2 Unscrew the securing screws.

3 Disconnect the cables and remove the assembly.

4 For operating cable renewal, separate the two plates (see **FIG 12 : 35**) for access to the cables.

5 The air channeling is removed by withdrawing the appropriate securing screws (see **FIG 12 : 36**).

Refitting of the control gear and channeling is a reversal of removal and dismantling procedure but remake the weatherproof seal on the air channeling when refitting.

Whenever the heating system (water section) has been dismantled and reassembled, bleed the system as described in **Chapter 4** after refilling with coolant.

If interior heating is insufficient, check the working of the thermostat, and bleed the system of air.

The thermostat should start to open at 84°C (183.2°F) and should be fully open at 94°C (201.2°F).

(e) Changes for the R1181 engine:

The direction of the water flow has been reversed on these models and the layout of the component parts of the system is according to **FIG 12 : 38**.

Identification letters **D** (droit=right) and **G** (gauche= left) are placed on the two radiators to show location and arrows to show the direction of circulation, and it will be noted that the entry pipe on each radiator is lower than the outlet pipe.

The bleed screw is on the righthand side instead of on the left as in R1180 engines.

12 : 6 Removal of the facia panel and parcels shelf

1 Remove the fresh air grille 1, the control knobs 2, the lighting switch lower cover fixed by five screws 3, the group of three switches with their supports 4 push fitted into the facia panel, all as indicated in **FIG 12 : 37**.

2 Disconnect the instrument panel (wiring harness, speedometer cable), the choke cable (on the carburetter), the ashtray (fixing screw 5).

3 Disconnect the gear control rod, the heater control 6, the steering wheel (see **Chapter 8**) and the rubber cover round the Neiman lock.

4 The facia panel is fixed at the five points as follows: At each end of the dash 7. Under fresh air grille 8. Inside the glove box 9.

5 The parcel shelf is fitted under the facia at five places in the righthand side and four places on the lefthand side, as arrowed. Three screws V secure the parcel shelf at each end and in the centre.

Recommended body sealing compounds:

The following are specified and should be obtained from your Renault distributor.

Mastic 297—for all sheet metal joints visible or not.

Mastic 306—for the replacement of detachable components, or for windscreen sealing.

Mastic 307—to finish off after fixing quarter lights, or rear window frames, etc.

Mastic 503—applied by hand for filling large or small holes.

APPENDIX

TECHNICAL DATA

       Engine   Cooling system   Fuel system   Ignition system
       Clutch   Transmission   Suspension   Brakes
       Electrical equipment   Capacities   Dimensions
       Torque wrench settings

WIRING DIAGRAM

HINTS ON MAINTENANCE AND OVERHAUL

GLOSSARY OF TERMS

INDEX

Inches		Decimals	Milli-metres	Inches to Millimetres		Millimetres to Inches	
				Inches	mm	mm	Inches
	1/64	.015625	.3969	.001	.0254	.01	.00039
	1/32	.03125	.7937	.002	.0508	.02	.00079
	3/64	.046875	1.1906	.003	.0762	.03	.00118
1/16		.0625	1.5875	.004	.1016	.04	.00157
	5/64	.078125	1.9844	.005	.1270	.05	.00197
3/32		.09375	2.3812	.006	.1524	.06	.00236
	7/64	.109375	2.7781	.007	.1778	.07	.00276
1/8		.125	3.1750	.008	.2032	.08	.00315
	9/64	.140625	3.5719	.009	.2286	.09	.00354
5/32		.15625	3.9687	.01	.254	.1	.00394
	11/64	.171875	4.3656	.02	.508	.2	.00787
3/16		.1875	4.7625	.03	.762	.3	.01181
	13/64	.203125	5·1594	.04	1.016	.4	.01575
7/32		.21875	5.5562	.05	1.270	.5	.01969
	15/64	.234375	5.9531	.06	1.524	.6	.02362
1/4		.25	6.3500	.07	1.778	.7	.02756
	17/64	.265625	6.7469	.08	2.032	.8	.03150
9/32		.28125	7.1437	.09	2.286	.9	.03543
	19/64	.296875	7.5406	.1	2.54	1	.03937
5/16		.3125	7.9375	.2	5.08	2	.07874
	21/64	.328125	8.3344	.3	7.62	3	.11811
11/32		.34375	8.7312	.4	10.16	4	.15748
	23/64	.359375	9.1281	.5	12.70	5	.19685
3/8		.375	9.5250	.6	15.24	6	.23622
	25/64	.390625	9.9219	.7	17.78	7	.27559
13/32		.40625	10.3187	.8	20.32	8	.31496
	27/64	.421875	10.7156	.9	22.86	9	.35433
7/16		.4375	11.1125	1	25.4	10	.39370
	29/64	.453125	11.5094	2	50.8	11	.43307
15/32		.46875	11.9062	3	76.2	12	.47244
	31/64	.484375	12.3031	4	101.6	13	.51181
1/2		.5	12.7000	5	127.0	14	.55118
	33/64	.515625	13.0969	6	152.4	15	.59055
17/32		.53125	13.4937	7	177.8	16	.62992
	35/64	.546875	13.8906	8	203.2	17	.66929
9/16		.5625	14.2875	9	228.6	18	.70866
	37/64	.578125	14.6844	10	254.0	19	.74803
19/32		.59375	15.0812	11	279.4	20	.78740
	39/64	.609375	15.4781	12	304.8	21	.82677
5/8		.625	15.8750	13	330.2	22	.86614
	41/64	.640625	16.2719	14	355.6	23	.90551
21/32		.65625	16.6687	15	381.0	24	.94488
	43/64	.671875	17.0656	16	406.4	25	.98425
11/16		.6875	17.4625	17	431.8	26	1.02362
	45/64	.703125	17.8594	18	457.2	27	1.06299
23/32		.71875	18.2562	19	482.6	28	1.10236
	47/64	.734375	18.6531	20	508.0	29	1.14173
3/4		.75	19.0500	21	533.4	30	1.18110
	49/64	.765625	19.4469	22	558.8	31	1.22047
25/32		.78125	19.8437	23	584.2	32	1.25984
	51/64	.796875	20.2406	24	609.6	33	1.29921
13/16		.8125	20.6375	25	635.0	34	1.33858
	53/64	.828125	21.0344	26	660.4	35	1.37795
27/32		.84375	21.4312	27	685.8	36	1.41732
	55/64	.859375	21.8281	28	711.2	37	1.4567
7/8		.875	22.2250	29	736.6	38	1.4961
	57/64	.890625	22.6219	30	762.0	39	1.5354
29/32		.90625	23.0187	31	787.4	40	1.5748
	59/64	.921875	23.4156	32	812.8	41	1.6142
15/16		.9375	23.8125	33	838.2	42	1.6535
	61/64	.953125	24.2094	34	863.6	43	1.6929
31/32		.96875	24.6062	35	889.0	44	1.7323
	63/64	.984375	25.0031	36	914.4	45	1.7717

UNITS	Pints to Litres	Gallons to Litres	Litres to Pints	Litres to Gallons	Miles to Kilometres	Kilometres to Miles	Lbs. per sq. In. to Kg. per sq. Cm.	Kg. per sq. Cm. to Lbs. per sq. In.
1	.57	4.55	1.76	.22	1.61	.62	.07	14.22
2	1.14	9.09	3.52	.44	3.22	1.24	.14	28.50
3	1.70	13.64	5.28	.66	4.83	1.86	.21	42.67
4	2.27	18.18	7.04	.88	6.44	2.49	.28	56.89
5	2.84	22.73	8.80	1.10	8.05	3.11	.35	71.12
6	3.41	27.28	10.56	1.32	9.66	3.73	.42	85.34
7	3.98	31.82	12.32	1.54	11.27	4.35	.49	99.56
8	4.55	36.37	14.08	1.76	12.88	4.97	.56	113.79
9		40.91	15.84	1.98	14.48	5.59	.63	128.00
10		45.46	17.60	2.20	16.09	6.21	.70	142.23
20				4.40	32.19	12.43	1.41	284.47
30				6.60	48.28	18.64	2.11	426.70
40				8.80	64.37	24.85		
50					80.47	31.07		
60					96.56	37.28		
70					112.65	43.50		
80					128.75	49.71		
90					144.84	55.92		
100					160.93	62.14		

UNITS	Lb ft to kgm	Kgm to lb ft	UNITS	Lb ft to kgm	Kgm to lb ft
1	.138	7.233	7	.967	50.631
2	.276	14.466	8	1.106	57.864
3	.414	21.699	9	1.244	65.097
4	.553	28.932	10	1.382	72.330
5	.691	36.165	20	2.765	144.660
6	.829	43.398	30	4.147	216.990

TECHNICAL DATA

Measurements and dimensions throughout this manual are given in Imperial with Metric equivalents unless otherwise stated

850 ENGINE

Type	800-02 (early), 800-03 (later)
Brake horse power	38 bhp at 5000 rev/min
Maximum torque	40 lb ft at 3000 rev/min
Bore	2.284 inch (58 mm)
Stroke	3.150 inch (80 mm)
Cubic capacity	51 cu in (845 cc)
Compression ratio	8:1

Crankshaft (three bearing):
  Journals:
    Nominal diameter ... ... — 1.57 inch (40 mm)
    Regrind diameters for repair size bearing shells ... — 1.565 inch (39.75 mm)
    Grinding tolerances ... ... — .00035 inch (.009 mm) to .001 inch (.025 mm)

  Crankpins:
    Nominal diameter ... ... — 1.496 inch (38 mm)
    Regrind diameters for repair size bearing shells ... — 1.486 inch (37.75 mm)
    Grinding tolerances ... ... — —.001 inch (—.025 mm) to —.0016 inch (—.041 mm)

Crankshaft end float ... ... — .002 to .010 inch (.05 to .25 mm)
Crankshaft end float flange thicknesses:
  Standard size ... ... — .079 inch (2 mm)
  Repair sizes ... ... — .081 inch (2.05 mm) to .083 inch (2.10 mm) and .085 inch (2.15 mm)

Cylinder liner projection ... ... — .003 to .006 inch (.08 to .15 mm)
Cylinder liner seal thickness availability ... ... — .038 inch (.95 mm), .040 inch (1 mm) and .042 inch (1.05 mm)

Valves:
  Inlet:
    Diameter of head ... ... — 1.110 inch (28.2 mm)
    Stem diameter ... ... — .276 inch (7 mm)
  Exhaust:
    Diameter of head ... ... — .984 inch (25 mm)
    Stem diameter ... ... — .276 inch (7 mm)
  Seat angle ... ... — 45 deg.
  Valve guides:
    Nominal size ... ... — .433 inch (11 mm)
    Repair size ... ... — .437 inch (11.10 mm) to .443 inch (11.25 mm)

Maximum valve seat width:
  Inlet ... ... — $\frac{1}{16}$ inch (1.5 mm)
  Exhausts ... ... — $\frac{5}{64}$ inch (1.8 mm)
Valve clearances:
  Clearances on a cold engine:
    Inlet ... ... — .006 inch (.15 mm)
    Exhaust ... ... — .008 inch (.20 mm)
Inlet and exhaust:
  Valve springs:
    Free length ... ... — $1\frac{19}{32}$ inch (40.4 mm)
    Length under a load of 47 to 51 lb ... ... — $\frac{15}{16}$ inch (24 mm)
Oil pressure ... ... — 17 lb/sq inch at 500 rev/min
 34 lb/sq inch at 4000 rev/min

1100 ENGINE

Type	688-10
Brake horse power	48 at 5300 rev/min
Maximum torque	60 lb ft
Bore	2.756 (70 mm)
Stroke	2.835 (72 mm)
Cubic capacity	67.6 cu in (1108 cc)
Compression ratio	7.25 or 8.0:1 (early), 9.5:1 (late)
Crankshaft (five bearing):	
Journals:	
Nominal diameter	1.811 (46 mm)
Regrind diameter	1.801 (45.75 mm)
Crankpins:	
Nominal diameter	1.731 (43.98 mm)
Regrind diameter	1.722 (43.75 mm)
End float	.002 to .006
Thrust washers	.109, .113, .115
Camshaft end float	.002 to .005
Cylinder liners:	
Base diameter	2.972
Projection above block	.002 to .005
Valves:	
Head diameter, inlet	1.319
exhaust	1.181
Stem diameter	.276
Seat angle	45 deg.
Seat width, inlet	.043 to .055
exhaust	.055 to .067
Valve guides:	
Diameter nominal	.433
Repair size, 1 groove	.437
2 grooves	.443
Valve springs:	
Free length	$1\frac{21}{32}$
Length under 80 lb load	$\frac{63}{64}$
Colour	Light green
Valve clearances:	
Cold, inlet	.006
exhaust	.008
Hot, inlet	.007
exhaust	.010
Oil pump pressure at 80°C	17 lb/sq in at 600 rev/min
	34 lb/sq in at 4000 rev/min

COOLING SYSTEM

Thermo-syphon, water pump assisted, fan cooled
Sealed system with expansion tank and air bleed screw

Thermostat opens at	80°C (early), 84°C (late)
Fan motor:	
Type	SEV-Marchal VR 12 or Paris-Rhone M7 C 1
Temperature switch:	
Points close at	90.5 to 93.5°C (195 to 200°F)
Points open at	80.5 to 83.5°C (177 to 182°F)

FUEL SYSTEM

Pump ... ... Mechanical, camshaft driven or SU electric (1108 cc)

Type ... ... SEV (mechanical)

Carburetter (845 cc):

    Type (early) ... ... Solex 32 PDIS 3, Mk 428, 451 or 467 with manual choke and accelerator pump

	428, 451	467
Choke tube	24	24
Main jet	120	122.5
Correction jet	150	145
Pilot jet	47.5	47.5
Needle valve with spring	1.2 mm	1.2 mm
Float	5.7 g	5.7 g
Pump injector	47.5	47.5
Accelerator pump stroke	3.5 mm	3.5 mm

    Type (later) ... ... Solex 32 EISA 4 Mk 570

Choke tube	22
Main jet	117.5
Air compensator	150 N4
Idling jet	45
Needle valve	1.5 mm
Accelerator pump	40

Carburetter (1108 cc):

    Type ... ... Solex 32.EISA.2, Mk 481, EISA.3, Mk 525, EISA 4, Mk 512 or 560

	481, 525	512	560
Choke	23	23	23
Main jet	132.5	120	120
Air compensator	175 LB	125 NA	125 NA
Idling jet	50	47	45
Needle valve	1.5 mm	1.5 mm	1.5 mm
Accelerator pump	35	40	40

Idling speed:

Early 845 cc	650 ± 25 rev/min
Later 845 cc	750 ± 25 rev/min
1108 cc	650 ± 25 rev/min
1108 cc with 9.5:1 CR	700 ± 25 rev/min

IGNITION SYSTEM

Sparking plugs:

    Make ... ... AC.42.FS (1108 cc), AC.43.FS (850 cc)
Marchal 35/36 (850 cc)
Champion L.87Y
Motorcraft AE.32 (850 cc)

    Gap ... ... .025 inch

Distributor 845 cc:

    Early ... ... SEV 27914, 27916, dustproof SEV 27915 or 27917
Ducellier 4226 or dustproof 4227

    Later ... ... SEV 4000 2002 or dustproof 4002 9002
Ducellier 4274 or dustproof 4275

Distributor 1108 cc:

Early	SEV 4030 3502 or dustproof 4032 9502
	Ducellier 4336 or dustproof 4337
Later	SEV 4030 3702 or dustproof 4032 9702
	Ducellier 4326 or dustproof 4327
9.5:1 CR...	Ducellier 4406 or dustproof 4410
Coil	SEV Type FC 91-685
Contact breaker gap	.016 to .020 inch (.4 to .5 mm)
Firing order	1-3-4-2
Timing	Pointer and flywheel mark

TRANSMISSION

Clutch :

Single dry plate—type 845 cc	160.DBIR.210
1108 cc	160.DBR.260
Friction disc with elastic hub, thickness	.291 inch (7.4 mm)

Clutch plate with diaphragm spring:

Clutch clearance at fork end, 845 cc	$\frac{1}{8}$ to $\frac{5}{32}$ inch (3 to 4 mm)
lever end, 1108 cc ...	$\frac{13}{64}$ inch (5 mm)

Gearbox and differential:

Type, 845 cc	334-04 (early), 354-28 or 29 (late)
1108 cc	354-000

Four synchromesh forward speeds—one reverse

Crownwheel and pinion	8 x 33
Speedometer drive	51 x 30

Reduction ratios 845 cc:				334-04		354-28
1st	...	...	...	3.80	3.67	
2nd	...	...	...	2.05	2.23	
3rd	...	...	...	1.36	1.45	
4th	...	...	...	1.03	1.03	
Reverse	..	..	3.80	3.23	

Reduction ratios 1108 cc:						TL
1st	...	...	...	3.66	3.67	
2nd	...	...	...	2.05	2.24	
3rd	...	...	...	1.36	1.46	
4th	...	...	...	1.03	1.03	
Reverse	...	...	3.07	3.23	

Drive shafts with 'BED' joints at the wheel end and 'SPIDER' or 'WEISS' joints at the gearbox end

Differential side cover adjustment shims:

Thickness availability	.004 inch (.10 mm)
	.006 inch (.15 mm)
	.008 inch (.20 mm)
	.020 inch (.50)
	.040 inch (1.0 mm)

Primary shaft end float shims:

Thickness availability	.004 inch (.10 mm)
	.006 inch (.15 mm)
	.008 inch (.20 mm)
	.020 inch (.50 mm)
	.038 inch (.95 mm)
	.079 inch (2 mm)
	.118 inch (3 mm)

FRONT AXLE AND SUSPENSION

Independent by upper wishbone, lower transverse arms and tie rods, longitudinal torsion bars and anti-roll bar

Track	50.4 inch (1.279 m)
Kingpin inclination	14° 40'
Camber: 845 cc early	1° 20' ±30'
845 cc later	0 to 1°
1108 cc	0 to 1°
Caster: 845 cc early	10° to 12°
845 cc later	9° to 11°
1108 cc	9° to 11°
Toe-out: 845 cc early	0 to .12 inch (0 to 3 mm)
845 cc later	0 to .2 inch (0 to 5 mm)
1108 cc...	0 to .2 inch (0 to 5 mm)
Diameter of torsion bars	.670 inch (17 mm)
Length of torsion bars	43.5 inch (1.106 m)
Identification: Lefthand	Two triangular symbols and yellow paint or a white/red mark
Righthand	Three triangular symbols and red paint or a white/yellow mark

REAR AXLE AND SUSPENSION

Independent by trailing arms and long transverse torsion bars, anti-roll bar on later models
Provision made for adjusting ground clearance

Track	49 inch (1.244 m)
Camber	0 to 1° 30'
Toe-in (each wheel)	0 to .08 inch (0 to 2 mm)
Diameter of torsion bars	.728 inch (18.5 mm)
Length of torsion bars	34.19 inch (868 mm)
Identification: Lefthand	Two triangular symbols and white paint or red paint
Righthand	Three triangular symbols and blue paint or yellow paint

BRAKING SYSTEM

Hydraulic brakes	Acting on all four wheels
Brake fluid	SAE.70.R3 specification
Brake limiting valve...	Acting on the rear wheels
Brake limiting valve setting with driver and full fuel tank, 845 cc (early)	340 to 425 lb/sq in
Brake limiting valve:	
Late 845 cc, limiter on lefthand side ...	385 to 470 lb/sq in
limiter on righthand side ...	345 to 415 lb/sq in
1108 cc	425 to 515 lb/sq in
Master cylinder diameter	.811 inch (20.6 mm) early, .748 inch (19 mm) later
Stroke of master cylinder	1 inch (25.4 mm)
Wheel cylinder diameters:	
Front:	
Drum	.937 inch (23.8 mm)
Caliper	1.772 inch (45 mm)
Rear:	
845 cc...	.812 inch (20.6 mm)
1108 cc	.867 inch (22 mm)

Brake drum diameters:
Front ... ... 9 inch (228.5 mm)
Rear:
845 cc ... ... 6.309 inch (160.25 mm)
1108 cc ... ... 7.096 inch (180.25 mm)
Brake lining width:
Front ... ... $1\frac{9}{16}$ inch (40 mm)
Rear:
845 cc ... ... $\frac{63}{64}$ inch (25 mm)
1108 cc ... ... $1\frac{3}{16}$ inch (30 mm)
Length of brake linings:
Front leading ... ... $9\frac{5}{8}$ inch (244 mm)
Front trailing ... ... $7\frac{7}{16}$ inch (189 mm)
Length of brake linings:
Rear leading ... ... 6 inch (152 mm)
Rear trailing ... ... $4\frac{5}{8}$ inch (118 mm)
Disc diameter ... ... 9 inch (228 mm)
thickness ... ... .393 inch (10 mm)
permitted wear thickness ... ... .353 inch (9 mm)
Pad thickness (including support) ... ... .551 inch (14 mm), minimum .27 inch
(7 mm)

Permissible wear ... ... $\frac{1}{16}$ inch
Pedal free-play ... ... $\frac{13}{64}$ inch (5 mm)

ELECTRICAL EQUIPMENT

Battery ... ... 12-volt 30 amp/hr
Starter:
Type:
845 cc, early ... ... Paris-Rhone D8E74
845 cc, later ... ... Ducellier 6185
1108 cc ... ... Paris-Rhone D8E81 or Ducellier 6187
Brush length, minimum:
Paris-Rhone ... ... $\frac{5}{16}$ inch (8 mm)
Ducellier ... ... $\frac{19}{64}$ inch (7.5 mm)
Dynamo:
Ducellier 7346 or 7352:
Output ... ... 22 amps
Paris-Rhone G-10 C-35 or G-10 C61:
Output ... ... 22 amps
Brush length minimum:
Paris-Rhone ... ... .315 inch (8 mm)
Ducellier ... ... .433 inch (11 mm)
Regulator:
Ducellier 8311A or 8314 ... ... 12-volt 22 amps
Paris-Rhone YD 216 ... ... 12-volt 22 amps
Windscreen wiper:
SEV 12-volt type ... ... 11 6007 or 521-208-11
Bosch 12-volt type ... ... WS.49 or WS4910 RE2A
Alternator:
SEV-Motorola ... ... 034838 or Ducellier 712.27912
Regulator:
Ducellier 8364
SEV-Marchal 33546

CAPACITIES

	845 cc	1108 cc
Engine sump (less filter)	4½ pints (2.5 litres)	5¼ pints (3 litres)
(with filter)	5 pints (2.84 litres)	5¾ pints (3.25 litres)
Gearbox/transmission	2¾ pints (1.5 litres)	3 pints (1.8 litres)
Cooling system	10 pints (5.6 litres)	11 pints (6.2 litres)
Expansion chamber	1¾ pints (1 litre)	—
Fuel tank (early 845 cc)	7 galls (32 litres)	8¾ galls (39 litres
(late 845 cc)	8¾ galls (39 litres)	—
Luggage boot	12 cu ft (.34 cu m)	—

DIMENSIONS

Overall length	12 ft 7½ inch (3.850 m)
Overall width	5 ft 4½ inch (1.536 m)
Overall height (laden)	4 ft 7½ inch (1.4 m) unladen 4 ft 11 inch (1.49 m)
Wheelbase: Righthand side	8 ft $\frac{7}{16}$ inch (2.450 m)
Lefthand side	7 ft 10½ inch (2.400 m)
Track: Front	4 ft 2$\frac{7}{16}$ inch (1.280 m)
Rear	4 ft 1 inch (1.244 m)
Ground clearance	5 inch (127 mm) laden
Weight (unladen) 845 cc	1653 lb (750 kg)
1108 cc	1807 lb (820 kg)

TIGHTENING TORQUES (lb ft)

(All nut and bolt sizes are metric)

Cylinder head bolts	40 to 50
Manifold nuts	10
Main bearing cap bolts:	
845 cc	50
1108 cc	40 to 50
Big-end cap nuts	25
Rocker shaft bolts, 1108 cc	10 to 15
Camshaft pulley hub, 1108 cc	35 to 45
Flywheel bolts:	
845 cc	30
1108 cc	40
Camshaft sprocket, 1108 cc:	
Bolts, $\frac{25}{32}$ inch (20 mm) long with .158 inch (4 mm) washer and lockplate	15
Bolts, $\frac{3}{16}$ inch (30 mm) long with .197 inch (5 mm) washer	20
Clutch to flywheel nuts	8
Gearbox BV.334:	
Halfhousing bolts	15 to 20
Intermediate plate bolts	15
Front cover bolts:	
7 mm diameter	15
8 mm diameter	15 to 20
Gearshift lever housing bolts	15
Differential cover bolts	15 to 20
Primary and secondary shaft end nuts	45 to 60
Crownwheel bolts	65 to 80

Gearbox BV.354:
Top cover bolts 10
Front cover bolts 15
Primary shaft bearing thrust plate bolts 15
Differential lockplate bolts 15
Gearbox casing to rear cover and clutch housing bolts:
    10 mm diameter 30
    8 mm diameter 15
Speedometer worm nut ... ... 75 to 85
Crownwheel bolts ... ... 65 to 80
Reverse gear swing lever bolt 20
Front axle upper pin 30
Front axle lower pin:
    12 mm diameter nut 35
    10 mm diameter nut 30
Steering wheel shaft UJ pins 25
Steering arm pin 25
Shock absorber 30
Anti-roll bar... 30
Steering ball joint nut 25
Suspension upper ball joint nut 25
Suspension lower ball joint nut 35
Steering wheel shaft flexible coupling 10
Steering wheel nut 35
Stub axle nut 85
Road wheel nuts ... ... 35 to 45
Rear suspension arm bearing bolts 20
Cam nuts 55
Rear shock absorber nut 34
Rear brake backplate nut 30
Bleed screws 7
Brake hose, front wheel, cylinder 15
Metal pipe line unions:
    Copper 9
    Steel 10
Caliper retaining bolts 50
Disc retaining bolts 20
Caliper bracket deflector bolts 15
Rear stub axle nut 90
Rear wheel nut ... ... 40 to 45
Master cylinder reservoir 6

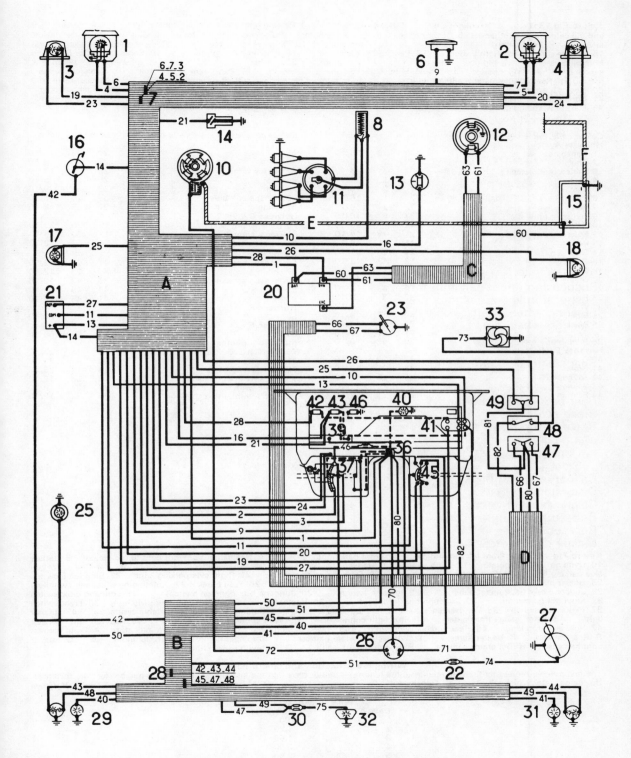

FIG 13:1 Early wiring diagram for 845 cc and 1108 cc

Key to Fig 13:1 1 Headlight left   2 Headlight right   3 Parking light and indicator front lefthand   4 Parking light and indicator, front righthand   5 Town hooter   6 Highway hooter   7 Cable connectors, front   8 Coil   9 Cold start device, electrical   10 Starter   11 Distributor   12 Generator   13 Oil pressure switch   14 Coolant temperature sender unit   15 Battery   16 Stoplight switch   17 Parking light lefthand   18 Parking light righthand   19 Cable connector on wiring from oil pressure switch and cold starter device   20 Regulator   21 Flasher unit   22 Connector on wiring from petrol tank sender unit   23 Wiper motor   25 Interior light   26 Ignition starter switch   27 Petrol tank sender unit   28 Cable connectors, rear   29 Rear light lefthand   30 Connector on wiring to number plate light   31 Rear light righthand   32 Number plate light   33 Heater blower   36 Connectors for instrument panel   37 Combination switch   39 Petrol gauge   40 Dashboard light   41 Connectors on instrument panel   42 Battery charge warning light   43 Coolant temperature gauge   45 Flasher switch   46 Flasher warning light   47 Switch for wipers   48 Switch for blower   49 Switch for parking light

Colour code, cable covers and cables	from	to	mm	Colour code, cable covers and cables	from	to	mm
Harness A				45 Yellow	37	28	12/10
1 Transparent. white	20	36	25/10	46 White	37	40	9/10
2 Grey	37	7	20/10	47 Yellow	28	30	12/10
3 Transparent. beige	37	7	20/10	48 Red	28	29	9/10
4 Blue	7	1	16/10	49 Red	30	31	9/10
5 Blue	7	2	16/10	50 Transparent. blue	36	25	9/10
6 Red	7	1	16/10	51 White	22	39	9/10
7 Red	7	2	16/10	**Harness C**			
9 Transparent. white	37	6	16/10	60 Transparent. white	15	20	25/10
10 Red	41	8	16/10	61 Transparent. black	12	20	25/10
11 Blue	21	45	16/10	63 Transparent green	20	12	12/10
13 Red	41	21	16/10	**Harness D**			
14 Grey	21	16	12/10	66 Transparent. grey	47	23	12/10
16 Grey	13	43	12/10	67 Green	47	23	12/10
19 Grey	45	3	12/10	80 Transparent. salmon	36	47	12/10
20 Green	45	4	12/10	81 Blue	47	49	9/10
21 Green	14	43	12/10	82 Red	41	48	16/10
23 Red	37	3	9/10	**Harness E**			
24 White	37	4	9/10	68	15	10	60/10
25 Black	49	17	9/10	**Harness F**			
26 Black	21	41	9/10	69	15	Earth	60/10
27 Salmon	21	41	9/10	**Individual cables**			
28 Blue, blue	20	42	9/10	70 White, black	36	26	25/10
Harness B				71 Red, black	26	41	20/10
40 Grey	45	29	12/10	72 Transparent. black	26	10	25/10
41 Green	45	31	12/10	73 Black, with outer cable	48	33	12/10
42 Salmon	16	28	12/10	74 White, with outer cable	22	27	9/10
43 Salmon	28	29	12/10	75 Black, with outer cable	30	32	12/10
44 Salmon	28	31	12/10				

Key to Fig 13:2 1 Front left turn indicator   2 Front park light   3 Horn   4 Headlamp   5 Front right turn indicator   9 Battery   10 Dynamo   11 Regulator   12 Earth strap   13 Starter   14 Water temperature transmitter   15 Distributor   16 Coil   17 Left side parking light   19 Connector (oil warning)   20 Oil warning transmitter   21 Right side parking light   22 Stop lamp switch   23 Heater blower fan resistor   24 Windscreen wiper   25 Instrument panel   26 Fuse block   27 Junction box (column switches)   28 Junction box (instrument panel)   29 Ignition switch   30 Junction box (ignition switch)   31 Lefthand door switch   32 Stoplight connector   33 Junction box (rear lights)   34 Heater fan   35 Righthand door switch   36 Light switch   37 Heater fan switch   38 Windscreen wiper switch   39 Flasher unit   40 Column switches   41 Cable connectors   42 Interior light   43 Petrol gauge transmitter   44 Rear light connectors   45 Wire connector (fuel gauge)   46 Rear left turn indicator   47 Rear and stop lamp   48 Rear number plate lights   49 Rear and stop lamp   50 Rear right turn indicator   **A** Front harness   **B** Rear harness   **C** Heater harness   **D** Windscreen wiper harness   **E** Stop light harness   **F** Column harness   **G** Interior light harness   **H** Generator harness   **P** Negative earth cable   **Q** Battery positive cable

Wiring identification and colour code

The first number represents the wire reference, the letter(s) —colour code and the last number is the code number for wire thickness:
Be Beige   **Bc** White   **B** Blue   **C** Transparent   **G** Orange   **J** Yellow   **M** Maroon   **N** Black   **S** Salmon   **R** Red   **V** Green

Wire thickness:

Code No.	Thickness (mm)
1	.90
2	1.20
3	1.60
4	2.00
5	2.50
6	3.00

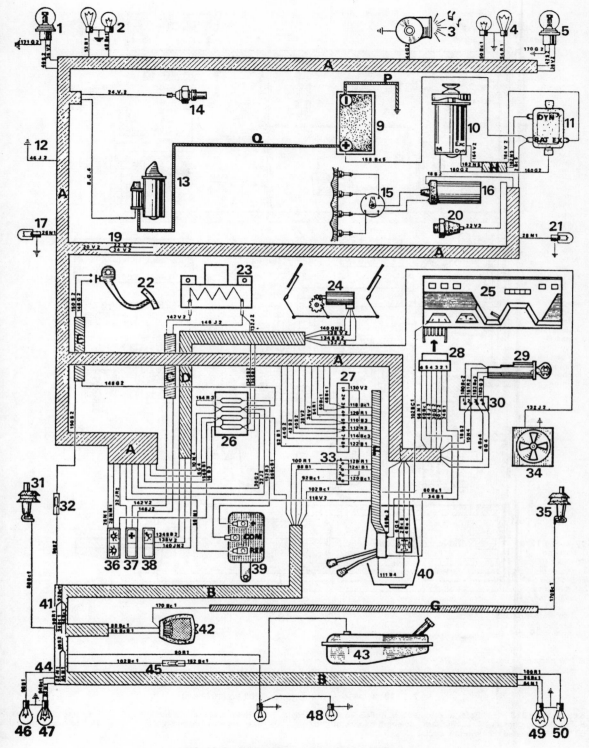

FIG 13:2 Wiring diagram for 850 cc (1971 on)

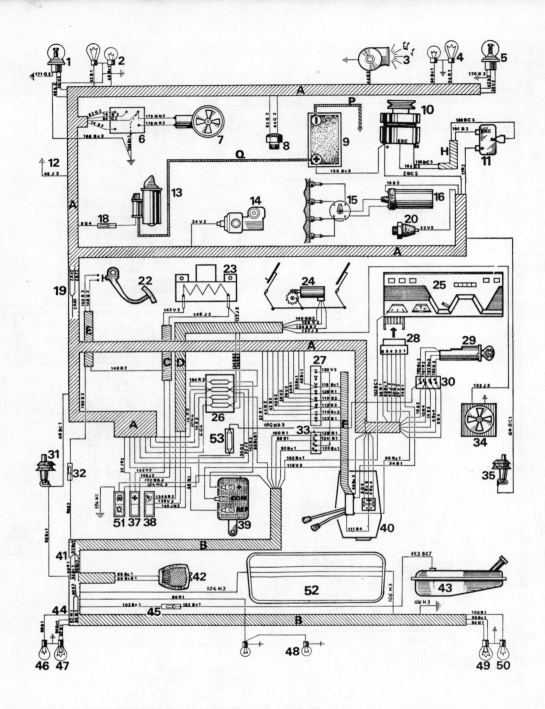

FIG 13:3   Wiring diagram for 1108 cc (1972 on)

Key to Fig 13:3   Refer to key numbers in **FIG 13:2** and add: 6 Relay for engine electric fan   7 Engine electric fan
8 Fan thermo contact   18 Starter solenoid connector clips   51 Rear window heater switch   52 Heated rear window
53 Fuse for heated rear window circuit

Refer to Fig 13:2 for wiring identification and colour code

HINTS ON MAINTENANCE AND OVERHAUL

There are few things more rewarding than the restoration of a vehicle's original peak of efficiency and smooth performance.

The following notes are intended to help the owner to reach that state of perfection. Providing that he possesses the basic manual skills he should have no difficulty in performing most of the operations detailed in this manual. It must be stressed, however, that where recommended in the manual, highly-skilled operations ought to be entrusted to experts, who have the necessary equipment, to carry out the work satisfactorily.

Quality of workmanship:

The hazardous driving conditions on the roads to-day demand that vehicles should be as nearly perfect, mechanically, as possible. It is therefore most important that amateur work be carried out with care, bearing in mind the often inadequate working conditions, and also the inferior tools which may have to be used. It is easy to counsel perfection in all things, and we recognize that it may be setting an impossibly high standard. We do, however, suggest that every care should be taken to ensure that a vehicle is as safe to take on the road as it is humanly possible to make it.

Safe working conditions:

Even though a vehicle may be stationary, it is still potentially dangerous if certain sensible precautions are not taken when working on it while it is supported on jacks or blocks. It is indeed preferable not to use jacks alone, but to supplement them with carefully placed blocks, so that there will be plenty of support if the car rolls off the jacks during a strenuous manoeuvre. Axle stands are an excellent way of providing a rigid base which is not readily disturbed. Piles of bricks are a dangerous substitute. Be careful not to get under heavy loads on lifting tackle, the load could fall. It is preferable not to work alone when lifting an engine, or when working underneath a vehicle which is supported well off the ground. To be trapped, particularly under the vehicle, may have unpleasant results if help is not quickly forthcoming. Make some provision, however humble, to deal with fires. Always disconnect a battery if there is a likelihood of electrical shorts. These may start a fire if there is leaking fuel about. This applies particularly to leads which can carry a heavy current, like those in the starter circuit. While on the subject of electricity, we must also stress the danger of using equipment which is run off the mains and which has no earth or has faulty wiring or connections. So many workshops have damp floors, and electrical shocks are of such a nature that it is sometimes impossible to let go of a live lead or piece of equipment due to the muscular spasms which take place.

Work demanding special care:

This involves the servicing of braking, steering and suspension systems. On the road, failure of the braking system may be disastrous. Make quite sure that there can be no possibility of failure through the bursting of rusty brake pipes or rotten hoses, nor to a sudden loss of pressure due to defective seals or valves.

Problems:

The chief problems which may face an operator are:
1 External dirt.
2 Difficulty in undoing tight fixings
3 Dismantling unfamiliar mechanisms.
4 Deciding in what respect parts are defective.
5 Confusion about the correct order for reassembly.
6 Adjusting running clearances.
7 Road testing.
8 Final tuning.

Practical suggestion to solve the problems:

1 Preliminary cleaning of large parts—engines, transmissions, steering, suspensions, etc.,—should be carried out before removal from the car. Where road dirt and mud alone are present, wash clean with a high-pressure water jet, brushing to remove stubborn adhesions, and allow to drain and dry. Where oil or grease is also present, wash down with a proprietary compound (Gunk, Teepol etc.,) applying with a stiff brush—an old paint brush is suitable—into all crevices. Cover the distributor and ignition coils with a polythene bag and then apply a strong water jet to clear the loosened deposits. Allow to drain and dry. The assemblies will then be sufficiently clean to remove and transfer to the bench for the next stage.

On the bench, further cleaning can be carried out, first wiping the parts as free as possible from grease with old newspaper. Avoid using rag or cotton waste which can leave clogging fibres behind. Any remaining grease can be removed with a brush dipped in paraffin. If necessary, traces of paraffin can be removed by carbon tetrachloride. Avoid using paraffin or petrol in large quantities for cleaning in enclosed areas, such as garages, on account of the high fire risk.

When all exteriors have been cleaned, and not before, dismantling can be commenced. This ensures that dirt will not enter into interiors and orifices revealed by dismantling. In the next phases, where components have to be cleaned, use carbon tetrachloride in preference to petrol and keep the containers covered except when in use. After the components have been cleaned, plug small holes with tapered hard wood plugs cut to size and blank off larger orifices with grease-proof paper and masking tape. Do not use soft wood plugs or matchsticks as they may break.

2 It is not advisable to hammer on the end of a screw thread, but if it must be done, first screw on a nut to protect the thread, and use a lead hammer. This applies particularly to the removal of tapered cotters. Nuts and bolts seem to 'grow' together, especially in exhaust systems. If penetrating oil does not work, try the judicious application of heat, but be careful of starting a fire. Asbestos sheet or cloth is useful to isolate heat.

Tight bushes or pieces of tail-pipe rusted into a silencer can be removed by splitting them with an open-ended hacksaw. Tight screws can sometimes be started by a tap from a hammer on the end of a suitable screwdriver. Many tight fittings will yield to the judicious use of a hammer, but it must be a soft-faced hammer if damage is to be avoided, use a heavy block on the opposite side to absorb shock. Any parts of the steering system which have been damaged should be renewed, as attempts to repair them may lead to cracking and subsequent failure, and steering ball joints should be disconnected using a recommended tool to prevent damage.

3 If often happens that an owner is baffled when trying to dismantle an unfamiliar piece of equipment. So many modern devices are pressed together or assembled by spinning-over flanges, that they must be sawn apart. The intention is that the whole assembly must be renewed. However, parts which appear to be in one piece to the naked eye, may reveal close-fitting joint lines when inspected with a magnifying glass, and, this may provide the necessary clue to dismantling. Left-handed screw threads are used where rotational forces would tend to unscrew a right-handed screw thread.

Be very careful when dismantling mechanisms which may come apart suddenly. Work in an enclosed space where the parts will be contained, and drape a piece of cloth over the device if springs are likely to fly in all directions. Mark everything which might be reassembled in the wrong position, scratched symbols may be used on unstressed parts, or a sequence of tiny dots from a centre punch can be useful. Stressed parts should never be scratched or centre-popped as this may lead to cracking under working conditions. Store parts which look alike in the correct order for reassembly. Never rely upon memory to assist in the assembly of complicated mechanisms, especially when they will be dismantled for a long time, but make notes, and drawings to supplement the diagrams in the manual, and put labels on detached wires. Rust stains may indicate unlubricated wear. This can sometimes be seen round the outside edge of a bearing cup in a universal joint. Look for bright rubbing marks on parts which normally should not make heavy contact. These might prove that something is bent or running out of truth. For example, there might be bright marks on one side of a piston, at the top near the ring grooves, and others at the bottom of the skirt on the other side. This could well be the clue to a bent connecting rod. Suspected cracks can be proved by heating the component in a light oil to approximately 100°C, removing, drying off, and dusting with french chalk, if a crack is present the oil retained in the crack will stain the french chalk.

4 In determining wear, and the degree, against the permissible limits set in the manual, accurate measurement can only be achieved by the use of a micrometer. In many cases, the wear is given to the fourth place of decimals; that is in ten-thousandths of an inch. This can be read by the vernier scale on the barrel of a good micrometer. Bore diameters are more difficult to determine. If, however, the matching shaft is accurately measured, the degree of play in the bore can be felt as a guide to its suitability. In other cases, the shank of a twist drill of known diameter is a handy check.

Many methods have been devised for determining the clearance between bearing surfaces. To-day the best and simplest is by the use of Plastigage, obtainable from most garages. A thin plastic thread is laid between the two surfaces and the bearing is tightened, flattening the thread. On removal, the width of the thread is compared with a scale supplied with the thread and the clearance is read off directly. Sometimes joint faces leak persistently, even after gasket renewal. The fault will then be traceable to distortion, dirt or burrs. Studs which are screwed into soft metal frequently raise burrs at the point of entry. A quick cure for this is to chamfer the edge of the hole in the part which fits over the stud.

5 **Always check a replacement part with the original one before it is fitted.**

If parts are not marked, and the order for reassembly is not known, a little detective work will help. Look for marks which are due to wear to see if they can be mated. Joint faces may not be identical due to manufacturing errors, and parts which overlap may be stained, giving a clue to the correct position. Most fixings leave identifying marks especially if they were painted over on assembly. It is then easier to decide whether a nut, for instance, has a plain, a spring, or a shakeproof washer under it. All running surfaces become 'bedded' together after long spells of work and tiny imperfections on one part will be found to have left corresponding marks on the other. This is particularly true of shafts and bearings and even a score on a cylinder wall will show on the piston.

6 Checking end float or rocker clearances by feeler gauge may not always give accurate results because of wear. For instance, the rocker tip which bears on a valve stem may be deeply pitted, in which case the feeler will simply be bridging a depression. Thrust washers may also wear depressions in opposing faces to make accurate measurement difficult. End float is then easier to check by using a dial gauge. It is common practice to adjust end play in bearing assemblies, like front hubs with taper rollers, by doing up the axle nut until the hub becomes stiff to turn and then backing it off a little. Do not use this method with ballbearing hubs as the assembly is often preloaded by tightening the axle nut to its fullest extent. If the splitpin hole will not line up, file the base of the nut a little.

Steering assemblies often wear in the straight-ahead position. If any part is adjusted, make sure that it remains free when moved from lock to lock. Do not be surprised if an assembly like a steering gearbox, which is known to be carefully adjusted outside the car, becomes stiff when it is bolted in place. This will be due to distortion of the case by the pull of the mounting bolts, particularly if the mounting points are not all touching together. This problem may be met in other equipment and is cured by careful attention to the alignment of mounting points.

When a spanner is stamped with a size and A/F it means that the dimension is the width between the jaws and has no connection with ANF, which is the designation for the American National Fine thread. Coarse threads like Whitworth are rarely used on cars to-day except for studs which screw into soft aluminium or cast iron. For this reason it might be found that the top end of a cylinder head stud has a fine thread and the lower end a coarse thread to screw into the cylinder block. If the car has mainly UNF threads then it is likely that any coarse threads will be UNC, which are not the same as Whitworth. Small sizes have the same number of threads in Whitworth and UNC, but in the $\frac{1}{2}$ inch size for example, there are twelve threads to the inch in the former and thirteen in the latter.

7 After a major overhaul, particularly if a great deal of work has been done on the braking, steering and suspension systems, it is advisable to approach the problem of testing with care. If the braking system has been overhauled, apply heavy pressure to the brake pedal and get a second operator to check every possible source of leakage. The brakes may work extremely well, but a leak could cause complete failure after a few miles.

Do not fit the hub caps until every wheel nut has been checked for tightness, and make sure the tyre pressures are correct. Check the levels of coolant, lubricants and hydraulic fluids. Being satisfied that all is well, take the car on the road and test the brakes at once. Check the steering and the action of the handbrake. Do all this at moderate speeds on quiet roads, and make sure there is no other vehicle behind you when you try a rapid stop.

Finally, remember that many parts settle down after a time, so check for tightness of all fixings after the car has been on the road for a hundred miles or so.

8 It is useless to tune an engine which has not reached its normal running temperature. In the same way, the tune of an engine which is stiff after a rebore will be different when the engine is again running free. Remember too, that rocker clearances on pushrod operated valve gear will change when the cylinder head nuts are tightened after an initial period of running with a new head gasket.

Trouble may not always be due to what seems the obvious cause. Ignition, carburation and mechanical condition are interdependent and spitting back through the carburetter, which might be attributed to a weak mixture, can be caused by a sticking inlet valve.

For one final hint on tuning, never adjust more than one thing at a time or it will be impossible to tell which adjustment produced the desired result.

GLOSSARY OF TERMS

Allen key   Cranked wrench of hexagonal section for use with socket head screws.

Alternator   Electrical generator producing alternating current. Rectified to direct current for battery charging.

Ambient temperature   Surrounding atmospheric temperature.

Annulus   Used in engineering to indicate the outer ring gear of an epicyclic gear train.

Armature   The shaft carrying the windings, which rotates in the magnetic field of a generator or starter motor. That part of a solenoid or relay which is activated by the magnetic field.

Axial   In line with, or pertaining to, an axis.

Backlash   Play in meshing gears.

Balance lever   A bar where force applied at the centre is equally divided between connections at the ends.

Banjo axle   Axle casing with large diameter housing for the crownwheel and differential.

Bendix pinion   A self-engaging and self-disengaging drive on a starter motor shaft.

Bevel pinion   A conical shaped gearwheel, designed to mesh with a similar gear with an axis usually at 90 deg. to its own.

bhp   Brake horse power, measured on a dynamometer.

bmep   Brake mean effective pressure. Average pressure on a piston during the working stroke.

Brake cylinder   Cylinder with hydraulically operated piston(s) acting on brake shoes or pad(s).

Brake regulator   Control valve fitted in hydraulic braking system which limits brake pressure to rear brakes during heavy braking to prevent rear wheel locking.

Camber   Angle at which a wheel is tilted from the vertical.

Capacitor   Modern term for an electrical condenser. Part of distributor assembly, connected across contact breaker points, acts as an interference suppressor.

Castellated   Top face of a nut, slotted across the flats, to take a locking splitpin.

Castor   Angle at which the kingpin or swivel pin is tilted when viewed from the side.

cc   Cubic centimetres. Engine capacity is arrived at by multiplying the area of the bore in sq cm by the stroke in cm by the number of cylinders.

Clevis   U-shaped forked connector used with a clevis pin, usually at handbrake connections.

Collet   A type of collar, usually split and located in a groove in a shaft, and held in place by a retainer. The arrangement used to retain the spring(s) on a valve stem in most cases.

Commutator   Rotating segmented current distributor between armature windings and brushes in generator or motor.

Compression ratio   The ratio, or quantitative relation, of the total volume (piston at bottom of stroke) to the unswept volume (piston at top of stroke) in an engine cylinder.

Condenser   See capacitor.

Core plug   Plug for blanking off a manufacturing hole in a casting.

Crownwheel   Large bevel gear in rear axle, driven by a bevel pinion attached to the propeller shaft. Sometimes called a 'ring gear'.

'C'-spanner   Like a 'C' with a handle. For use on screwed collars without flats, but with slots or holes.

Damper   Modern term for shock-absorber, used in vehicle suspension systems to damp out spring oscillations.

Depression   The lowering of atmospheric pressure as in the inlet manifold and carburetter.

Dowel   Close tolerance pin, peg, tube, or bolt, which accurately locates mating parts.

Drag link   Rod connecting steering box drop arm (pitman arm) to nearest front wheel steering arm in certain types of steering systems.

Dry liner   Thinwall tube pressed into cylinder bore

Dry sump   Lubrication system where all oil is scavenged from the sump, and returned to a separate tank.

Dynamo   See Generator.

Electrode   Terminal, part of an electrical component, such as the points or 'Electrodes' of a sparking plug.

Electrolyte   In lead-acid car batteries a solution of sulphuric acid and distilled water.

End float   The axial movement between associated parts, end play.

EP   Extreme pressure. In lubricants, special grades for heavily loaded bearing surfaces, such as gear teeth in a gearbox, or crownwheel and pinion in a rear axle.

Fade	Of brakes. Reduced efficiency due to overheating.
Field coils	Windings on the polepieces of motors and generators.
Fillets	Narrow finishing strips usually applied to interior bodywork.
First motion shaft	Input shaft from clutch to gearbox.
Fullflow filter	Filters in which all the oil is pumped to the engine. If the element becomes clogged, a bypass valve operates to pass unfiltered oil to the engine.
FWD	Front wheel drive.
Gear pump	Two meshing gears in a close fitting casing. Oil is carried from the inlet round the outside of both gears in the spaces between the gear teeth and casing to the outlet, the meshing gear teeth prevent oil passing back to the inlet, and the oil is forced through the outlet port.
Generator	Modern term for 'Dynamo'. When rotated produces electrical current.
Grommet	A ring of protective or sealing material. Can be used to protect pipes or leads passing through bulkheads.
Grubscrew	Fully threaded headless screw with screwdriver slot. Used for locking, or alignment purposes.
Gudgeon pin	Shaft which connects a piston to its connecting rod. Sometimes called 'wrist pin', or 'piston pin'.
Halfshaft	One of a pair transmitting drive from the differential.
Helical	In spiral form. The teeth of helical gears are cut at a spiral angle to the side faces of the gearwheel.
Hot spot	Hot area that assists vapourisation of fuel on its way to cylinders. Often provided by close contact between inlet and exhaust manifolds.
HT	High Tension. Applied to electrical current produced by the ignition coil for the sparking plugs.
Hydrometer	A device for checking specific gravity of liquids. Used to check specific gravity of electrolyte.
Hypoid bevel gears	A form of bevel gear used in the rear axle drive gears. The bevel pinion meshes below the centre line of the crownwheel, giving a lower propeller shaft line.
Idler	A device for passing on movement. A free running gear between driving and driven gears. A lever transmitting track rod movement to a side rod in steering gear.
Impeller	A centrifugal pumping element. Used in water pumps to stimulate flow.
Journals	Those parts of a shaft that are in contact with the bearings.
Kingpin	The main vertical pin which carries the front wheel spindle, and permits steering movement. May be called 'steering pin' or 'swivel pin'.
Layshaft	The shaft which carries the laygear in the gearbox. The laygear is driven by the first motion shaft and drives the third motion shaft according to the gear selected. Sometimes called the 'countershaft' or 'second motion shaft.'
lb ft	A measure of twist or torque. A pull of 10 lb at a radius of 1 ft is a torque of 10 lb ft.
lb/sq in	Pounds per square inch.
Little-end	The small, or piston end of a connecting rod. Sometimes called the 'small-end'.
LT	Low Tension. The current output from the battery.
Mandrel	Accurately manufactured bar or rod used for test or centring purposes.
Manifold	A pipe, duct, or chamber, with several branches.
Needle rollers	Bearing rollers with a length many times their diameter.
Oil bath	Reservoir which lubricates parts by immersion. In air filters, a separate oil supply for wetting a wire mesh element to hold the dust.
Oil wetted	In air filters, a wire mesh element lightly oiled to trap and hold airborne dust.
Overlap	Period during which inlet and exhaust valves are open together.
Panhard rod	Bar connected between fixed point on chassis and another on axle to control sideways movement.
Pawl	Pivoted catch which engages in the teeth of a ratchet to permit movement in one direction only.
Peg spanner	Tool with pegs, or pins, to engage in holes or slots in the part to be turned.
Pendant pedals	Pedals with levers that are pivoted at the top end.
Phillips screwdriver	A cross-point screwdriver for use with the cross-slotted heads of Phillips screws.
Pinion	A small gear, usually in relation to another gear.
Piston-type damper	Shock absorber in which damping is controlled by a piston working in a closed oil-filled cylinder.
Preloading	Preset static pressure on ball or roller bearings not due to working loads.
Radial	Radiating from a centre, like the spokes of a wheel.

Radius rod	Pivoted arm confining movement of a part to an arc of fixed radius.
Ratchet	Toothed wheel or rack which can move in one direction only, movement in the other being prevented by a pawl.
Ring gear	A gear tooth ring attached to outer periphery of flywheel. Starter pinion engages with it during starting.
Runout	Amount by which rotating part is out of true.
Semi-floating axle	Outer end of rear axle halfshaft is carried on bearing inside axle casing. Wheel hub is secured to end of shaft.
Servo	A hydraulic or pneumatic system for assisting, or, augmenting a physical effort. See 'Vacuum Servo'.
Setscrew	One which is threaded for the full length of the shank.
Shackle	A coupling link, used in the form of two parallel pins connected by side plates to secure the end of the master suspension spring and absorb the effects of deflection.
Shell bearing	Thinwalled steel shell lined with anti-friction metal. Usually semi-circular and used in pairs for main and big-end bearings.
Shock absorber	See 'Damper'.
Silentbloc	Rubber bush bonded to inner and outer metal sleeves.
Socket-head screw	Screw with hexagonal socket for an Allen key.
Solenoid	A coil of wire creating a magnetic field when electric current passes through it. Used with a soft iron core to operate contacts or a mechanical device.
Spur gear	A gear with teeth cut axially across the periphery.
Stub axle	Short axle fixed at one end only.
Tachometer	An instrument for accurate measurement of rotating speed. Usually indicates in revolutions per minute.
TDC	Top Dead Centre. The highest point reached by a piston in a cylinder, with the crank and connecting rod in line.
Thermostat	Automatic device for regulating temperature. Used in vehicle coolant systems to open a valve which restricts circulation at low temperature.
Third motion shaft	Output shaft of gearbox.
Threequarter floating axle	Outer end of rear axle halfshaft flanged and bolted to wheel hub, which runs on bearing mounted on outside of axle casing. Vehicle weight is not carried by the axle shaft.
Thrust bearing or washer	Used to reduce friction in rotating parts subject to axial loads.
Torque	Turning or twisting effort. See 'lb ft'.
Track rod	The bar(s) across the vehicle which connect the steering arms and maintain the front wheels in their correct alignment.
UJ	Universal joint. A coupling between shafts which permits angular movement.
UNF	Unified National Fine screw thread.
Vacuum servo	Device used in brake system, using difference between atmospheric pressure and inlet manifold depression to operate a piston which acts to augment brake pressure as required. See 'Servo'.
Venturi	A restriction or 'choke' in a tube, as in a carburetter, used to increase velocity to obtain a reduction in pressure.
Vernier	A sliding scale for obtaining fractional readings of the graduations of an adjacent scale.
Welch plug	A domed thin metal disc which is partially flattened to lock in a recess. Used to plug core holes in castings.
Wet liner	Removable cylinder barrel, sealed against coolant leakage, where the coolant is in direct contact with the outer surface.
Wet sump	A reservoir attached to the crankcase to hold the lubricating oil.

INDEX

NOTES

Alfa Romeo Giulia 1600,
1750, 2000 1962 on
Aston Martin 1921-58
Auto Union Audi 70, 80,
Super 90, 1966-72
Audi 100 1969 on
Austin, Morris etc.
1100 Mk. 1 1962-67
Austin, Morris etc. 1100
Mk. 2, 3, 1300 Mk. 1, 2, 3
America 1968 on
Austin A30, A35, A40
Farina 1951-67
Austin A55 Mk. 2, A60
1958-69
Austin A99, A110 1959-68
Austin J4 1960 on
Austin Allegro 1973 on
Austin Maxi 1969 on
Austin, Morris 1800
1964 on
Austin, Morris 2200 1972 on
Austin Kimberley, Tasman
1970 on
Austin, Morris 1300, 1500
Nomad 1969 on
BMC 3 (Austin A50, A55
Mk. 1, Morris Oxford
2, 3 1954-59)
Austin Healey 100/6,
3000 1956-68
Austin Healey, MG
Sprite, Midget 1958 on
Bedford CA Mk. 2 1964-69
Bedford CF Vans 1969 on
Bedford Beagle HA Vans
1964 on
BMW 1600 1966 on
BMW 1800 1964-71
BMW 2000, 2002 1966 on
Chevrolet Corvair 1960-69
Chevrolet Corvette V8
1957-65
Chevrolet Corvette V8
1965 on
Chevrolet Vega 2300
1970 on
Chrysler Valiant V8
1965 on
Chrysler Valiant Straight
Six 1963 on
Citroen DS 19, ID 19
1955-66
Citroen ID 19, DS 19, 20,
21 1966 on
Citroen Dyane Ami 1964 on
Daf 31, 32, 33, 44, 55
1961 on
Datsun Bluebird 610 series
1972 on
Datsun Cherry 100A, 120A
1971 on
Datsun 1000, 1200 1968 on
Datsun 1300, 1400, 1600
1968 on
Datsun 240C 1971 on

Datsun 240Z Sport 1970 on
Fiat 124 1966 on
Fiat 124 Sport 1966 on
Fiat 125 1967-72
Fiat 127 1971 on
Fiat 128 1969 on
Fiat 500 1957 on
Fiat 600, 600D 1955-69
Fiat 850 1964 on
Fiat 1100 1957-69
Fiat 1300, 1500 1961-67
Ford Anglia Prefect 100E
1953-62
Ford Anglia 105E, Prefect
107E 1959-67
Ford Capri 1300, 1600 OHV
1968 on
Ford Capri 1300, 1600,
2000 OHC 1972 on
Ford Capri 2000 V4, 3000 V6
1969 on
Ford Classic, Capri
1961-64
Ford Consul, Zephyr,
Zodiac, 1, 2 1950-62
Ford Corsair Straight
Four 1963-65
Ford Corsair V4 1965-68
Ford Corsair V4 2000
1969-70
Ford Cortina 1962-66
Ford Cortina 1967-68
Ford Cortina 1969-70
Ford Cortina Mk. 3
1970 on
Ford Escort 1967 on
Ford Falcon 6 1964-70
Ford Falcon XK, XL
1960-63
Ford Falcon 6 XR/XA
1966 on
Ford Falcon V8 (U.S.A.)
1965-67
Ford Falcon V8 (Aust.)
1966 on
Ford Pinto 1970 on
Ford Maverick 6 1969 on
Ford Maverick V8 1970 on
Ford Mustang 6 1965 on
Ford Mustang V8 1965 on
Ford Thames 10, 12,
15 cwt 1957-65
Ford Transit V4 1965 on
Ford Zephyr Zodiac Mk. 3
1962-66
Ford Zephyr Zodiac V4,
V6, Mk. 4 1966-72
Ford Consul, Granada
1972 on
Hillman Avenger 1970 on
Hillman Hunter 1966 on
Hillman Imp 1963-68
Hillman Imp 1969 on
Hillman Minx 1 to 5
1956-65
Hillman Minx 1965-67

Hillman Minx 1966-70
Hillman Super Minx
1961-65
Jaguar XK120, 140, 150,
Mk. 7, 8, 9 1948-61
Jaguar 2.4, 3.4, 3.8 Mk.
1, 2 1955-69
Jaguar 'E' Type 1961-72
Jaguar 'S' Type 420
1963-68
Jaguar XJ6 1968 on
Jowett Javelin Jupiter
1947-53
Landrover 1, 2 1948-61
Landrover 2, 2a, 3 1959 on
Mazda 616 1970 on
Mazda 808, 818 1972 on
Mazda 1200, 1300 1969 on
Mazda 1500, 1800 1967 on
Mazda RX-2 1971 on
Mazda R100, RX-3 1970 on
Mercedes-Benz 190b,
190c, 200 1959-68
Mercedes-Benz 220
1959-65
Mercedes-Benz 220/8
1968 on
Mercedes-Benz 230
1963-68
Mercedes-Benz 250
1965-67
Mercedes-Benz 250
1968 on
Mercedes-Benz 280
1968 on
MG TA to TF 1936-55
MGA MGB 1955-68
MGB 1969 on
Mini 1959 on
Mini Cooper 1961-72
Morgan Four 1936-72
Morris Marina 1971 on
Morris (Aust) Marina
1972 on
Morris Minor 2, 1000
1952-71
Morris Oxford 5, 6 1959-71
NSU 1000 1963-72
NSU Prinz 1 to 4 1957-72
Opel Ascona, Manta
1970 on
Opel GT 1900 1968 on
Opel Kadett, Olympia 993 cc
1078 cc 1962 on
Opel Kadett, Olympia 1492,
1698, 1897 cc 1967 on
Opel Rekord C 1966-72
Peugeot 204 1965 on
Peugeot 304 1970 on
Peugeot 404 1960 on
Peugeot 504 1968 on
Porsche 356A, B, C 1957-65
Porsche 911 1964 on
Porsche 912 1965-69
Porsche 914 S 1969 on
Reliant Regal 1952-73

Renault R4, R4L, 4 1961 on
Renault 5 1972 on
Renault 6 1968 on
Renault 8, 10, 1100 1962-71
Renault 12, 1969 on
Renault 15, 17 1971 on
Renault R16 1965 on
Renault Dauphine
Floride 1957-67
Renault Caravelle 1962-68
Rover 60 to 110 1953-64
Rover 2000 1963-73
Rover 3 Litre 1958-67
Rover 3500, 3500S 1968 on
Saab 95, 96, Sport
1960-68
Saab 99 1969 on
Saab V4 1966 on
Simca 1000 1961 on
Simca 1100 1967 on
Simca 1300, 1301, 1500,
1501 1963 on
Skoda One (440, 445, 450)
1955-70
Sunbeam Rapier Alpine
1955-65
Toyota Carina, Celica
1971 on
Toyota Corolla 1100,
1200 1967 on
Toyota Corona 1500 Mk. 1
1965-70
Toyota Corona Mk. 2
1969 on
Triumph TR2, TR3, TR3A
1952-62
Triumph TR4, TR4A
1961-67
Triumph TR5, TR250,
TR6 1967 on
Triumph 1300, 1500
1965-73
Triumph 2000 Mk. 1, 2.5 PI
Mk. 1 1963-69
Triumph 2000 Mk. 2, 2.5 PI
Mk. 2 1969 on
Triumph Dolomite 1972 on
Triumph Herald 1959-68
Triumph Herald 1969-71
Triumph Spitfire, Vitesse
1962-68
Triumph Spitfire Mk. 3, 4
1969 on
Triumph GT6, Vitesse
2 Litre 1969 on
Triumph Stag 1970 on
Triumph Toledo 1970 on
Vauxhall Velox, Cresta
1957-72
Vauxhall Victor 1, 2, FB
1957-64
Vauxhall Victor 101
1964-67
Vauxhall Victor FD 1600,
2000 1967-72

Continued on following page

Vauxhall Victor 3300,
Ventora 1968-72
Vauxhall Victor FE
Ventora 1972 on
Vauxhall Viva HA 1963-66
Vauxhall Viva HB 1966-70

Vauxhall Viva, HC Firenza
1971 on
Volkswagen Beetle 1954-67
Volkswagen Beetle 1968 on
Volkswagen 1500 1961-66

Volkswagen 1600 Fastback
1965-73
Volkswagen Transporter
1954-67
Volkswagen Transporter
1968 on

Volkswagen 411 1968-72
Volvo 120 series 1961-70
Volvo 140 series 1966 on
Volvo 160 series 1968 on
Volvo 1800 1960-73